Glimpses of God

from the writings of
J. Wash Watts

Professor of Old Testament Interpretation
New Orleans Baptist Theological Seminary
1930-1968

collected and edited
by
John D.W. Watts

Memorial
By
J. Hardee Kennedy, Dean
New Orleans Baptist Theological Seminary

Jameson Press
1833 Bushell Avenue
South Pasadena, CA 91030

D1212641

pietas filii

Copyright © 1977 by John D. W. Watts
1833 Bushnell Avenue., South Pasadena, CA 91030

Library of Congress Cataloging in Publication Data

Watts, James Washington, 1896-1975.
    Glimpses of God from the writings of J. Wash Watts.

    Bibliography: p.
    1. God-Biblical teaching--Collected works.
I. Watts, John D.W.   II. Title.
BS1192.6.W37 1977   231   77-15526
ISBN 0-87808-954-3

PRINTED IN THE UNITED STATES OF AMERICA

Contents

Preface

One can lay no claim on time. Productive life may end before the fruit of labor can be presented for the benefit and delight of friends and students.

So it was with my father. He was actively engaged in writing and arranging his papers when he was cut down by a stroke in August 1970. He passed on to his reward in October 1975 unable to return to his work.

It seems unfair to those who prized his teaching to leave to dusty archives the papers which reflect his Christian devotion and best scholarship. The two works among his papers which were most complete are published in this volume. Reflection on the academic development of the Seminary is preserved in another chapter.

The editor's personal gratitude, scholarly dependence, and spiritual debt to the author are reflected in the publication of this volume.

JOHN D. W. WATTS

This biographical sketch was prepared by John D.W. Watts, the author's son and editor of this book. He is Associate Professor of Old Testament in the Fuller Theological Seminary, Pasadena.

Important information and confirmation of details were provided by Mrs. J. Wash Watts, the author's companion for fifty-four years who now makes her home at the Bethea Baptist Home, Darlington, S.C.

Biographical Sketch

John D.W. Watts
and Mrs. J. Wash Watts

James Washington Watts III was born February 26th, 1896, the only child of John Drayton Williams Watts and Clara Dial Watts, at the Watts' home in the Chestnut Ridge community near Laurens, South Carolina.

The family was of Anglo-Saxon stock and had lived in the Piedmont of South Carolina since 1772. Wash's great-great grandfather, James Williams, was appointed Representative to the South Carolina Provincial Congress and later was Colonel of Independent Militia and hero of several important battles of the Revolution including Ninety-Six, Musgrove Mill, and King's Mountain. At King's Mountain, after he had already taken his place, he was killed in action. A grandfather, James Washington Watts, served as a reserve colonel in the War Between the States. He was a staunch supporter of the South Carolina State Fair in Columbia and was credited with keeping it alive single-handedly through at least one lean year of that war.

His father, John D.W. Watts, a farmer and breeder of fine live-stock, later turned to county politics. He served as county supervisor for over twenty years and as sheriff for one term. He was a high-spirited man who loved fox hunting all his life and was known in younger days to be a good fiddler for square dances. During the last two decades of his life he was a staunch church-member and Sunday School superintendent at the Chestnut Ridge Baptist Church.

His mother, Clara Dial Watts, came from a substantial family in the community. Her nephew later built and operated

the Laurens Glass Factory. A deeply spiritual woman, Clara
organized one of the first Sunbeam Bands in the state and was a
leader in every aspect of church life.

Wash grew up in the Chestnut Ridge Baptist Church, which
strongly shaped his life and thought. It was a missionary
church and its service flag already had eleven stars to com-
memorate missionaries and pastors who had gone out from the
church before Watts' own star was placed there. At the age of
nine, he suffered an attack of polio which completely inca-
pacitated him for three years. His right leg was paralyzed and
useless. However, the tireless patience and massage treatment
of his mother and his own indomitable courage and determination
over those years brought renewed strength to that withered limb.
He not only walked again, albeit with a limp, but became a tennis
player able to hold his own in almost any group of men his age.

He made his profession of faith in the Chestnut Ridge
Baptist Church and was baptized there about 1908.

His early schooling was in the one-teacher Chestnut Ridge
school. At fifteen years of age he entered Furman University
where he majored in mathematics and for two years was a member
of the debating team. He graduated with honors in 1915 and was
chosen as speaker at his graduation exercises. His mother always
insisted that he would have been valedictorian of his class if
he had not been manager of the Furman football team in his senior
year. But he never regretted one moment of that happy association with a game that he never ceased to love. His *alma mater*
honored him with the Algernon Sidney Sullivan award in 1961.

While in college he came under the strong influence of the
Student Missionary Movement. He attended two of its National
Conferences, once while in college and again in the Seminary.
For two or three years he struggled with the question of what
his life's work should be. He was drawn toward teaching, being
a Y.M.C.A. secretary, or a minister. 1916 proved to be an auspicious year for him. He finally committed himself to the ministry, he met a Limestone College student, Mattie Leila Reid,
who would in time become his wife, and that fall he entered the
Southern Baptist Seminary in Louisville, Kentucky. But in 1917
his studies were interrupted by a stint in Y.M.C.A. army work
which led to an appointment as Army Chaplain and a commission as
First Lieutenant just weeks before the war came to a close.

Mattie Leila Reid's college career was also interrupted for
two years by illness which the doctor feared might bring permanent blindness. But almost miraculously healing came, and she
graduated in 1918 with Bachelor of Arts and Bachelor of Music
(piano) degrees. She and Wash were engaged in August 1917. But

she graduated from college in 1918, taught school a year, and spent a year at the Woman's Missionary Union Training School while he completed his military service, his second year at the Seminary, and an interim pastorate, his first, at the First Baptist Church of Sumter, South Carolina.

Wash's Seminary mates included men like Ellis Fuller, M.T. Rankin, Hubert Hester, and Kyle Yates. Reunions in later years were occasions for recounting student pranks in old New York Hall and in "The House Beautiful."

On June 30, 1920 Wash and Mattie Leila were married in the First Baptist Church in Spartenburg and in the fall they return- ed to Louisville for a final year. But the study was interrupt- ed by the illness of Wash's mother which made it necessary for them to return to Laurens to be with her for a year. There on August 9, 1921 John Drayton Williams Watts was born.

At a Missionary Day service at the Seminary in the spring of 1920, before their marriage, both had volunteered for Foreign Mission work. Dr. and Mrs. Eugene Sallee of China urged the vol- unteers to join them in China as soon as possible. So applica- tion had already been made to the Foreign Mission Board before they returned to Louisville with a six-weeks old baby for their final year. Wash graduated in the spring of 1922, expecting appointment to China where several of his classmates did go.

But the Lord and the Foreign Mission Board directed other- wise. They were appointed in May 1922, but their field of service was to be Palestine. They sailed for Jerusalem, Pales- tine with Fred B. and Ruth Pearson of Alabama in February 1923. The Pearsons soon had to return home, and Wash and Mattie Leila were left alone, the first Southern Baptist Missionaries in Palestine. (Cf. Mrs. J. Wash Watts, *Palestinian Tapestries*. The Foreign Mission Board, Richmond, VA., 2nd ed. 1936, p. 18ff.)

The next five years were spent in strengthening work already begun by nationals in Nazareth and in Lebanon, in exploring possibilities for new work, in buying property and building in Nazareth and Jerusalem, and in an attempt to found a new work in Tel-Aviv. The signs of foundations well-laid still show in Southern Baptist mission work in Isarel and Lebanon five decades later. One of the results of that work was the translation and collection of a hymn book in Hebrew.

In the summer of 1928 the Watts came home on furlough. They spent their furlough year in Laurens at the Watt's large country home. There were now three children: Bryson Reid born in Jer- usalem February 12, 1925 and Betty Jane also born there December 12, 1926, in addition to John. At the end of the year they were not able to return to the field. The illness of Wash's mother, his own physical condition, and the Foreign Mission Board's depleted financial state because of the Depression - all these prevented their return.

Wash served as assistant pastor of the First Baptist Church, Greenville, South Carolina in 1929-30 while remaining indecisive about returning to Palestine. Then the family sold some stock inherited from Mattie Leila's parents and undertook graduate work in Hebrew Old Testament at the Southern Baptist Seminary in Louisville. Just two weeks after the semester began the banks closed with all the money they had.

Wash had a double fellowship for junior and senior Hebrew under Dr. Kyle Yates and Dr. John R. Sampey. With income from these, occasional preaching engagements, and the help of mission-minded churches, the family survived. The Seminary granted credit for language study in Palestine so residence requirements were met in one year and a summer school session. But it would be two more years before the thesis on *The Meaning of Yahweh in Exodus* would be complete and the degree Doctor of Philosophy conferred in May 1933.

In the spring of 1931 Wash was approached by President W.W. Hamilton with an invitation to join the faculty of the Baptist Bible Institute in New Orleans. Despite the advice of friends, he felt impelled to accept. In the fall of that year he moved his family to a house on the campus in New Orleans at 1230 Sixth Street to begin a career that would last thirty-six years.

Six months later the financial situation of the Baptist Bible Institute, caught by the Depression with large debts, was so desperate that radical measures were necessary. The faculty and staff were cut to five. Seven others were released. But Watts was one of those retained. For nearly seven years almost no salary could be paid, but the professors and their families received free board in the Institute's dining room. (Cf. Park H. Anderson, *New Orleans Baptist Theological Seminary*. A Brief History. (mimeographed) 1949; R.Q. Leavell, "New Orleans Baptist Theological Seminary," *Southern Baptist Encyclopedia* vol. II p. 970).

During 1932 Professor Watts served as pastor of the newly-organized Calvary Baptist Church of 65 members in Algiers, Louisiana. The small change of Sunday's offerings were often the only "cash money" the family had - and that was more than many had in those days.

Watts was active in shaping the curriculum of the Institute and carried major responsibility in the strengthening of the

Biographical Sketch

Institute's academic program which would lead a decade and a half later to its full accreditation as a Seminary.

During this period he wrote about the history and work of the Annuity Board of the Southern Baptist Convention in *The Living of the Gospel*. He was developing methods of study for Hebrew syntax and translation which would lead to his most fruitful work.

His older son attended Mississippi College and returned to study in the Institute in 1941, a mission volunteer. His second son attended one year at Louisiana State University before volunteering for the Army Air Corps in February 1943 - just days after his eighteenth birthday. The war cast its shadow over this family as over all others at that time. Reid went on to finish flight training in December 1943 and advanced training as a B-24 co-pilot. On June 6th 1943 he flew to Europe by way of North Africa where he joined the Fifteenth Air Force in southern Italy. He flew thirty combat missions over central and eastern Europe during the next four months and was promoted to First Lieutenant. He was honored with the Air Medal with two oak leaf clusters and with the Distinguished Flying Cross. September 24th, on his forty-fifth mission, his plane was hit by anti-aircraft fire over Salonika, Greece and he was killed.

Reid's loss brought a sadness in Dr. Watts' life that was noted by generations of students. But his faith and determination held firm. He missed no appointment or duty. If anything, his interpretations of scripture, especially his beloved twenty-third Psalm, took on deeper meaning.

John finished the Institute in 1944 and served two years as a Navy Chaplain before going to Southern Baptist Seminary in Louisville to do graduate work in Old Testament. He was granted the Th.D. degree in 1948 and married Winifred Williams in 1946. Betty Jane graduated from Blue Mountain College and married Elmer Stone West, Jr. in 1947.

During the decade of the forties Dr. Watts was twice called upon to serve as acting president of the Institute: in the 1942-43 interim between the administrations of W.W. Hamilton and Duke K. McCall, and again in 1946 for a few months before Roland Q. Leavell assumed office.

In 1947 his two-volumed *A Survey of Old Testament Teaching* was published by Broadman Press. It went through several printings over the next fifteen years, being used extensively in New Orleans seminary classes as well as in other schools. It continued to be used by the Seminary Extension Department even after that.

By the end of the decade his son was a missionary teacher in Switzerland and had presented him with his first grand-child, a girl named Cheryl. Wash and Mattie Leila were in Europe in that May 1949 to greet the new arrival. His sabbatical, the first in eighteen years of teaching, was spent at Oxford University and provided a treasured period of study under Prof. G.R. Driver. The year was largely spent in writing *A Survey of Syntax in the Hebrew Old Testament* which was published by Broadman Press in 1951. It would be reprinted by Wm. Eerdmans Publishing Company in 1964.

The fifties were years of building at the Seminary. Its name had been changed to New Orleans Baptist Theological Seminary by Convention action in 1946. A beautiful new campus was built in Gentilly. The Seminary was reorganized as three schools, each with a dean. Watts served as Administrative Dean for the Seminary until his 1962 sabbatical which was spent at the Arab Baptist Seminary in Beirut, Lebanon. The New Orleans Seminary prospered greatly, being strengthened in every way. His particular contribution was in the growing academic quality.

In 1958 Watts was again called upon to serve as acting president. His report to the Convention in that year recorded 39 faculty members with 1,087 students. The chapel was completed during his term of service. (Cf. *Southern Baptist Encyclopedia* III p. 1863).

The decade of the sixties provided opportunity to record the mature fruit of a lifetime of scholarly work. Unfortunately, only a small part found its way into print.

In 1964 Wm. B. Eerdmans Company took over the publication of a second enlarged edition of the *Survey of Syntax in the Hebrew Old Testament* to support the publication of *A Distinctive Translation of Genesis* which had been published in 1963. This was intended to be a pilot volume for a translation of the entire Old Testament according to the principles outlined in the *Syntax*. Several of his former students were to join in the translation. But the reader response was insufficient for Eerdmans to continue with the project.

Dr. Watts continued with his own work and produced translations of Exodus and Isaiah which were produced in mimeographed form on the New Orleans campus. The translation of these three books, along with the *Syntax* which provided their explanation and foundation, are surely his most mature and lasting contribution to Old Testament scholarship.

Short articles from his pen appeared in the *Wycliffe Bible Encyclopedia* and in the *Southern Baptist Encyclopedia*. In 1967 a revision into one volume of his Old Testament Survey appeared with the title, *"Old Testament Teaching: An Introduction to the Old Testament,* Broadman Press, 1967. A booklet on the twenty-third Psalm appeared with the title, "In the House of the Lord." And a tract called "The Light of the World," was prepared for the Home Mission Board.

Watts' work always looked beyond translation and exegesis to teaching and preaching. This was particularly evident in a series of studies which he prepared on the Book of Genesis. He named them "Glimpses of God." They provide the title for this collection of some of his unpublished works.

In 1965 an annual scholarship for a ministerial student was established in his honor.

In 1968, being seventy-one years old and having served thirty-six years in New Orleans, J. Wash Watts retired. The announcement was heard with regret by students and colleagues. Students crowded the largest classroom available for his last course. He and Mattie Leila, who had so selflessly served with him, were honored with dinners, gifts and plaques.

They moved to Mars Hill, N.C. to be near their daughter. There he suffered a slight stroke in 1968. Except for a little more difficulty in walking, he recovered within a few months. Later in 1969 he enjoyed a semester as guest professor at Golden Gate Theological Seminary in California. In the winter of 1969-70 he led a seminar for about twenty pastors in Nashville, where they had moved.

In August 1970 just after greeting John and his family on their return from Switzerland and on the eve of a trip to his granddaughter's wedding in Richmond, Virginia, he was stricken again. From that date until his death October 16th 1975, he was unable to move well or communicate clearly. But all who cared for him during the long illness of five and a half years marveled at his courtesy and the sweetness and gentleness of his manner toward all.

On October 18, 1975, J. Wash Watts was buried in the family plot of the Chestnut Ridge Cemetary near Laurens, South Carolina. The funeral was attended by his wife, his daughter, his son and their families: eight grandchildren and one great-great grandchild. The services were conducted by his son and son-in-law. They praised God for his life and service, thanking Him for the release to great reward that was now his.

Almost all of the hundreds of letters that came at that time from friends and former students expressed gratitude, not only

for his teaching or preaching, but also for his concern for the
individual, for his compassion and kindness, for his patience and
humor, for his sympathy and understanding. He loved to preach
in small country churches like the one in which he was reared.
There and in the beloved First Baptist Church of New Orleans,
where he held his membership for more than twenty hears, his
major ministry was teaching the Word.

A Bibliography of Books by J. Wash Watts

The Meaning of Yahweh in Exodus. Ph.D. dissertation, Southern
    Baptist Theological Seminary, Louisville, KY, 1933.
    Typescript: 188 pp.
Living the Gospel. The History and Purpose of the Relief and
    Annunity Board of the Southern Baptist Convention. ca.
    1938.
"The Syntax of the Verb," in Kyle Yates, *Essentials of Biblical
    Hebrew.* New York, Harper Brothers, 1938, pp. 121-150.
A Survey of Old Testament Teaching. 2 vols., Nashville,
    Broadman Press, 1947, 295 and 304 pp.
    revised and replaced by: *Old Testament Teaching: An Intro-
    duction to the Old Testament.* Nashville, Broadman Press,
    1967, 358 pp.
A Survey of Syntax in the Hebrew Old Testament. Nashville,
    Broadman Press, 1951.
    2nd revised edition: Grand Rapids, Wm.B. Eerdmans, 1964,
    164 pp.
A Distinctive Translation of Genesis. Grand Rapids, Wm.B.
    Eerdmans, 1963, 154 pp.
In the House of the Lord: Psalm 23. Nashville, Broadman Press,
    1965.
Exodus - A Distinctive Translation with Interpretative Outline.
    South Pasadena, Jameson Press, 1977, 156 pp.
Isaiah - A Distinctive Translation with Interpretative Outline.
    South Pasadena, Jameson Press, 1977, 172 pp.
Glimpses of God. J.D.W. Watts, ed., South Pasadena, Jameson
    Press, 1977, 200 pp.

This Memorial to Dr. J. Wash Watts was delivered at a special service in the Roland Q. Leavell Chapel of the New Orleans Baptist Theological Seminary, February 10, 1976. It is printed with permission.

Dr. J. Hardee Kennedy is the Dean of Academic Affairs, New Orleans Baptist Theological Seminary. He was the student and colleague of Dr. Watts for more than twenty-five years.

Memorial

J. Hardee Kennedy

Hear some very brief and familiar passages from the Role of Isaiah, as translated by Dr. J. Wash Watts.

Why should you say, O Jacob, yea why should you speak,
    O Israel,
"My way is hidden from Yahweh, and my right continues
    to be disregarded by my God?"
Have you not known? Have you not heard? *The God of*
    the ages is Yahweh, the creator of the ends of the
    earth. He does not become faint or grow weary.
There is no searching out of his understanding.
The one giving *to the weary* strength [is he],
Yea for the one who has no might he is accustomed to
    multiply might.
Though youths will grow weary and faint,
And *young men* will indeed stumble,
Yet *those who wait for Yahweh* will renew their strength,
    they will mount up with wings like the eagles,
They will run and not grow weary, they will walk and
    not become faint.

Who can give credence to our report?
And *The Arm of Yahweh to whom* can it be revealed?
For he will grow up as a tender plant before him, and
    as a root out of dry ground, having no such form
    and no such beauty,
That we should observe him, and no such appearance that
    we should desire him;
One despised and forsaken of men, a man of sorrows and

acquainted by experience with grief.
Yea, *as one who causes faces to be hidden from him,* he
      will be continuously despised, and we will not esteem
      him.
Verily our sicknesses he shall bear, and *our* griefs
      he shall carry [on his own person],
While we will consider him one stricken, smitten by God,
      and afflicted.
But *he* will be thrust through for our transgressions,
      crushed for our iniquities,
The discipline necessary to secure our peace will be his
      responsibility, and *by reason of his stripes* there
      shall be healing for us.
All of us like sheep go astray, *each one to his own*
      way turns,
And *Yahweh* shall cause to fall on him the iniquity of
      us all.

Evangelist Billy Graham tells us that he remembers the
speech of President Dwight Eisenhower at Valley Forge. Mr. Eisenhower described the ragtag army of General Washington. He told
of the bitter cold, the hunger, the illness, the suffering, and
the sacrifice of that brave band of soldiers. When he had
spoken of their singular devotion, of their gallant dedication
to the cause of bringing to birth a new nation of freedom, he
added: "This is where they got it for us."

In sober reflection on Mr. Graham's report I want to exclaim: What a noble and inspiring heritage for all of us who
are citizens of the United States of America in this bicen-
tennial year! We are challenged, and sometimes baffled, by the
staggering difficulties of the present. But we are inspired by
a noble heritage as we look toward the future. Whether at Valley
Forge or elsewhere, whether in that earlier period or in more recent years, noteworthy achievement has been linked with heroic
struggle in the history of our Republic. We have ample reason
to remember, to acknowledge again and again: ."This is where they
got it for us!"

On October 16 last, Dr. J. Wash Watts died in a nursing home
in Darlington, South Carolina. Dr. Watts retired from the faculty of our Seminary in 1967, having served for 36 years as Professor of Old Testament and Hebrew. During most of that extensive period of service his heavy assignments included both
administrative tasks and teaching responsibilities. On two
occasions he served as Acting President. When the news of his
death reached the campus, I felt glad in my heart. The long illness and final comatose state had ended.

In the days of the Great Depression, in those bitter and desperate times, when it seemed that the doors of this institution surely would be closed, Dr. Watts shared the strong resolve of the administration and faculty. This school would not close if he could prevent it, if through total devotion and dedication the work could be sustained and continued. When the financial resources of the institution were utterly inadequate, his teaching ministry did not falter. When funds necessary to meet the meager salaries were not forthcoming, he and his family took their meals in the dining hall. Somehow he and the others who made up the leadership of the institution kept the doors open, and in so doing they ushered this Seminary into a golden future.

In contemplating the life and work of Dr. Watts, I have reflected not only with sober heart, but also with tears. In recalling the extraordinary measure of his courage and commitment, I want to exclaim: O, what a heritage is ours! What an inspiring and noble heritage belongs to those who make up the Seminary family at this time! At the present auspicious juncture in the history of the institution, with new leadership, redesigned educational programs, enlarged student enrollment, and increased physical resources, there are new and compelling reminders of our heritage. There are added reasons to remember gratefully and humbly: "This is where they got it for us!"

But I am keenly aware that Dr. Watts continued the getting. As I have thought about the continuation of that getting across the years of his distinguished ministry as a member of the faculty and administration of the Seminary, I have attempted to identify the main components of the goodness of his life and the greatness of his achievements. For one thing (This is first!), Dr. Watts committed himself to Jesus Christ. As a lad in South Carolina he met the Lord in a personal experience of salvation. Some years later he answered the call of the Lord to preach the gospel. These experiences basically account for his spiritual ministry during World War I when he served in the Y.M.C.A. They account for his distinguished service, along with that of his devoted wife, in Old Palestine under appointment of the Foreign Mission Board. They explain why he gave himself with such singular devotion to the Seminary and to the cause of theological education. They point up the reason for his concern for the equipping of God-called men and women who would share the message of Christ across the world. No reasonable and perceptive person was left in doubt concerning Dr. Watts' calling and commitment. His experience with Jesus Christ was rich and real, and the warmth and the glow of the Divine presence was convincingly manifest in his life.

Dr. Watts was a diligent student of the Holy Scriptures. As many in this audience will recall, the focus of his scholarly

study was a superb blending of reverent spirit and critical
mind. For him, a critical apparatus for the Hebrew text was
no mere collection of dead mechanics. For him, the principles
of syntax could not be confined to statements in a textbook. He
had a way of insisting that his students understand the distinction between an infinitive construct and an infinitive absolute.
And there was serious trouble unless that distinction was understood.

     Dr. Watts' meticulous concern for technical matters related
to the Hebrew Old Testament was only the means to an end: an
accurate and meaningful interpretation of the Scriptures. His
paramount concern was that the message of the Lord might go out
across the world, reaching the hearts and minds of people,
changing them and changing the human society. In recent days I
have thought anew of the evangelical spirit and purpose of his
preaching. For example, on one occasion he turned to the beautiful passage with which the book of Hosea is brought to a close.
Pointing to the striking figures of the dew and the fruit, he
developed the message in this way: "Yea, it is the dew drops
in the dry season that help the languishing plant to flourish
again. Yea, it is the dew drops in the dry season that help
the tender plant to take root. Yea, it is the dew drops in the
dry season that help the plant to get ready for spreading out.
Yea, it is the dew drops in the dry season that help the plant
to develop vigor. Yea, it is the dew drops in the dry season
that help the plant to be fragrant again." And then he concluded, "The dew drops in the dry season become the flowers
and the fruit of heaven in the springtime."

     Dr. Watts was fervent in prayer. In fact, while he was
active in his ministry at the Seminary many of the students and
faculty responded with eagerness, almost with excitement, when
someone in charge of the chapel service called on Dr. Watts to
lead the congregation in prayer. We wanted to hear him pray.
Ah, in his words were the fervor of the eighth century prophets
and the poetical cadence and soul-stirring imagery of the
psalmists. He prayed not only with great moving of heart in
public worship, but his life reflected the strength and glow of
his daily devotion. I have thought many times of that crisis
hour when Reid, the younger son of Dr. and Mrs. Watts, was lost
during World War II. Long, suspenseful months of waiting ensued,
and then there came the message. The plane had been shot out of
the skies over Greece, and Reid had died in the flower of his
youth. But when someone questioned Dr. Watts about his personal
trauma and suffering, the man of fervent prayer and faith
answered with confident decisiveness: "It will be all right.
We make no demands on God."

Dr. Watts was a disciplined teacher. I have known very
few teachers in my lifetime who so superbly combined in their
ministry both technical scholarship and great spiritual warmth.
He would not be pushed around. His standards were high, and
I thought they were inflexible. With the index finger of his
right hand pointed toward heaven (There seemed to be some kind
of extension!) and his voice lifted to high C, he would exclaim,
"Ah, yes, you want an A. Well, get with it, work, that's the
way to get it." And he meant every word of it. But if the
demands of Dr. Watts' classwork were great, the dividends for
his students were immeasurably greater. When he taught the
famous 23rd Psalm the number of students absent from other
classes was abnormally large. (I can tell it now, but I dared
not do so then.) On some occasions when every available chair
in the classroom was occupied, many of the "visiting" students
stood at the doors and along the walls in order to listen to
the magnificent exposition of Psalm 23. My life could never be
the same after hearing Dr. Watts teach and preach the famous
Pastoral Psalm.

Dr. Watts was a zealot for theological education. In a
sense we may say that he devoted his life to this cause. Clearly aware of the breadth of what I am saying, I would affirm that
few other people have contributed so significantly to the
character of this Seminary, to the shaping of its lofty spiritual ideals and its demanding academic standards. He wanted to
see this institution make a maximal contribution to young men
and young women, God-called and committed, who need to be
equipped for Christian service across the world. He was steadfastly convinced that the corollary to the divine call is the
best possible educational preparation for the fulfilling of that
call.

Dr. Watts, the distinguished former professor of Old Testament and Hebrew in this institution, and my beloved teacher,
left us a great heritage. Today I can think of the marble
plaque on the porch of this chapel and remember that he drew
the plans for it. I can look again at the magnificent furniture
here in this pulpit and remember that he designed it. I can re-
read portions of the books which he wrote in the areas of Old
Testament Introduction and Exegesis and in Hebrew Syntax and
hear the resounding voice of the teacher. All of these are reminders. But the deeper, more meaningful, reminders are en-
shrined in my heart. And as surely as I may say this, a host
of others also may attest to the same kind of experience. The
impact of his life and ministry upon hundreds of his students
and upon others has reached across the world and blessed a
multitude.

I would conclude this message by referring to a simple yet profoundly expressive couplet that has come to us from the poet Reddings.

Nothing that is memorable ever passes,
    for in memory the past is ever present.

Founders Day Address

October 7, 1954

Dr. Watts was interested in the curriculum and standards of the Baptist Bible Institute and of the Seminary from the beginning of his association with the school. He was registrar and then dean, becoming Dean of Academic Affairs when the Seminary was organized as three schools.

It was appropriate that he survey the development of the school in terms of its academic goals. This he did in this Founder's Day Address, October 7th 1954. It is recorded here as a reminder of the Seminary's heritage and of Dr. Watts' part in it.

The Achievement of Accredited Status by the Theological School

J. Wash Watts

"What mean ye by these stones?" is ever the inquiry of the young when former generations are wise in setting up memorials.

Baptists have often been accused of being so busy making history that they overlook the value of recording it. George Sokolsky, the columnist, recently upbraided Americans in general for neglecting their memorials. He said we are about to forget who Paul Revere was. Let us remember, therefore, that Founders' Day is the time for setting up memorials.

On this Founders' Day we are going back along the trail of the past to look for signs of something often forgotten, often unknown, very seldom celebrated, yet as essential to the life of an institution like ours as is a backbone to a human body -- *its academic standards*.

These stones we would set up today do not memorialize the wonder-working of God. We look today at man's side of the picture.

These stones do not memorialize purchase of property, erection of buildings, or provision of equipment. The record of these will be found on cornerstones or bronze tablets. We would that we never fail in our gratitude for them. Nevertheless, those that speak of such things are the first to say that

campuses and presidents without faculty and alumni to give
living demonstration of worthy academic standards are like a
mirage promising water when there is nothing but sand and sun.

These stones we would set up today are memorials of visions
in advance of their day and labors that often accomplished no
more than keeping open the door of opportunity. These visions
and labors were born of insights into the future that kept hope
alive when the hard realities of the immediate present forbade
implementation. They arose out of an understanding of God's
call that clung tenaciously to ideals when the opportunism of
majorities stifled even the confession of them. The evidence
of these things remains as a rule in old files of correspondence,
in scattered catalogue paragraphs and statistics, in the hearts
of friends who have survived many years and many trials, or in
prayers recorded only in heaven.

There were visions of an accredited status for the theological courses in the very beginning of the school's history. The
first stone we would set up today tells of the planning, the
second of the maintaining, and the third of the attaining of an
accredited status for the theological school.

I.   Planning the Possibilities of the Future School

The word *school* is used here because it was the common
understanding at the time the institution was founded that it
was to be a Bible School, not a seminary.

The following excerpt from a news item in one of the New
Orleans papers in 1918 reflects this understanding:

> Having purchased ... the buildings of the Sophie
> Newcomb College, ... The Baptist Bible Institute
> ... will open its doors for the regular session
> September 23.

> The purpose of the school is to equip Christian
> workers, both men and women, for a fuller service
> to humanity. It is not meant to make a theological
> seminary but to provide adequate academic and
> biblical knowledge for those who desire to become
> efficient Christian workers and cannot or do not
> care to take a theological course.[1]

---

[1] From a clipping in the files of the president, the name
of the paper is not included.

The occasion for this understanding was the wording of the
action taken by the Southern Baptist Convention in authorizing
the founding of the school. The memorial proposing the founding described the school as "a Baptist Missionary Training
School."[2] The instruction of the Convention concerning its
founding described it as follows:

> ... the English Bible at the heart ..., with
> missionary training courses, personal workers'
> courses, pastoral training courses, Sunday
> School training and gospel music courses,
> grouped around that center ....[3]

Furthermore, the name Baptist Bible Institute was chosen
by the first Board of Directors (the Trustees of the school were
at that time called Directors) in accord with these directions.

On the other hand, *prior conceptions* of the role to be
played by this school had included more than a Bible school.

In the decade immediately following the establishment of
the Southern Baptist Convention, the wisdom of establishing one
central theological school was being debated throughout its
territory. In 1849, right in the midst of that period, Dr.
Basil Manly Sr.,[4] the man who was later president of the
Educational Convention that recommended its establishment, wrote
to his son, Basil Manly, Jr. as follows:

> What do you think of a great Baptist college for
> the Southwest to be located in New Orleans? The
> idea seems to me to be very rational, feasible, and
> eligible. That is, and is to be, the place of chief
> commercial importance through the whole region drain-
> ed by the Mississippi.
>
> When we have once gotten our great college
> established there, endowed, officered, and in
> full motion we will then place by its side a
> first-rate theological institution, for profound
> requirements in that line. This must be on its
> own separate basis and governed by a different set
> of trustees.

---

[2]Minutes of the Southern Baptist Convention for 1917, pp.
30, 31.

[3]Minutes of the Southern Baptist Convention for 1917, p. 83.

[4]Catalogue for 1927-28, p. 9.

Dr. Manly's statement has frequently been followed by the following one:

> There was never an agitation for the founding of
> a theological seminary in the South that New Orleans
> was not prominently mentioned as the location. Per-
> haps the only reason a theological school was not
> founded here long ago was the occasional prevalence
> of yellow fever, but owing to the triumphs of med-
> ical science and the improvement of hygienic
> conditions New Orleans has become one of the
> healthiest cities of its size in the United States.
> Fall, winter, and spring months are particularly
> attractive to both tourists and students.[5]

In 1914, Dr. P.I. Lipsey,[6] editor of the Baptist record, wrote a word concerning the value of a theological seminary in New Orleans. He was active in discussions concerning the founding of the school, he became vice-chairman of its Board of Directors for the first session, president the following year, and he continued in that position until failing health shortly before his death forced his retirement in 1947. Thus, through 30 years, through "thick and thin," he served this institution. It never had a more loyal or a wiser friend. His judgment stood steadfastly with these others concerning the need for a theological seminary.

To this list of prior conceptions may be added those of the original three on the faculty, Drs. B.H. DeMent, president, James E. Gwatkin, and W.E. Denham. Their testimony and influ-ence leave it as a matter of record that they came anticipating growth into a theological seminary.

It needs to be understood, therefore, that there were two lines of throught from the beginning as to what the school should be. The action of the Convention in founding it did not say, seemingly was not intended to say, that it must remain a Bible school only. Instead it was agreed by all concerned that it should start that way.

Accordingly, the statement of purpose written by the first Board of Directors began with this sentence, "This institution

---

[5] Catalogue for 1927-28, p. 9.

[6] Catalogue for 1924-25, p. 9.

shall center around the study of the Bible as the Word of God."[7] This uses the word *Bible* rather than *English Bible*, leaving the door open for developments. It is exceedingly interesting, therefore, to observe that this statement of purpose has appeared in every catalogue and has fitted those published under the name New Orleans Baptist Theological Seminary as well as those published under the name Baptist Bible Institute.

Inner developments, arising out of the lessons of experience, led from the very beginning toward fulfillment of these prior conceptions. Among these inner developments, there were four main ones, as follows:

(1) The need of students for higher courses came to be increasingly evident. One man who "began his work on the opening day"[8] was the first to qualify for studies leading to the Master of Theology degree and to a Doctor of Theology degree.

(2) From 1922 onward courses of study leading to theological degrees were added, that for a Bachelor of Theology in 1922, that for a Master of Theology in 1923, and that for a Doctor of Theology in 1924.

(3) The faculty was built up in the period of 1924-27 with the specific intention of meeting the needs of students qualifying for theological courses. Therefore, the 1927-28 catalogue adds this bit of information:

> It is interesting to note that the four younger members of the faculty, J.E. Dean, L.G. Cleverdon, E.F. Haight and L.B. Campbell, alumni of Howard College, Tulane University, Furman University and Mississippi College, respectively, were among the first to take the degree of Doctor of Theology in the Baptist Bible Institute.[9]

(4) Contemporary catalogues carried a new historical sketch which began with this statement, "The Baptist Bible Institute is a south-wide Theological school. . . ." This new description appeared first in 1924. Previously the word *theological* was not used at any place in the catalogues.

-----

[7] Records of the Baptist Bible Institute, Vol. 1 (1918), pp. 60-61.

[8] Catalogue of 1924-25, p. 11.

[9] Catalogue for 1927-28, p. 11.

The new historical sketch was expanded from year to year
in the period 1924-27, as indicated by the quotations already
cited, with the obvious intention of justifying these developments. When, why, and how the debate within the inner circle
of Faculty and Trustees was settled is indicated by this record:

> At the meeting of the Board of Trustees in 1926
> the faculty was instructed to offer the degree of
> Doctor of Theology under the definite and rigid
> conditions of a Bachelor of Arts degree from a
> standard college or university, a Master of Theology
> degree, or its equivalent, requiring at least
> three years of Greek and two of Hebrew, from a
> theological institution of recognized standing,
> and two years of graduate study, including a major
> and two minors, and a scholarly thesis showing
> original research. The Baptist Bible Institute
> has thus progressively realized the ideals of the
> founders of the institution; *namely*, to give the
> best possible training to preachers, laymen and
> women, for different types of service at home
> and abroad.[10]

Outside as well as inside the Institute family there was
much questioning as to what was the wise course for the future.
Inside there were those who feared that emphasis on the weight-
ier elements of theological education like Greek and Hebrew
would stifle the missionary passion and practical activities
of the school. Outside there were those who believed that the
Southern Baptist Convention ought to strengthen existing seminaries for the purpose of giving higher forms of theological
training and to use this school as an enlarged Bible school,
at most as a junior seminary. "Junior Seminary" meant a school
not doing graduate work, not even giving the Th.M. or B.D. degree, merely a feeder or preparatory school for real seminaries.
Such advice was often heard in the inner councils of the Southern Baptist Convention and sometimes spoken openly in state
convention speeches.

The opposition in this case should not be interpreted as
partisanship or enmity. It was mistaken judgment about two
great issues.

One of these issues was the missionary dream of winning
and training, quickly and continuously, a great number of
leaders for the half-million French-speaking people in Southern

---

[10]Catalogue for 1927-28, p. 11.

Louisiana and the hundred thousand or two hundred thousand people of Italian and Spanish extraction in Louisiana. Such great
hopes were entertained in the beginning that one "Professor of
French,"[11] Dr. L.O.F. Cotey, and one "Professor of Italian,"[11]
Reverend Lawrence Zarilli, were brought into the faculty to lead
in this work. These were good and able men, but French and Italian preachers were not won and trained fast enough to build the
school around them. These professorships disappeared after a
time as a result of the following lesson learned from experience:
missionary progress among these peoples, who were without a
background in Baptist teaching and Baptist church life would
depend upon close co-operation between the few local preachers
and the missionary hearted, well trained men and women out of
the Baptist homes and churches in Louisiana, Mississippi, and
surrounding states; moreover, the patient and persistent labor,
the wise and strong leadership of such co-operative workers could
be produced only by the thorough training of a seminary, including in many cases Greek and Hebrew.

The other great mistake of this opposition was in doubting
the possibility of a sufficiently great and rapid increase in the
number of college trained candidates for the ministry to warrant
the establishment of a third Southern Baptist Seminary at that
time. In that day there was a sea of missionary need in front
of the school, a morass of Landmark confusion about organized
co-operation behind it, and big mud-puddles of niggardly church
support in its own backyard. Moreover, not even seminary presidents of that day could dream of the nearly 3000 theological
students, not to mention religious education and music students,
in five Southern Baptist seminaries in 1954-55.

Establishment of the seminary goal in the face of these
conditions was a triumph of vision and zeal of a rare order.

II. Maintaining the Seminary Goal

Maintaining the seminary goal was more difficult than setting it up.

The first and main reason for this difficulty was financial
distress. The initial success of the seventy-five million dollar
campaign put on by Southern Baptists immediately after the First
World War brought expectation of a million dollars for the
Baptist Bible Institute. One effect was the floating of a heavy
bonded indebtedness to secure houses and apartment buildings
adjoining the Sophie-Newcomb College property for faculty and

---

[11]Catalogue for 1918-19, p. 3.

married students. When the five year program of the seventy-
five million campaign failed to live up to expectations, the
appropriations for the Institute became insufficient to pay off
that indebtedness, and it became a millstone around the neck of
the school. Finally, in 1932, under the pressure of the severe
depression existing throughout the United States, the Institute
defaulted on its bonded indebtedness. It was kept open only
because bank officials had confidence in the determination of
the President and faculty to continue in its service and in the
ability of Southern Baptists to pay eventually the whole of its
indebtedness.

This period of years 1927-32 produced uncertainty, rest-
lessness, the moving of various professors to more promising
fields, and gradual reduction of the teaching force. All tutors
and other aids were dropped. Separate lists of teachers for
the Department of Religious Education and the Department of
Sacred Music, which appeared in the 1926-27 catalogue, were
dropped; and all teachers were listed as one small faculty. The
number of full-time professors in that small faculty was gradually reduced from thirteen to ten; then, in view of the financial
crisis of 1931-32, it was drastically cut to five including the
president. These five were W.W. Hamilton, President, E.F. Haight,
John W. Shepard, J. Wash Watts, and A.E. Tibbs.[12]

These facts, however, serve to highlight an important
decision. That part of the school which the trustees and faculty determined to keep at all costs was the theological course.
Let us observe with care their line of reasoning, as given in
these words:

> The Theological Course has been made necessary by
> the demands of preachers who in most cases because
> of proximity, or because they have pastorates, or
> because they have families, must get their train-
> ing here or never be able to secure it, and the
> trustees feel that those who do come to the Bible
> Institute should receive the best we are able to
> furnish them. It would be impossible in most cases
> for these married men to resign and take their
> families elsewhere without becoming a liability.
> Here they are an asset and a positive mission force.
>
> The ministerial students are many of them pastors
> in charge of nearby churches, and they are render-
> ing most valuable service in preaching the gospel

---

[12]Catalogue for 1932-33, pp. 16,17.

in New Orleans and carrying forward the work of
our Lord Jesus in the vast mission fields near by.
The preachers are the ones who are establishing
missions, organizing congregations, strengthening
churches, presenting our denominational causes,
and lengthening the cords among the many nation-
alities in these almost foreign fields.[13]

This directive from the trustees was implemented by the
setting up of plans for the tightly dovetailed schedules of a
theological course and a minimum of Christian Training courses
which could be handled by the one small faculty that existed.
The close coordination of schedules and teaching forces, with
the warm fellowship resulting between all groups of students,
has continued until this day. Suggestions made by this author
led to his being charged with responsibility for drafting these
plans, and he has never been able since then to escape that particular responsibility. This is important merely because it has
been continuously a part of those efforts that have maintained
the seminary goal.

The seminary dream did live, and the most important step
toward realization was the lifting of standards for the theological courses. Admission standards, grading standards, library
standards, teaching hours, teaching preparation, and sabbatic
years were gradually brought toward the seminary level. For
instance, through the 1933-34 session only two years of college
work were required for admission as a candidate for the Th.M.
degree, which is now the B.D. degree. In 1934-35, right in the
midst of this long, hard pull, the prerequisite was lifted to a
B.A. degree or equivalent.

Another important step was the formation of the Southern
Baptist Inter-Seminary Council. In those years, transfer of
credit depended upon recognition by the other school involved
of the work of each teacher. In some cases it was accepted; in
some it was not. Naturally our faculty hoped to establish more
thoroughly regulated relations, at least between Southern Baptist Seminaries. With the approval of President Hamilton, this
author approached Dr. John R. Sampey, then president of the
Southern Baptist Convention in 1937. Conversations followed between the three presidents, Sampey, Scarborough, and Hamilton,
which resulted in the calling together of a group in December
1937 that organized the Conference of Seminary Faculties, now
the Inter-Seminary Council. It has continued to meet every year

---

[13]Catalogue for 1932-33, pp. 17,18.

since in order to discuss matters of mutual concern to our seminaries.   Through constant exchange of information and the
working out of agreements for reconciliation of unseemly differences, a thorough exchange of credits was brought about.
Thus it has served to help this school prepare for accreditation
in the full sense of the word.

An Outline
of Old Testament
Theology

Dr. Watts taught theology through exegesis. He read the Old Testament to feed and instruct his faith. He structured his doctrine according to that study.

Cardinal Lines of Teaching in the Old Testament is an outline of Old Testament Theology, rich in suggestion and deep in insight.

Cardinal Lines of Teaching in the Old Testament

J. Wash Watts

Propulsion of the spirit of man by the Spirit of God is a cardinal teaching of all portions of the Scriptures. In the Old Testament four great stages of this Spirit-propulsion are described. First, God's self-revelation, moving man to a faith-response, led to the making of mutual covenants between God and men. Second, the covenants, imparting to man by the aid of the Spirit assurance concerning the future, led to inspired prophecy. Third, prophecy, giving men inspired insight and understanding concerning the purposes of God for all mankind, led to Messianic hope. Fourth, Messianic hope, involving Spirit-given assurance concerning the certainty and extent of the personal aid God would give in the fight against Satan and sin, led to anticipation of the Kingdom of God on Earth.

The marvelous ballistic programs of our day furnish an illustration that applies with a peculiar force to the Old Testament picture of Spirit-propulsion. The great rockets are lifted from the ground by a limited and ingeniously compounded portion of the propellant, called "the grain." Then they are propelled into outer space by the full power of the propelling fuel. Afterwards, speed, direction, and range are regulated by regulation of the fuel power. Finally, with the power of the propellant cut gradually according to an exact design, the cone is allowed to return earthward to do its designated work at a designated spot.

Revelation, the covenants, prophecy, and the Messianic hope rise like the multiple sections of a rocket capable of transversing the heavens. Each arises out of the other or others.

Each gains impetus and velocity from spiritual powers preceding it.   Each finds fulfillment in that which follows.   Man is marvelously propelled into that spiritual realm called in the New Testament "the heavenlies in Christ Jesus."

Even in the Old Testament the outline of development takes shape as follows:

I.   Revelation Gave Rise to The Covenants

    1.   By God's Revelation of Himself as Elohim, The Transcendent and Sovereign God, Ruler of Heaven and Earth

    2.   By God's Revelation of Himself as Yahweh, The Immanent, Saving, and Covenant-Making God

    3.   By God's Revelation of Himself as The One True God, The God Whose Providential Control Guarantees Fulfillment of The Covenants

II.   The Covenants Gave Rise to Prophecy

    1.   By The Revealed Purpose of Miraculous Interventions and Unilateral Covenants

    2.   By The Covenant Yahweh Sought to Make with National Israel

    3.   By The Covenant Yahweh Actually Made with National Israel

    4.   By The Relation of Both Covenants to The Remnant of Believers

III.   Prophecy Gave Rise to Messianic Hope

    1.   By Spirit-Inspired Ecstacies That Produced Preachers and Teachers

    2.   By Truth Received Directly from God through The Mind and Heart

    3.   By Ethics Linked with Evangelistic Zeal

    4.   By Assurance That Believers will be Kept and Glorified by Yahweh Acting as Messiah

IV.   Messianic Hope Gave Rise to Visions of The Kingdom

    1.   By Previews in The Pentateuch

       (1)   Warfare Against Satan by Yahweh Himself
       (2)   'Watchcare' Over Believers by The Angel of Yahweh
       (3)   Inspiration of Faith by *El Shaddai*

(4)   The King's Claim to The Kingdom in The "Shiloh" of Genesis 49:10
(5)   The Offer of The Covenant of The Kingdom by The Eagle of The Exodus
(6)   The Glory Revealed in Fire and Cloud
(7)   The Administrator of The Kingdom, The Angel of Whom Yahweh said, "My Name Is In Him"

2.   By Crystalized Views in The Psalms

(1)   The Identification of Yahweh and The Anointed in Their Relations With The Nations
(2)   The Identification of Yahweh and Messiah in Earthly Authority

3.   By Analytical Views in The Eighth Century Prophets

(1)   The One Who Will Raise Up The Tabernacle of David
(2)   The Holy One Who Will Accomplish Redemption by Unfailing Love for His People
(3)   The Judge Who Decrees Redemptive Judgment Upon Judah and Jerusalem
(4)   The Babe of Bethlehem Who Controls Israel's History
(5)   The One Using World Judgment to Establish His Kingdom
(6)   The One Using The Restoration from Captivity to Make Israel Serve Him
(7)   The Servant Sent to Save The Servant That Failed
(8)   The Glory of Zion Who Makes Heaven His Throne and Earth His Footstool

4.   Summary Views in The Later Prophets

(1)   Yahweh, The King of Israel, Who Will Make a New Covenant
(2)   Lord Yahweh, Who Will Put His Spirit in The Hearts of The People
(3)   The Glory That Will Return to Zion
(4)   The Fountain for Sin and Uncleanness in New Jerusalem

I.   REVELATION GAVE RISE TO THE COVENANTS

1.   God's Revelation of Himself as Elohim, The Transcendent and Sovereign God, Ruler of Heavens and Earth

(1)   In the heavens and the earth

Genesis 1:1-19.   The use of Elohim only as subject of "create," not only in Genesis 1:1 but everywhere in the

Bible, declares the biblical interpretation of creation
as a supernatural act, revealing the transcendent nature
of God. The use of all other verbs in the jussive form
reveals God's use of his sovereign power to overrule all
developments in the inanimate realm of the heavens and
the earth.

(2) In the animal kingdom

Genesis 1:20-25. Creation of animal souls by Elohim
reveals his sovereignty yet more fully by showing his
power to intervene in natural processes and to implant
in a physical body capacity for learning, emotion, and
choice. The use of imperatives in dealing with the
animals reveals personal concern and influence in dir-
ecting their development.

(3) In the human soul

Genesis 1:26 - 2:3. Creation of mankind "in the image
of God," reveals a sovereignty that finds its highest
expression in the impartation of moral capacity. This
involves moral intelligence or understanding of right
and wrong in mutual relationships, mutual moral attraction or influence, and independent moral will power of
decision. The blessing upon dominion over all created
things by being endowed with capacity for a moral
dominion, yet apart from any account of man's actual
response, is an introduction to the stupendous moral
struggle related in the remainder of the Bible.

2. God's Revelation of Himself as Yahweh, The Immanent, Saving,
and Covenant-Making God

Introduction: The name Yahweh was first used by Eve after
the birth of Cain. It was first used in worship by Adam,
Eve, Seth, Enoch, and others after Cain slew Abel and violence began to spread. According to evidence furnished by
the biblical account of these developments, it appears that
the individuals named here drew upon their experiences with
God in giving him a personal name and later invoking God's
protection and blessing through the use of that name in
worship. Those experiences as evidence of God's revelation
of himself to them are outlined in the following:

(1) By endowment of man with moral faculties

Genesis 2:4-7. In Genesis 2:7a, the use of these words,
"out of the ground," in connection with the formation
of man's body distinguishes it from the "breath of life"
which God breathed into him afterwards. The breath of
life, therefore, corresponds to the soul God created in
him according to Genesis 1:27. Moreover, this soul

created in the image of God is described by what follows
as that which endowed man with moral faculties.

(2)   By instruction concerning moral responsibility

Genesis 2:8-17. In Genesis 2:9, the phrase "out of the
ground" is placed emphatically to distinguish the trees
made to grow out of the ground from those not made to
grow out of the ground. Thus the trees in the second
group are made, even as their names imply, to symbolize
moral and spiritual experience. Accordingly, the story
goes on to teach that moral responsibility, leading to
spiritual life or death, is involved in man's stewardship over possessions placed in his care by God. Thus
the Garden of Eden was an object lesson, and Yahweh was
man's teacher concerning the meaning of life.

(3)   By giving a helpmeet in moral experience

Genesis 2:18-25. In Genesis 2:19, a third use of the
phrase "out of the ground," places it emphatically. It
distinguishes all animals from the helpmeet, the helper
corresponding to Adam, which Yahweh prepared by building her out of a portion of Adam's own body. Thus Eve
is a part of mankind, created with a soul like Adam,
and endowed with equal spiritual capacity to be a helpmeet for him in moral experience.

(4)   By taking the initiative in efforts to save mankind from
moral ruin

Genesis 3:1-19. As soon as Eve and Adam were enticed
into sin, Yahweh started his search for them and the
counsel intended to show them the door of hope. In
other words, Yahweh took the initiative in salvation. In
the great judicial statement of Genesis 3:14-19 there
was nothing to close the door of hope for them. There
was a remarkable diagnosis of the effects of sin, given
in such a way to lead them back to Yahweh for saving
help.

(5)   By providences that led to the beginning of the worship
of Yahweh

Genesis 3:20 - 4:26. In each scene of Yahweh's dealing
with these first sinners there was a demonstration of
Yahweh's way with sinful men calculated to lead all who
would to turn to him in spirit and in truth. His first
act was one of kindness, as he made clothing to meet
their need, and this showed that he still cared for
them. His second act was one of discipline, as he drove
them out of the Garden of Eden. This taught that separation from God is an inevitable penalty upon all sin.
His acceptance of Abel's offering and his rejection of

Cain's taught that renewal of fellowship could come only
upon condition of faith. His reasoning with Cain and
his protection of Cain from enemies who would slay him,
though failing to win Cain, taught others the merciful
forbearance and the intense desire of Yahweh to bring
sinners back to him and to forgive them. Therefore, the
coming of a little band to worship Yahweh and to trust
him for salvation was a result of the providential
'watchcare' and the teaching of Yahweh.

3. God's Revelation of Himself as The One True God, The God
Whose Providential Control Guarantees Fulfillment of the
Covenants

(1) To Enoch and Noah

Genesis 5:22,24, 6:2,4,9,11. Corrupt thinking among men
gave occasion for this distinctive description of Yahweh.

(2) To Shem and Eber

Genesis 9:26, 10:21,25, 11:5-9. The confusion at Babel
continued for the occasion for distinction.

(3) To Abraham

Genesis 17:1,18. The covenant assurances concerning the
giving of an heir as the child of Abraham and Sarah gave
occasion for this distinction.
Genesis 18:27,30,31,32. Abraham's use of the title
"Lord" to indicate his conviction that The Angel of Yahweh was God supports the distinction.
Genesis 20:6,17. God's assurance to Abilemech that
Abraham would pray for him and he would be forgiven
supports the distinction.
Genesis 22:1,3,9. The care taken by the author of Genesis to indicate that the place where Abraham offered
Isaac was designated by The One True God, i.e. not a
place of heathen sacrifice, strongly supports the dis-
tinction.

(4) To Isaac and Jacob

Genesis 27:28,29,33,39,40, 28:21, 31:11, 32:30, 48:15,16.
By chastening and providential control. Yahweh brings
both these heirs to the promises to recognize him as The
One True God.

(5) To Judah and Joseph

Genesis 41:25,28,32, 42:18, 44:16. Both of these are led
to recognize him as The One True God, sharply distinguish
ed from the many gods of Egypt.

II. THE COVENANTS GAVE RISE TO PROPHECY

1. By Miraculous Intervention and Unilateral Covenants

   (1) The earliest theophanies

   Genesis 2:16,17. These were, according to the context, means for the spiritual development of man in the likeness of God.

   (2) Yahweh's initiative in dealing with sinners

   Genesis 4:25,26. Yahweh's discipline and concern led a little band to seek preservation of life, both physical and spiritual, from him.

   (3) Yahweh's unilateral covenant with Noah

   Genesis 6:8,9, 9:8-17. The deliverance of Noah preserved an opportunity for fulfillment of God's purposes concerning mankind. The covenant with Noah guaranteed time for this fulfillment.

   (4) Yahweh's intervention on behalf of Israel in Egypt

   Exodus 3:14, 6:2-8. Yahweh interpreted his faithfulness to the promises made to Abraham, Isaac, and Jacob as means of inspiring faith.

   (5) Yahweh's intervention at the Red Sea

   Exodus 15:6,11,13,17,18. Moses interpreted this as evidence that Yahweh is glorious in power, holiness, and loving kindness, using his miracles to promote a spiritual kingdom.

2. By the Covenant Yahweh Sought to Make with National Israel

   (1) This covenant was conditioned upon faith and obedience

   Exodus 19:5a. The literal meaning of "If you will obey my voice" is "If you will indeed harken unto me," and this described trust of faith.
   Exodus 19:5b. "And keep my commandments" describes acts of obedience.

   (2) The first blessing Yahweh offered was election of believers

   Exodus 19:5c. This covenant was described as a mutual covenant between Yahweh and those who would trust him; accordingly, all the results assured by it were spiritual blessings, the first and immediate one being that believers were Yahweh's "peculiar treasure" or elect people.

(3)   The second blessing Yahweh offered was his "kingdom of priests"

Exodus 19:6a. "And you will be" is literally "and you will become." The spiritual rule of Yahweh as King over this Kingdom is a spiritual development in the hearts of believers.

(4)   The third blessing Yahweh offered was holiness

Exodus 19:6b. "And a holy nation" is governed by the same verb as the second blessing; thus its full meaning is "and you will become a holy nation." Man's character is the climactic development in Yahweh's kingdom.

(5)   This kingdom growth includes the keeping of the Law

Exodus 20:1 - 23:19. The Law includes both the great moral principles of the Ten Commandments and the obligations of civil and ritual ordinances that vary according to changing circumstances of time and place.

(6)   This kingdom growth is assured by The Angel of Yahweh

Exodus 23:20-33. The Angel of whom Yahweh said, "My name is in him," can be no other than The Angel of Yahweh. Cf. Exodus 33:14 and Isaiah 63:9.

(7)   This kingdom growth is symbolized in the Tabernacle

Exodus 28:1 - 31:11. The priests represented the people in their approach unto God, securing a covering for sin (cf. the sin offering for atonement), communion with God (cf. the altar of incense), and holiness (cf. the mercy seat on the ark and the table of the Law in the Ark).

3.   By The Covenant Yahweh Actually Made with Israel

(1)   This covenant was conditioned upon a mere reprieve

Exodus 32:9-14, 33:1-6,12-17, 34:8-9. Yahweh had already consented to grant mercy but refused to grant forgiveness for all; Moses had moved the Tent of Meeting so that those who truly sought Yahweh should signify their seeking by going out to it; so the renewal of covenant relation was a mere pardon or temporary reprieve with warning added that sinners must face a final judgment.

(2)   This covenant added certain laws merely as commands

Exodus 34:1-27. All Israelites, believers and unbelievers, were commanded to obey but given no assurance, apart from the previous offer of a covenant, that this covenant would result in faith, obedience, and salvation.

(3) This covenant made necessary "the blessings and the curses"

Exodus 34:10c; Deuteronomy 27:11 - 28:68. The "terrible thing" that Yahweh did with national Israel at this time was to give Israel the promised land by visiting a terrible judgment upon the reprobates already there, giving at the same time a most solemn warning that he would make their plagues "wonderful" if they also turned to the abominations of these reprobates.

4. By The Relation of Both Covenants to the Remnant of Believers

(1) Protection of the nation

Isaiah 8:13,14a,16,17, 65:8-10. According to the covenant of Exodus 34, Yahweh guaranteed the settling of Israel in the land of Canaan. Yahweh's protection of Israel was continued through the judges and the kings who were anointed according to God's will. As the nation turned more and more to idolatry, withdrawal of protection was predicted by the prophets. Gradually, however, and from this time onward the attention of the prophets was concentrated upon the remnant. Explanations of various restorations of the nation to its own land show that the nation is to be preserved for the sake of the remnant.

(2) Preservation of a remnant

Amos 9:14,15; Hosea 3:4,5; Isaiah 10:20-23; Micah 4:6-8; Jeremiah 31:31-37, 33:18-26; Ezekiel 36:22-28; Daniel 9:27; Zechariah 13:1,2. According to the covenant of Exodus 19, Yahweh guaranteed both preservation and salvation to believers. The prophets described the remnant to be preserved permanently as a remnant of believers. Therefore, they are unequivocal in their assertions concerning the continued existence, the preservation, and the blessing of such a spiritual remnant out of national Israel.

(3) Separation between the godly and the wicked

Amos 9:7-10; Isaiah 65:11-16; Jeremiah 24:1-10; Ezekiel 34:20-22; Zechariah 14:20,21. The assurances given to the believing remnant out of Israel involve all that is involved in modern interpretations of "a regenerate church membership" in any true church of the Lord Jesus Christ. Yahweh says that he will make it to be so.

(4)   Cleansing and glorification of the believing remnant

Hosea 2:19,20; Isaiah 4:2-6, 28:5,6, 35:5-10; Jeremiah
30:18-22.   In accord with the preceding definitions of
the remnant of Israel, the prophets foresaw far more
than deliverance and regeneration for that remnant.
Their visions included glorification of character and
use of all members as means of extending spiritual
blessings to all peoples, as promised in the call of
Abraham.

(5)   Final Location of the believing remnant

Isaiah 11:11-16, 27:12,12, 49:22,23, 66:20; Jeremiah
32:6-15,36-42; Zechariah 12:1-10, 13:8,9.   Fulfillment
of the far reaching prophecies concerning the remnant
are linked by the prophets with the return of Israelites in the later days to their own land, with a
titanic world struggle in which only a third of them is
delivered by the personal intervention of Yahweh from
utter destruction at the hand of the nations.   At this
time, according to the word of Yahweh, the remnant will
recognize the Messiah whom they rejected and violently
cut off long before.   These words likewise locate this
believing remnant in the land of Judah and locate it
there permanently.

(6)   Inclusion of other believing remnants

Isaiah 2:1-4, 16:1-5, 45:22-25, 60:1-3, 56:6-8; Ezekiel
47:1-12; Zechariah 14:8.   Believers out of other nations
were invited by Yahweh, welcomed by Yahweh, and blessed
by Yahweh as surely as those out of Israel.   The spiritual salvation of all believers is the same.   Together
these composed a spiritual Israel within the nation of
Israel.

(7)   Inclusion of all believing remnants in the Kingdom

Hosea 11:8,9, 14:4; Isaiah 9:7, 59:20,21, 66:18-21;
Jeremiah 31:40, 33:14-18; Daniel 12:3.   As the understanding of the prophets laid hold upon the fact that
Messiah was to rule in human hearts rather than over
bodies politic, their understanding of the relations
between the remnants composing the spiritual kingdom of
Messiah clarified.   They saw these things dimly and afar
off, but they did begin to see a spiritual, universal,
everlasting kingdom in which there would be no distinction between a Jew and a Gentile.   Believing Israelites
in this kingdom would be merely a part of a great spiritual Israel composed of remnants out of all nations.
In these, in all of these, the covenant of Exodus 19
would find fulfillment.

III. PROPHECY GAVE RISE TO MESSIANIC HOPE

Four characteristic elements of true prophecy appear in the biblical record. These are as follows: (1) an *ecstatic zeal* inspired by the Spirit of God that moves a man to be a spokesman for God, (2) a *spiritual understanding* communicated by the Spirit of God directly to the spirit of a man, (3) an *evangelistic passion* that empowers a man to persuade others to accept the will of God as their standard of right and wrong, (4) a *messianic hope* that sees Yahweh as the Messiah who guarantees the safety and glory of believers.

The consistency of these four elements gives great strength to each point in the message of true prophecy. All four appear in the words of every prophet of Yahweh. It follows naturally, therefore, that no man is called a prophet of Yahweh when any one of these elements is lacking.

Thus the inspiration of the prophets of Yahweh gave rise to messianic hope. Their consciousness of guidance by the Spirit lifted them from height unto height, up to this summit of hope. They looked back on their own experiences to see in every phase evidence of the energizing and guiding influence of the Spirit. They observed that from the beginning Yahweh had intervened in the struggle of believers, now in one form or mode of being now in another, doing what was needed to assure these believers of spiritual victory over themselves and over their enemies. Accordingly, their hopes were brightened and enlarged to include the coming of Yahweh himself as a man to lead believers into fulfillment of all their hope.

1. By Spirit-Inspired Ecstacy that Produced Preachers and Teachers

    (1) Ecstacies arising out of delusion, fear, fanaticism, or desires for selfish gain produce false prophets

    I Kings 18:25-29. The frenzied cries of the worshippers of Baal were mocked by silence and they were left to despair. Here, as in all examples of Baal worship, self-stirred ecstacies produced emotional and moral excesses that led to disintegration of personality.

    (2) Ecstacy alone, even when caused by the Spirit, does not make one a prophet

    Numbers 11:25. Yahweh put the Spirit upon the seventy men appointed to aid Moses, and they "prophesied" for one day only, but they were not called prophets. The noun "prophet" is not applied to these men. The verb "prophesied" without an object, without any indication of a message delivered, a lesson taught, appears to describe mere emotional reactions. This is true wherever it appears in this way. Those who are said to have prophesied in this way are never called prophets of Yahweh. The fact that they were believers in Yahweh is not denied, but prophecy reflects an integration of faith with other great spiritual developments.

I Samuel 19:22-24. Saul is another example. In this instance, the Spirit came upon him in a way to prevent his doing injury to David. At various times the Spirit came upon him in a way to stir him up for battle. But, he is never called a prophet.

(3)   In addition to Spirit-Inspired ecstacy or holy zeal, the experience of all true prophets included messages communicated by the Spirit, ethics preached with evangelistic zeal, and hope based on Yahweh as Messiah.

Genesis 5:22,24; Hebrews 11:5,6; Jude 14-16. Enoch walked with God; in a day when men all around him were corrupt no one charged him with evil; he was "well-pleasing unto God"; his message is recorded in Jude; accordingly, we may list him as the first prophet.

Genesis 6:8,9; Hebrews 11:7; II Peter 2:5. Noah was "a righteous man"; Yahweh spoke to Noah and used him to predict and to interpret the Flood; so Peter called him "a preacher of righteousness."

Genesis 12:1-3, 17:4-8, 20:7; Hebrews 11:8-10. Abraham received the promises concerning a promised land, a promised heir, and a promised blessing in his call, and he inculcated these promises in the heart of Isaac. He received from Yahweh detailed and marvelous information about his posterity as a part of the covenant, and he passed it on to succeeding generations. Therefore, God himself called Abraham a prophet.

Exodus 6:2-8, 20:18-20; Deuteronomy 18:15-19. Moses was used to apply the covenant with Abraham to Israel as a nation. Through him the Law and the worship associated with the national covenant was received and explained to the people. Through him was brought the great assurance of a prophet like unto him who would guarantee fulfillment of this covenant. Thus he is presented as one of the greatest of the prophets.

2.   By Truth Received Directly from God Through the Mind and the Heart

(1)   Messages from God received through another person, information received through impersonal means of revelation, or wisdom acquired by mere human learning

and reason are never called prophecy.

Exodus 4:14-16, 7:1. Aaron's messages were second hand, received through Moses. He is called Moses' prophet, but not Yahweh's prophet.

Numbers 27:21. Eleazar, as the ordained priest, used the Urim (with the Thummim probably) as ordained means of securing for Joshua information concerning God's will. Their use is thought to have involved chances in the casting of lots. Whatever the nature of the means and the results, they were controlled and used by Yahweh. Personal understanding and interpretation, however, were not involved. The fact is significant, therefore, that no priest depending upon the Urim and the Thummim for revelation of information was ever called a prophet.

(2) Spiritual understanding imparted by the Spirit but not expressed in open and effective persuasion of others to fear God is not prophecy.

I Kings 19:18. The seven thousand in Elijah's day who had not bowed the knee to Baal were secret believers. They knew the truth about Yahweh. They were taught by the Spirit and remained faithful in times of persecution. They did not, however, stand openly with Elijah to declare the Truth, and they were not prophets.

(3) In addition to inspired zeal, understanding, and hope, a prophet's heart was moved by a passion to preach and to win others in the name of Yahweh.

II Kings 2:4-12. Elijah was told by Yahweh at Sinai to anoint Elisha as his successor. He did so immediately after that. Elisha left home and family to accompany him and minister to him. Still Elijah was the prophet and Elisha his servant. Then, on the day set for Elijah's translation, Elisha refused to be left behind, either at Gilgal or at Bethel or at Jericho or at the Jordan. Beyond Jordan and upon request he expressed the great longing of his soul to receive a double portion of the spirit of Elijah. Elijah gave assurance that his request would be granted if he should see him when taken from him. So he did, and picking up the mantle of Elijah he returned to his people, speaking out for God wherever there was occasion. Thus he became his master's successor in the prophetic office.

3. By Evangelistic Passion to Win Men for God

(1) Prediction not intended or received as persuasion to trust God pushes the speaker deeper and deeper into the abominations of sin.

Numbers 24:17-19. Balaam was forced by Yahweh (cf.
Numbers 23:20,21, 24:1,2,10-14) to utter this prophecy
concerning the future "star out of Jacob." Nevertheless, he did not love Yahweh. He loved "the hire of
wrongdoing" (II Peter 2:15). He was morally rotten, for
he remained among the Midianites who seductively induced
Israel into the abominations committed at Shittim (Cf.
Numbers 25:1-18; Revelation 2:14), and he died with
them under the curse of God (Cf. Numbers 27:18). Balaam
was not a prophet of Yahweh but a soothsayer (Cf.
Numbers 23:23; Joshua 13:22).

(2)   Even great wisdom that lacks an evangelistic note is not
      prophecy

      Proverbs 1--31. Solomon acquired wisdom above all
      others in his day. He wrote proverbs containing
      inspired interpretation of ethical principles. Proverbs
      8:22-31 is attributed to him, and that passage portrays
      Wisdom in the abstract with a perfection fulfilled only
      in Jesus. Yet one great essential of prophecy is
      lacking. The zeal, the passion, the preaching that make
      a teacher of ethics to be an evangelist are not found
      in Solomon's life or writings. In all of Proverbs
      there is nothing about the impassioned determination of
      Yahweh to redeem, to preserve, and to honor believing
      sinners. There is *much* about the kindness men may show
      to men, *nothing* about the loving-kindness of Yahweh
      which makes a gospel theme in the prophets. *And Solomon
      is not called a prophet.*

(3)   All true prophecy makes the song of redemption to be the
      flower that springs in beauty from its inspiration, its
      teaching, and its ethics.

      Psalms 16:10, 18:2, 43--50, 51:13; Acts 2:29-36, 13:22,
      23,32-37. David is called a prophet by Peter because
      David's prediction concerning the preservation of his
      soul in the life after death is seen as fulfilled
      through Jesus, the son of David, whom God raised from
      the dead. Paul likewise saw David's words fulfilled
      through Christ. We in turn look for fulfillment of
      David's prophecy concerning the establishment of his
      kingdom as a universal kingdom through Jesus his son
      and his savior. These scriptures bear witness, there-
      fore, to his inspiration, his teaching, and his
      prediction. As for his evangelism, this word speaks
      eloquently, "Then will I teach transgressors thy ways,
      and sinners shall be converted unto thee." The fact
      that God's providence lifted David out of a period of
      terrible confusion, due to exceedingly serious sin, made
      his testimony and his influence afterwards to be a

constant praise of Yahweh's unfailing love. He adds
many impassioned pleas to sinners to trust Yahweh and
accept his righteousness. As surely as Proverbs lacks
this song of redemption, so Psalms is filled with it.

4.   By Messianic Hope in Yahweh as the Messiah

   (1)   All hope apart from Yahweh is hopeless

      Isaiah 7:9b, 8:20. For all who would not believe, all
      those unwilling to accept the assurance contained in the
      law and the testimony, there is "a night without a
      morning."

   (2)   Faith in Yahweh that lacks hope based on expectation of
         his coming as messiah is not prophecy.

      Ezra 7:1-10. Ezra was a Spirit-led and wise teacher.
      He lived an exemplary life and he pleaded with the
      people to do the same. There was, however, no word in
      his message about the coming of Yahweh as Messiah. He
      is called "a ready scribe" but not a prophet.

      Ecclesiastes 1--12. The author of Ecclesiastes,
      whoever he was, was wise in many ways. Having turned
      his back upon earthly pleasures, intellectual shrewd-
      ness, and mere human achievement, he recognized the
      fear of God as the beginning of wisdom. That reverence
      of Yahweh was to him the chief thing, the fountainhead
      of wisdom. Accordingly, he anticipated the return of
      the spirit of man to God who gave it, and he pleaded
      fervently with his fellows that they remember their
      creator in the days of their youth. Nevertheless, even
      as in the words of Solomon, there was no vision and no
      preaching of a personal Messiah. And, he is not called
      a prophet.

   (3)   Those called prophets of Yahweh anchored their
         assurance concerning their inspiration, their under-
         standing, and their preaching to the hope in a personal
         messiah, to Yahweh as the Messiah.

      Isaiah 7:14; Micah 5:2. When Isaiah used the name
      Immanuel, God-With-Us, as a name for the future ruler
      of Judah, and when Micah described the ruler to be born
      in Bethlehem as "one whose goings forth are from of
      old," both were speaking of Yahweh.

      Isaiah 9:6,7; Micah 7:7, 18-20; Jeremiah 23:5,6;
      Ezekiel 24:23,24; Daniel 7:13,14; Zechariah 6:12,13,
      14:9; Malachi 3:1. In addition to using personal names
      and descriptions for Messiah, these prophets predicted
      personal roles, personal influences, and personal
      triumphs for Messiah. In doing so they credited to him
      the attributes of deity. To them the Messiah expected

by their spiritual fathers became the unique God-man,
The Messiah.   Thus to a sublime height of hope prophecy
lifted them.

IV.   MESSIANIC HOPE GAVE RISE TO VISIONS OF THE KINGDOM

1. By Previews in The Pentateuch

   (1) Warfare Against Satan by Yahweh Himself
      Introduction: The "I" of Genesis 3:15
      A propaganda warfare in Yahweh's declaration of the
         "cursed" character of Satan. Genesis 3:14a
      A psychological warfare in Yahweh's prediction of the
         ultimate and utter defeat of Satan. Genesis 3:14b
      A personal warfare in Yahweh's promise to inspire
         the will of Eve and her seed to fight Satan.
         Genesis 3:15

   (2) 'Watchcare' Over Believers by The Angel of Yahweh
      His protection of an ignorant believer. Genesis 16:7-14
      His preservation of a weak believer. Genesis 19:29
      His perfection of the faith of Abraham. Genesis
         22:16-18
      His aid in perpetuating the line of believers.
         Genesis 24:7

   (3) Inspiration of Faith by *El Shaddai*
      His control of nature to fulfill his promises.
         Genesis 17:2
      His control of history to fulfill his covenants.
         Genesis 17:4-8
      His control of the inheritance of Abraham's blessing--
        By the faith that made Isaac the "only son"
          of Abraham . . . Genesis 17:19, 22:2,16
        By the faith that made Isaac bless Jacob rather
          than Esau . . . Genesis 27:33
        By the faith that warranted the scepter of Judah and
          the strength of Joseph. Genesis 49:10,24

   (4) The King's Claim to The Kingdom in The "Shiloh" of
         Genesis 49:10
      This claim locates the Kingdom in the hearts of men.
         Genesis 49:4,6,9,15,26
      This claim reveals a progressive possession of the
         Kingdom. Genesis 49:17,18
      This claim predicts a full possession in the latter days.
         Genesis 49:1

   (5) The Offer of The Covenant of The Kingdom of The Eagle
         of The Exodus

Introduction: The eagle of Exodus 19:4b
He called the people of Israel to Sinai, or
He pushed the little eagles out of the nest.
   Exodus 19:4a
He delivered the people of Israel at the Red Sea, or
He bore the little eagles on his wings. Exodus 19:4b,c
He spoke the offer of the covenant at Sinai, or
He showed the little eagles how to fly. Exodus 19:5,6

(6) The Glory Revealed in Fire and Cloud

Yahweh used the cloud to make it possible for men to see
   God in a limitation of his glory. Exodus 24:9-11
Yahweh used the degrees of fiery brightness to make
   possible the gradual approach of believers to his
   glory. Exodus 33:7
Yahweh used the filling of the Tabernacle by his glory
   to signify his final meeting with believers in the
   Holy of Holies. Exodus 40:17-34

(7) The Administrator of The Kingdom, The Angel of Whom
Yahweh Said, "My Name Is In Him"

He possesses the prerogative of forgiving sin.
   Exodus 23:20,21
He will inflict the curses on those who hate the Lord.
   Exodus 20:5; Deuteronomy 27:15-26, 28:15-68
He will bring the blessings on those who love the Lord.
   Exodus 20:6; Deuteronomy 28:1-14
He will bring, after the curses and the blessings,
   restoration and fullness of blessing to those who
   return unto the Lord. Deuteronomy 4:25-31, 30:1-10

2. By Crystallized Views in The Psalms

Introduction: Indirect messianic prophecies, as in
   Ps. 18:43,50 and 72:8-11, 17-18, paved the way for
   the messianic person of Ps. 2 and Ps. 110.

(1) The Identification of Yahweh and The Anointed in Their
Relations With the Nations

a. In their struggle against the nations. Ps. 2:1-3
b. In their establishment of Zion despite the nations.
   Ps. 2:4-6
c. In their possession of the place of the nations.
   Ps. 7--9
d. In their receiving of remnants out of the nations.
   Ps. 10--12

(2) The Identification of Yahweh and Messiah in Earthly
Authority

Introduction: In Psalm 110a, Yahweh speaks from his
   throne to the one David calls "my Lord" and tells him

to sit on his right hand. Thus they are identified
as a king and his appointed premier and identified in
the exercise of authority in the Kingdom. Jesus
cited this passage as evidence of his authority as
Messiah to cleanse the temple of Yahweh (Cf.
Matt. 21:23-27, 22:41-45).

    a.   While the conquest of enemies proceeds. Ps. 110:1
    b.   With extension from Jerusalem as a center.
        Ps. 110:2
    c.   With support by an army of volunteers. Ps. 110:3
    d.   Characterized by the rule of a priest-king.
        Ps. 110:4
    e.   Warranting recognition of the one "at thy right
        hand" as "The Lord." Ps. 110:5
    f.   Leading to final victory over all earthly powers.
        Ps. 110:6
    g.   Leading to victory after a desperate struggle.
        Ps. 110:7

Con. "All authority hath been given unto me . . ." Mt. 28:18

3. By Analytical Views in the Eighth Century Prophets

    (1)   The One Who Will Raise Up The Tabernacle of David

        a.   In which will be no favoritism. Amos 9:7
        b.   In which will be a remnant of Jacob. Amos 9:8
        c.   In which will remain only those tested and proved.
           Amos 9:9,10
        d.   Which will be built as in the days of old. Amos 9:11
        e.   Which will contain remnants out of the nations.
           Amos 9:12
        f.   Which will enjoy peace and prosperity. Amos 9:13,14
        g.   Which will no more be plucked up. Amos 9:15

    (2)   The Holy One Who Will Accomplish Redemption by Unfailing
        Love for His People

        a.   Who loved them when Israel was a child.
           Hosea 11:1-4
        b.   Who refuses to give them up, despite sins that bring
           on the exile. Hosea 11:5-11
        c.   Who will correct them as their father Jacob was
           corrected. Hosea 11:12--12:6
        d.   Who will send prophets to condemn their deceitful-
           ness. Hosea 12:7-14
        e.   Who will visit the fierce wrath of God upon their
           idolatry. Hosea 13:1-8
        f.   Who is determined, nevertheless, to redeem them
           from death and Sheol. Hosea 13:9-14
        g.   Who will heal their backsliding and love them
           freely. Hosea 13:15--14:9

(3) The Judge Who Decrees Redemptive Judgment Upon Judah
     and Jerusalem

   a. By an Invitation that Cuts Two Ways Like a Two-edged
       Sword
       The invitation opens the possibility of forgiveness
           for scarlet sins, with the result depending upon
           the human response. Isaiah 1:18
       The invitation assures the blessing of those who
           become willing and shall harken. Isaiah 1:19
       The invitation assures the destruction of those who
           remain unwilling and shall rebel. Isaiah 1:20

   b. By a Prediction that the Glory will Return and Abide
       in Zion
       The glory will become the teacher of the nations by
           being both the branch of Yahweh and the fruit of
           the land. Isaiah 2:1-4, 4:2
       The glory will wash and purge the remnant by elimi-
           nation of pride. Isaiah 2:5--4:1, 4:3,4
       The glory will sanctify and protect the remnant by
           creating again the evidences of the divine
           presence over its homes and its assembly.
           Isaiah 4:5,6

   c. The Owner Who Will Prove His Righteousness by
       Condemning the Vineyard for Unfruitfulness
       Who gave it every care necessary to assure the
           expectation of fruit-bearing. Isaiah 5:1,2
       Who is forced by its unfruitfulness to withdraw his
           care and to permit trampling by invaders.
           Isaiah 5:3-7
       Who declares its woes as a justification of his
           righteousness. Isaiah 5:16

   d. The Lord of the Whole Earth Who Will Make the
       Prophet's Ministry a Test of Judah's Guilt
       Who admits his own failure hitherto to cure the
           spiritual blindness of Judah. Isaiah 6:9
           (A cohortative of acquiescence signifies this
           admission.)
       Who decrees that the prophet's ministry be used to
           confirm this spiritual blindness. Isaiah 6:10
       Who pronounces a sentence--
           That the land be utterly wasted.--Isaiah 6:11
           That the people be removed far away.--Isaiah 6:12
           That any surviving remnant in the land be
               destroyed.--Isaiah 6:13

   e. Immanuel, The One to Cut and to Continue The Line of
       David
       As the supremely wonderful sign offered to inspire

the faith of Ahaz, he was anticipated as the
great divine aid of believers, Messiah. Isaiah
7:10,11

As the sign rejected by Ahaz but given nevertheless
by Yahweh, he was anticipated as the divine
judgment that would bring to an end the line of
David through Solomon. Isaiah 7:12,13

As the God-man to be born of a virgin daughter of
David, he was anticipated both as Yahweh coming
in human form to save believers and as Yahweh
coming in wrath to condemn unbelievers . . . .
Isaiah 7:14

f. The Prince of Peace to Establish and to Uphold The
Throne of David

As the rule of God in the hearts of men, he will
establish it:

By a miraculous counsel that will make this rule
a miracle of God and a counsel (a persuasion)
of man; Isaiah 9:6

By the might of God that will make this rule the
rule of a mighty man or hero and of a being
who is God; Isaiah 9:6

By an everlasting fatherhood that will manifest
the immediate care of a human father and the
eternal character that belongs only to God;
Isaiah 9:6

By an administration of peace that will rule like
a human prince and also as the giver of that
peace which is the supreme gift of God.
Isaiah 9:6

As the ruler of the Kingdom of God on earth, he will
uphold it:

By a peace that will not end.--Isaiah 9:7

By justice and righteousness for evermore.--
Isaiah 9:7

By the zeal of Yahweh of hosts.--Isaiah 9:7

g. The Holy One Who Will Finally Establish Himself as
The God of The People of Israel

As the shoot to come out of the stock of David.
Isaiah 11:1

As the one upon whom shall rest the Spirit of Yahweh.
Isaiah 11:2

As the righteous judge who will protect the poor and
needy of the earth. Isaiah 11:3-5

As the little child that shall lead the beasts into
ways of peace. Isaiah 11:6-9

As the ensign unto whom the nations shall seek.
Isaiah 11:10

As the one who shall use the nations to restore

Israel, remove the strife between Ephraim and
Judah, and make the remnant victorious. Isaiah
11:11-16

As Yahweh of whom the saved ones shall sing, "Behold,
God is my salvation." Isaiah 12:1-6

(4) The Babe of Bethlehem Who Controls Israel's History

a. Who will be born in time to come, yet whose "goings
forth" (earthly activities) were "from of old, from
everlasting." Micah 5:2

b. Who will give up Israel, "until the time that she
(Zion) who travaileth hath brought forth." Micah
5:3

c. Who shall feed his flock in the strength of Yahweh
and make them to abide. Micah 5:4

d. Who shall deliver his people from the Assyrian.
Micah 5:5,6

e. Who shall make the remnant a marvelous work of
Yahweh, as refreshing as dew on grass and as mighty
as a lion among the beasts. Micah 5:7-9

f. Who shall cut off militarism from the midst of his
people. Micah 5:12-14

g. Who shall cut off idolatry from his people. Micah
5:12-14

(5) The One Using World Judgment to Establish His Kingdom

a. Who shall reduce all nations to remnants. Isaiah
24:13

b. Who shall thus bring Israel into the dust as a
means of accomplishing the forgiveness of Jacob.
Isaiah 27:9

c. Who shall use this judgment to make himself a crown
of glory to the residue of his people. Isaiah 28:5

d. Who shall preserve the city of David through all of
this as Ariel, the (altar) hearth of God, whose
sacred testimony to the covenant will never be
allowed to remain permanently unanswered and
unfulfilled. Isaiah 29:21,22,23, 30:18-33, 31:4-9

e. Who shall use all this to establish Zion as a Kingdom where rulers are a blessing, where citizens
serve their fellows, and where Yahweh himself is
king. Isaiah 32:1-8, 33:5, 17-24

f. Who shall use all this to devote to destruction the
nations, with Edom the people of his curse as

typical of them. Isaiah 34:1-5

g. Who shall use all this to bring back the redeemed
to Zion, the Kingdom where his glory is revealed.
Isaiah 35:1-10

(6) The One Using The Restoration from Captivity to Make
Israel Serve Him

Introduction: The voice proclaiming restoration and
revelation of Yahweh's glory. Isaiah 40:3-5

a. The One delivering Israel, his servant, that Israel
may learn to glory in the Holy One of Israel.
Isaiah 41:8-16

b. The One who called his servant in righteousness that
he might hold onto him, preserve him, and give him
to be a light to the Gentiles. Isaiah 42:6-8

c. The One who will open the blind eyes of his servant
to see that he has preserved and shall continue to
preserve Israel from the nations in order that his
servant may provide witnesses to the salvation of
Yahweh the King. Isaiah 43:8-13

d. The one who will do all this to prove that Yahweh,
the king of Israel and his redeemer, is God and he
alone, that he alone can save. Isaiah 44:1,2,6-8,21,
22, 45:1-7

e. The one who shall save Israel with an everlasting
salvation that remnants out of all nations,
including "all the seed of Israel," may see in him
a universal salvation. Isaiah 45:17-19,22-25

f. The One who will take vengeance on Babylon in order
to bring his salvation near to the remnant of Israel.
Isaiah 46:3,13, 47:1-4

g. The One who declared these things before they
happened in order to prevent false Israelites saying
later, "Mine idol hath done them," and to inspire
true Israelites to sing, "Yahweh hath redeemed his
servant Jacob." Isaiah 48:1-5, 17-22

(7) The Servant Sent to Save the Servant That Failed

Introduction: the first servant's confession of failure
appears in Isaiah 49:4; the second servant's
commission appears in Isaiah 49:5,6

a. Who will solve the problem of Israel's failure by
suffering contempt and abhorrence as a means of
proving the faithfulness of Yahweh to his choice of
Israel. Isaiah 49:7

   b. Who will solve the problem of Zion's fear that
       Yahweh has forsaken her by calling upon the nations
       to restore to Zion her children. Isaiah 49:22,23,26

   c. Who will solve the problem of Israel's failure to
       respond to Yahweh's efforts to save by using the
       tongue of an inspired teacher, able to sustain with
       words him that is weary. Isaiah 50:4

   d. Who will solve the problem of Zion's cry for
       intercession by Yahweh with the command that Zion
       clothe herself with strength by accepting the
       wisdom to be revealed in Yahweh's sacrifice of
       himself as an atonement for his people's sin.
       Isaiah 51:9,17, 52:1,13--53:12

   e. Who will solve the problem of Zions' childlessness,
       widowhood, and oppression by a free gift of
       salvation that will bring believers out of the
       nations as well as from among the outcasts of
       Israel, with all of whom Yahweh will make an
       everlasting covenant, even the sure mercies of
       David. Isaiah 54:1,4,14, 55:1-3, 56:6-8

   f. Who will solve the problem of moral delinquency
       among blind watchmen, greedy shepherds and idola-
       trous people by a spiritual revival that will bring
       the high and lofty One that inhabits eternity to
       dwell with the humble and the contrite of heart.
       Isaiah 56:10,11, 57:5,14,15

   g. Who will solve the problem of religious formalism
       which substitutes strife for service, self-will for
       God's will, and violence for justice by the inter-
       cession of Yahweh himself as a kinsman-redeemer who
       visits vengeance on his enemies, brings redemption
       to the repentant, and perpetuates the covenant.
       Isaiah 58:4-7,13-14, 59:7,8, 15a-21

(8) The Glory of Zion Who Makes Heaven His Throne and Earth
     His Footstool

     Introduction: Isaiah 60:1,19, 66:1

   a. Who will be glorified by imparting the glory of his
       character to all who dwell in Zion. Isaiah 60:1-3,
       9,14,19-21

   b. Who will bring glory by preaching to the poor and
       making them priests of Yahweh, whom men out of the
       nations will call "Ministers of our God." Isaiah
       61:1,6,9,11

   c. Who will be the glory of salvation to Zion by giving
       her a new name, Hephzibah (My delight is in her) in

the land of Beulah (Married One), because her people
are the redeemed of Yahweh and she is One-Sought-Out.
Isaiah 62:1,4,12

d. Who will manifest his glory by inflicting a
    righteous vengeance on his enemies and delivering
    thereby the redeemed as in the days of old. Isaiah
    63:1-4,7-9

e. Who has refused for the sake of the remnant to let
    the nation of Israel be destroyed, as a cluster of
    grapes with a blessing in it, and who will bring out
    of it a seed to inherit his mountains and to dwell
    there. Isaiah 65:8-9

f. Who will create a new earth and a new heavens,
    creating Jerusalem a rejoicing and her people a joy,
    blessed with old age, prosperity, and peace; like-
    wise, creating new heavenlies wherein the old
    heavenlies with a temple made with hands and animal
    sacrifices shall have passed away and the condition
    for receiving the King's look of favor will be a
    poor and a contrite heart. Isaiah 65:17-25, 66:1-2

g. Who shall bring Zion to her appointed glory through
    the travail of repentance, with both Israelites and
    Gentiles serving as her priests, and with a people
    enjoying eternal life that will make other men, dead
    in trespasses and sins, an abhorrence to them,
    because those men will be doomed to an unending
    punishment. Isaiah 66:7-9,18-21,23-24

4. Summary Views in the Later Prophets

    (1) Yahweh, the King of Israel, who will make a New Covenant

         Introduction: the identification of Yahweh with the
         King, the branch of Righteousness. Jeremiah 30:9,
         33:15-17

         a. He promises to restore Israel and Judah from
             captivity. Jeremiah 30:3,11

         b. He promises to be the God of all the families of
             Israel, making a new, spiritual, and everlasting
             covenant with them. Jeremiah 31:1,31,33,36

         c. He promises to settle them in their own land as a
             united people. Jeremiah 32:39

         d. He promises to be a branch of Righteousness, execut-
             ing justice and righteousness in the land, and he
             takes an oath to affirm the fulfillment of his
             promise. Jeremiah 33:15,19-26

(2) Lord Yahweh, Who Will Put His Spirit in the Hearts of the People

Introduction: emphasis on "my Spirit" in Ezekiel 36:27

a. He swears to pour out his wrath upon the nations which claim the land of Israel for themselves. Ezekiel 36:7

b. He promises to bless Israel in that land more than ever before and to prevent forever afterward their being cast out. Ezekiel 36:11,15

c. He explains that he dispossessed Israel in order to vindicate his name, but even in captivity Israel continues to profane his name because the nations see the sinful, disgraced Israel as his people. Ezekiel 36:18,20

d. He explains furthermore that, as means of vindicating his name, he shall do the following:

(a) bring Israel back to the land; Ezekiel 36:24
(b) give them new hearts; Ezekiel 36:26
(c) put his Spirit in their hearts; Ezekiel 36:27
(d) make them truly his people; Ezekiel 36:28
(e) make their land, after their cleansing, to be like the garden of Eden; Ezekiel 36:35
(f) make the nations round about to know that he, Yahweh, promised it and did it; Ezekiel 36:36
(g) make Israel to seek his aid and to know that he is Yahweh; Ezekiel 36:37,38

(3) The Glory that Will Return to Zion

Introduction: The Glory seen coming "from the way of the east" and entering the courts of the house of Yahweh by way of the East Gate was the same Glory seen reigning over the Jewish captives in Babylonia, by the River Chebar (cf. Ezekiel 1:26-28 and 43:2,3). It was also the same seen departing from the Holy of Holies by way of the threshold of the Temple, the East Gate of its courts, and the Mount of Olives (cf. Ezekiel 8:4, 9:3. 10:18,19, 11:23 and 43:3). Recognition of the Glory of a person appears in these words, "his voice was as the sound of many waters," and the same statement appears in the Revelation 1:15 as a description of the Lord Jesus Christ as he appeared to John on Patmos. Ezekiel saw the Glory returning in the same way it departed. Jesus followed this way at the time of his ascension, and both Zephaniah 14:4 and Acts 1:11 refer to it as the way for his return.

a. He will return to dwell in the midst of his people forever setting up his throne in the place of worship, the center of his spiritual reign. Ezekiel 43:7,9

b. He will return to bring the presence of Yahweh into their midst and to remain there. Ezekiel 44:1-3

c. He will return to sanctify his people and prevent the house of Israel to continue bringing the ungodly into the house of Yahweh. Ezekiel 44:5-8

d. He will return to sanctify the priesthood in service and life and teaching. Ezekiel 44:9ff

e. He will return to sanctify the princes in administering justice, in making offerings for their sins, even the sins of "the prince," the prince reigning over the political life of the people, providing for the various offerings including a sin-offering, and for inheritances due his sons and servants. Ezekiel 45:9,22, 46:12,15,16

f. He will return that healing waters may flow from the house of Yahweh, even from its altar, the place of sacrifice, becoming deeper and deeper, producing food and healing wherever they go. Ezekiel 47:1,5, 9,12

g. He returns to restore the tribes of Israel to their lands with the sanctuary in the center. Ezekiel 47:14, 48:8,35

(4) The Fountain for Sin and Uncleanness in New Jerusalem

Introduction: evidences of correlation between all events foreseen in Zechariah 12--14

a. The fountain will be opened in that day when Yahweh intervenes to deliver a remnant of Judah from annihilation by its enemies out of the nations. Zechariah 12:3,8

b. The fountain will be opened when Yahweh shall pour upon the house of David and the inhabitants of Jerusalem the spirit of conciliation and of supplication. Zechariah 12:10a

c. The fountain will be opened when those who rejected Messiah at his first coming look unto him whom they pierced. Zechariah 12:10b

d. The fountain will be opened when the people shall repent, with a repentance exceeding all that has occurred in the nation's history,--repent that awful shame visited upon Messiah by their rejection of him, their God, their Savior. Zechariah 12:10c-14

e. The opening of the fountain shall remove the spirit of false prophecy from the land. Zechariah 13:2

f. The opening of the fountain shall be accompanied by the deliverance of a third part of the people from their enemies and the spiritual conversion of them by their acceptance of Yahweh as their God. Zechariah 13:8,9

g. The opening of the fountain shall be accompanied by the return of the Glory to the Mount of Olives. Zechariah 14:4

h. The opening of the fountain shall be accompanied by a miraculous deliverance of the believing remnant. Zechariah 14:5-7

i. The opening of the fountain shall be accompanied by the going out of living waters from Jerusalem eastward and westward, summer and winter. Zechariah 14:8

j. The opening of the fountain shall be accompanied by the reign of Yahweh over all the earth and the recognition of Yahweh as one and his name as one. Zechariah 14:9

(5) The Keeper of The Book of Life

Introduction: the figure "book of life," as God's record of all who trust in Messiah for salvation, ties together the following Old Testament and New Testament passages, and it reveals the Messiah as the one who determines the eternal destiny of all mankind.

a. The one like unto a son of man to whom is given prerogatives and honors due to deity, even the dominion and glory in a kingdom that is universal and everlasting. Daniel 7:10,13,14

b. The rejected Messiah whose death is made to be ground of atonement for the sins of his people and the means whereby he shall make a covenant to prevail for the believing remnant, "the many" of Isaiah 53:12 and Daniel 9:27. Daniel 9:24-27

c. The man with the voice of a multitude who assures Daniel that the indignation of God against his people will be brought to a glorious end at End-Time for the remnant of Daniel's people, even those written in the book. Daniel 10:6,14, 12:1-4

d. The lamb that had been slain, who is declared worthy to receive worship due to God alone. The

Revelation 4:8-11, 5:11-17

e. The one worthy to open the seals of the book because
    of these crowning achievements in the establishment
    of his kingdom:
    Purchasing unto God with his blood men out of
        every tribe, tongue, people, and nation. The
        Revelation 5:9
    Making them a kingdom of priests. The Revelation
        5:10a
    Making them to reign on earth. The Revelation
        5:10b

f. The judge on the great white throne, who will
    administer final judgment for all who ever lived
    according to the book. The Revelation 20:11-15

g. God himself on the throne of the New Jerusalem, who
    admits only those written in the Lamb's Book of
    Life, and who makes those who serve him to reign
    for ever and ever. The Revelation 21:2,3,6,27,
    22:1-5

Glimpses of God
in Genesis

Dr. Watts delighted to teach the Book of Genesis. Familiar stories yielded gems of doctrine through his instruction.

Glimpses of God in Genesis is an enlarged and reworked form of these lectures. In 1957 a first form of them covered the first eleven chapters of Genesis and was produced in mimeographed form for the use of the Seminary Extension Department, Jackson, Mississippi, which graciously granted permission for reproduction.

Glimpses of God in Genesis

J. Wash Watts

1. GLIMPSES OF GOD AS YAHWEH

Shared by Adam and Eve

Introduction: God is Called Yahweh God, and He Deals with Man as an Individual

In Genesis 2:4-25 three glimpses of God appear, and in each case something he made out of the ground is closely associated with something not made out of the ground. In Genesis 2:7, it is man's body and spiritual life that are thus distinguished. In Genesis 2:9, it is trees made to satisfy man's physical needs and those describing his spiritual and moral experience. In Genesis 2:19ff., it is animals and Adam.

The close association of material with spiritual elements in each case may provide an explanation of the heading "Generations of The Heavens and The Earth." The material or physical is made in each case to furnish occasion or stimulus for exercise of spiritual faculties. Thus the physical universe, which is "the heavens and the earth" of these early chapters of Genesis, furnishes a stimulating environment in which all the generations occur.

Moreover these associations of the physical and spiritual give glimpses of God that are highly significant. Yahweh God breathed into man's body the breath of life and thereby endowed him with the faculties for moral discernment. Yahweh God planted the Garden of Eden and made man keeper of it, giving instruction in the use of his spiritual faculties. Yahweh God sought for man a helpmeet and finally presented to him Eve as the finest possible aid in the use of the spiritual faculties. The use of the name "Yahweh God" is quite deliberately and purposely related to these matters. Thus we are given three very significant glimpses of God. To these we shall now devote our attention.

1. Yahweh Breathed into Man's Body the Breath of Life, the Spiritual Faculties that Made Him a Man

"Formed man of the dust of the ground" (Gen. 2:7a) refers to the development of man's body. The verb "formed" describes development. Also the phrase "of the dust" describes those material elements found in a human body when it is analyzed in a chemical laboratory. We are told that they are approximately as follows: oxygen, 65%; carbon, 18%; hydrogen, 10%; nitrogen, 3%; calcium, 1.5%; phosphorus, 1%; potassium, .35%; sulphur, .25%; sodium, .15%; chlorine, .15%; magnesium, .05%; iron, .004%; and iodine, .00004%. These facts help us to understand the statement made later, " . . . for dust you are, and unto dust you shall return" (Gen. 3:19).

The action of the verb "formed" is progressive. The verb might well be translated "proceeded to form," but the length of time covered by that development is not indicated in any way.

It is definitely said that God formed this body, not that it developed by mere chance. The treatment is very brief. These facts combined with the extensive treatment of spiritual development that follows immediately makes it clear that the Bible is interested supremely in man's spiritual nature. Whatever may have been the facts concerning the time or nature of the body's formation, those facts are insignificant as compared with the facts concerning man's spiritual being.

"Breathed into his nostrils breath of life" (Gen. 2:7b) indicates that the source of the breath of life was in God, not in the ground, or in the flesh formed out of the dust of the ground. Spirit and flesh are distinguished here in the same way they are distinguished in the introduction. The inbreathing of the spirit, therefore, was the act of creation wherein God acted alone and apart from all material forces.

"Breath of life" gives a fresh and soul-stirring vision of the wonders involved in God's creation of the human soul. The word "life" is in the plural, signifying the unlimited possibilities for development of this soul. There is no occasion in this context for thinking that this plural may describe several different lives. Hebrew plurals are frequently used to describe fullness, completeness, plenitude. The word "God" in Hebrew is a plural of this kind. It is used regularly with singular verbs; so it cannot be construed as a plurality. Instead it describes a unity wherein there is an unlimited fullness of power. The word "face" is likewise a plural, not because a man has many faces to be put on like masks, but because a man's face is capable of expressing such a variety and richness of feeling, mood, or attitude. Thus "life" describes the rich possibilities of spiritual growth imparted to man by the creation of a soul in the image of God.

We see, therefore, in Gen. 2:4-7 man's endowment with spiritual capacity and with unlimited opportunity for spiritual growth and dominion.

2. Yahweh Provided the Garden of Eden as an Object Lesson in the Use of His Spiritual Faculties

The planting of the Garden of Eden (Gen. 2:8) and the placing of man in it "to dress it and keep it" (Gen. 2:15) were steps in an object lesson for man. Thus Yahweh God became man's instructor. He walked and talked with man as a teacher does with a pupil whose development he desires to watch and guide. He guided man in ways planned to help him learn great lessons from his own efforts.

For this purpose of instruction, Yahweh God "made to grow *out of the ground* every tree that is pleasant to the sight and good for food" (Gen. 2:9a). The words "out of the ground" are italicized in translation because the author of Genesis placed them emphatically. In other words, he made the chief characteristic of these trees to be the fact that they grew out of the ground. The descriptions "pleasant to the sight" and "good for food" show that all members of this group ministered to the body of man. No matter whether they served to give pleasure or to give food, they served the body.

The second group included only two trees, "the tree of life" and "the tree of the knowledge of good and evil" (Gen. 2:9b). The word "life" used here is exactly the same as the word "life" in "breath of life." This associates the tree of life with development of the breath of life. This tree symbolized the growing spirit of man, even before he sinned. The words "good" and "evil" obviously associate the other tree with moral experience of two different and contrary kinds. The word "knowledge," therefore, means "experience" rather than mere "mental perception." In this story the word stands for actual experience of good and evil. In this way both trees are representative or symbolical. They stand for two possible developments in moral experience, one involving only obedience to God's will, the other involving both good and evil. Thus these

two trees are definitely set in contrast with those that represent satisfaction of the body.

The clearly defined contrast between the two groups of trees
is sufficient cause for raising a question about our English
translation. The translation in the Authorized or King James
Version does not differ essentially from other English translations. It reads as follows: "the tree of life also in the midst
of the garden, and the tree of knowledge of good and evil." The
problem in this translation is that it makes the second group to
be made out of the ground like the first. The original clause
does not bear that meaning. There is no object before "the tree
of life," as there would be in this passage if it were a direct
object. "The man" in verse 8 has it. Hebrew authors quite
frequently left the verb "to be" to be understood rather than
written. Observe this usage in 2:4 and in 5:1. This was the
usual way when calling attention to the existence of something.
Thus interpreted, the clause reads this way: "also the tree of
life was in the midst of the garden and the tree of the knowledge
of good and evil." This translation sustains the contrast noted
above, and it is thus demanded by the entire context.

The suggested translation presents clearly the following
lesson: out of man's use of fruit trees, shade trees, and the
like, there arises necessity for a moral choice, a conscientious
decision whether to use possessions as God wills or as a selfish
nature desires. This lesson makes the first group of trees to be
objects used to stimulate man's conscience and the second group
to be symbols of the spiritual experiences involved in man's
exercise of his conscience.

This lesson helps readers to understand the connection
between the heading "Generations of The Heavens and The Earth"
and such a generation or production as the emergence of moral
consciousness. Only God could create the capacity, but earth's
resources and creatures challenged the use of that capacity. To
subdue the earth and exercise dominion over its creatures, man
must face the moral responsibilities involved.

Immediately following the naming of the trees, Genesis
2:10-14 describes features of the garden and Genesis 2:15 adds a
command "to dress it and to keep it." These duties are cited as
illustrations of the responsibilities symbolized by the trees.

Every soul comes face to face with this responsibility as
soon as he reaches "the age of accountability." That age cannot
be fixed by the number of years. It arrives as soon as there is
awareness of questions of moral right and wrong. Again let us
say that these questions are not matters of physical welfare or
misfortune, not thoughts about being punished or rewarded, not

hopes of praise or fears of disapproval, but questions raised by one's conscience, questions that weigh what ought to be done or ought not to be done, questions that inquire into the meaning of duty toward God.

The stewardship of possessions, of time, and of self brings us, even while we are yet children, face to face with these questions. When we earn our first dollar, even our first dime, the question arises as to whether or not we have the right to use it selfishly or in the fear of God. Our use of time raises this question; likewise our response to the opportunity to go to school, the possibilities in the use of a good body, an alert mind, a capacity for leadership, a need for helping others, and many, many similar responsibilities. God gave us moral faculties to use in spiritual development of ourselves that will make us daily to be more like God. A moral imperative rests upon us, and the soul that rebels must reap what it sows.

An illustration that lies close to people of today is found in the situation of a son who comes into possession of a great and good business by inheritance. Immediately great moral questions arise, like the following: Is there an obligation resting upon him to see that its great possibilities for production and service are fulfilled in some way? Does he have the right to utterly neglect it, neither managing it himself or allowing anyone else to do so, simply because he does not like it? Does he have the right to dissipate its resources to satisfy his own debased appetites? In other words, stewardship of life and possessions raises moral questions. Always and for every soul made in the image of God, it is so.

After the scriptural illustration, the eternal consequences of man's choices are set forth in solemn commands. Permission to enjoy the trees of the garden, including "the tree of life," is given in Genesis 2:16. Then "death" is said in Genesis 2:17 to be the terrible and immediate consequence of eating of the other tree. Since "life" in this story is spiritual life, "death" is spiritual death. Later scriptures show that death of the body also comes to man as a result of disobedience, but the death described as occurring in the day of disobedience is spiritual. Thus spiritual life and spiritual death are set before man as results of his moral choices. Also it appears that both are eternal consequences.

Each boy and girl that goes out to face the world, at school, at work, at play, making decisions for one's self, knows the struggle involved in this experience. Can one profit by trying all sides of life, the evil as well as the good? Can one know what is best without having experience of both? Remember that God tells us what is best. Moreover, he says that eating of the tree of the knowledge of good and evil means death in the very day of eating.

3. Yahweh who Provided a Helpmeet in the Use of the Spiritual Faculties

The statement "It is not good that man should be alone"[1] expressed the solicitude of Yahweh God for man's welfare. It reflects another side of his providential care for man. Not only did he create him with moral capacity and challenge him to use it; he earnestly sought to give him the benefit of every good and perfect gift that would enable him to succeed. As his benefactor, therefore, he proceeded to provide the finest of all possible aids in the moral struggle.

"I shall make for him a helpmeet for him"[2] was God's answer to the problem. His answer required "a helpmeet for him" or "a help corresponding to him." Such help is fittingly described as help "equal and adequate to himself,"[3] a helper who is a companion endowed with equal spiritual capacities and with a nature so corresponding to his as to enable the two of them to fill a perfect sphere of life. As his life alone would fill only half a sphere, so would hers; but as equal and opposite halves they make a perfect sphere.

The statement in Genesis 2:19 that God formed animals and birds and brought them to the man does not say that these creatures were formed after man was formed. The first part should be translated this way: *"out of the ground* Yahweh God continued to form . . . ."* The main point of Genesis 2:19,20 is that God and man failed to find a "helpmeet" among existing creatures because no other living creature possessed a nature corresponding to that of this man. This man, with a spirit inbreathed by God, needed a companion with a soul like him.

Man is dignified by a proper name for the first time in Genesis 2:20b. Prior to this point, the common noun *adham* was used to describe him, either without an article (Gen. 1:26, 2:5) as typical of a species, or with the definite article "the" (Gen. 1:27, 2:7,8,15,16,18,19,20a) as designating the one

---

1. The author's translation.

2. The author's translation.

3. Francis Brown, S.R. Driver, and Charles A. Briggs, *A Hebrew and English Lexicon* (Houghton Mifflin Co., Boston and New York, 1906), p. 617.

already mentioned in these stories. In this verse, though the
noun still designates the one mentioned before, the definite
article is dropped and the noun serves as a proper name. It
appears that this is done to dignify the man who is now conscious
of himself as a being created in the image of God. Under the
tutoring of God, he had observed the animals and the birds, he
had given names to identify them, and he had realized that no one
of them could be a helpmeet for him. Now he could be fittingly
identified by a proper name and by a name that would distinguish
him from any other kind of creature. As we sometimes say, he
became "a person."

Having failed to find a helpmeet among creatures of other
kinds, Yahweh God took "one of his ribs," a part of Adam himself,
and built it into a woman (Genesis 2:21,22). This time Adam
explained, "This is the time . . .!" This one whom Yahweh God
brought as his bride, Adam called "a woman" (an *ishshah*). Adam
recognized this *ishshah* as like unto the *ish* in himself for he
said, ". . . *out of man (ish)* was this one taken." The words
appear to have been chosen by Adam to distinguish beings created
in the image of God. Recognition of this vital truth also
appears in Genesis 9:5,6, where it is said, ". . . *at the hand
of men*, at the hand of every man *(ish)* (one who is) *their
brother*, I shall require the life of man. *Whosoever sheds the
blood of mankind*, by mankind shall his blood be shed, *for in the
image of God* he made mankind."[4] Thus it is clear that consciousness of a Godlike nature in Eve and in himself motivated Adam's
love song at the time of the first wedding. Not till that
consciousness emerged was he an *ish*, a God-like man.

LIFE on November 7, 1955, in a special supplement entitled
"The Epic of Man: Part I, Man Inherits The Earth," traced the
development of creatures it called men through hundreds of
thousands of years. The author took care to say in the second
paragraph of his article, "The physical attributes which relate
man to the ancient and epic line of animal organisms, and the
technology and social behavior which have helped him develop high
cultures are the subject matter of anthropology. The spiritual
qualities which differentiate man from the brutes are the
concern of philosophers and theologians." By the very terms of
this statement, those creatures called by anthropologists,
Proconsul, Pithecanthropus, Peking Man, Kanjera Man, Florisbad
Man, Solo Man, Rhodesian Man, Neanderthal Man, Fontechevade Man,
Swanscombe Man, Cro-magnon Man, and the like were "brutes," not
"men" in the high Biblical sense of the word. Accordingly, our
people, our children, our pupils need to have pointed out to them
the fact that in no part of LIFE's pictorial extravaganza, or in

---

4. The author's translation.

any other account of these matters, is there evidence that the
"breath of life" that belongs to moral consciousness, created
and instructed by Yahweh God, was in these creatures.

God's plan for the home of an ish and an ishshah sets up an
ideal for human relations that has ever challenged the very best
in man's moral make-up. One man and one woman, facing the
responsibilities of life together, have opportunity for mutual
understanding, appreciation, and support that furnishes incom-
parable encouragement to the development of the soul. This kind
of companionship makes the home to be the first unit of society,
and it gives to the word "home" that inexpressibly tender and
immeasurably powerful meaning that it bears among Jewish and
Christian peoples. As someone has happily said of woman, "God
did not make you out of his head to rule over him, or out of his
feet to be trampled upon by him, but out of his side to be equal
to him, under his arm to be protected by him, and close to his
heart to be loved by him."

God's plan for the home was what Jesus referred to when he
said concerning divorce as permitted by the Mosaic law, ". . . but
from the beginning it hath not been so" (Mtt. 19:8). Therefore
Jesus went on to indicate that he did not permit either party to
the marriage covenant to take the initiative in breaking it. As
indicated in Mtt. 5:32, he considered the innocent party free
when the other had already broken it. It remains true, however,
that whoever takes the initiative in breaking this union, by act
or by law, is violating the will of God. God's word and will is
recorded thus: "Because it is so, let a man leave his father
and his mother, and he shall cleave unto his wife: and they
shall be as one flesh" (Gen. 2:24 in the author's translation;
cf. Mtt. 19:5).

The blessing of this ideal for the home has been beautifully
illustrated by many a chapter in Jewish and Christian life.
Among these there have been homes such as that where Moses was
taught the meaning of faith in God, such as that where Jesus
"advanced in wisdom and stature, and in favor with God and man"
(Luke 2:52).

In societies influenced by such ideals for the home, many
women have been ennobled and exalted in influence over their
children and neighbors. Among these women there have been
Jochebed who taught her son Moses about God despite the rigors of
slavery in Egypt, Deborah who was a wife, a mother, a judge, and
a prophetess even in the backward days of the judges, Hannah who
reared Samuel in the fear of the Lord despite the vexations of a
home that was not ideal, a prophetess who married the prophet
Isaiah, Mary the mother of Jesus, and Elizabeth the mother of
John the Baptist. The boys and girls taught by fathers and

mothers who aided the teachers of the law in diligently teaching
their children have become, as a rule, the men who blessed their
people with godly leadership. Down through the centuries the
messengers of the cross of Christ have come, as a rule, out of
such homes.

2. GLIMPSES OF GOD

AS

THE BUILDER OF HOPE FOR SINNERS

Genesis 3:1-19; Luke 15:3-32; 19:10

Introduction: God's Search for Sinners

When Adam and Eve were seized by a sense of guilt and shame
(Gen. 3:7), Yahweh God started a search for them (Gen. 3:8). His
call "Where are you?" was heard immediately in the Garden of Eden.
Though their shame made them hide from him, he kept on calling.

The following translation of this story makes these facts
very clear: "Afterwards they heard the voice of Yahweh God, who
was walking in the garden at the breezy time of the day; so the
man and his wife hid themselves from the face of Yahweh God in
the midst of the trees of the garden. But Yahweh continued to
call and to say *to them* 'Where are you?'"[1]

On down through the days, the years, and the ages since,
whenever a soul has been gripped by the conviction of sin, Yahweh
God has called, saying, "Where are you?" He does not ask because
he is ignorant of the sinner's location and condition. He would
make a sinner recognize his real trouble, not laying the blame on
others. He would make a sinner acknowledge his sin. He does not
ask in order to trap or mock or condemn. He wants a sinner to
know that there is help at hand. He takes the initiative in
dealing with sinners lest despair engulf them. He asks for
confession and repentance that he may build upon these the hope
of salvation.

"As in creation, so also in redemption, the fundamental
truth is expressed in the language of Genesis 1:1, 'In the
beginning God.' The motive, the method, and the end of human
salvation all arose out of the nature of the infinitely holy God.

----

1. The author's translation.

The initiative was with God, not with man . . . ."[2]

Three glimpses of Yahweh God, as the builder of hope for sinners, are revealed in Genesis 3:1-19. First, in a declaration of the Devil's doom (Gen. 3:14,15), he was laying a foundation of hope for all sinners. Second, in a diagnosis of sin's effects on Eve (Gen. 3:16), he was building hope for women. Third, in a diagnosis of sin's effects on Adam (Gen. 3:17-19), he was building hope for men. In it all he was foreshadowing what Jesus saw fulfilled in himself when he said, ". . . for the Son of man came to seek and to save that which was lost" (Luke 19:10; cf. Luke 15:3-32).

The original text of Genesis presents these glimpses of God in poetic form. Because the parallelism of the poetry, particularly a comparison of the emphases in parallel lines, furnishes evidence essential to the interpretation of these lines, a translation of the whole passage, with poetic form and emphases indicated, is given here. This translation of Genesis 3:14-19 is as follows:

Then Yahweh God said *to the serpent:* "*Because you have done this,*

> *Cursed* are you more than all the cattle / and more
>   than the beasts of the field; /
> *Upon your belly* you will go, / and *dust* you will
>   eat all the days of your life; /
> And *enmity* shall I put between you and the woman /
>   and between your seed and her seed; /
> *He* will attack you at the head, / and *you* will
>   attack him at the heel." /

Unto the woman he said:

> "I shall greatly increase your pain and your preg-
>   nancy; / *in pain* you will bear children; /
> Yet *for your husband* you will have desire, / and *he*
>   will rule over you." /

And *to Adam* he said: "*Because you hearkened to the voice of your wife, and you proceeded to eat from the tree concerning which I commanded you, saying, 'You shall not eat of it,'*

---

2. E. Y. Mullins, *The Christian Religion in its Doctrinal Expression*, (Philadelphia: Roger Williams Press, 1917), p. 338.

>   *Cursed* is the ground for your sake; / *in toil*
>   will you eat of it all the days of your life; /
>   And *thorns* and *thistles* will it produce for you, /
>   while you eat the herb of the field; /
>   By *the sweat of your brow* will you eat bread, /
>   until you return unto the ground, / for *from it*
>   you were taken; /
>   For *dust* you are, / and *unto dust* you will return." /

1. Proclamation of the Devil's Doom

The one described in Genesis 3:1 as "the serpent" is described in Revelation 20:2 as "the dragon, the old serpent, which
is the Devil, and Satan." It is unmistakably clear, therefore,
that the serpent which deceived Eve and Adam was the Devil. The
story never turns aside to answer questions concerning the form
of his appearance, but it does make it quite clear that the serpent was the Devil. We learn, therefore, that the tempter was
the one described by later scriptures as the archangel who fell
because of pride and self-will, being cast out of heaven because
he had set himself against God.

In God's word to the Devil, Genesis 3:14,15, three things
are emphasized: his offense, his curse, and his defeat. The
poetic parallelism and the emphatic words in these verses help us
greatly in our observation of these three points. The poetry
reveals four main lines. The preceding word stands alone because
it alone looks backward at what had already happened. It is
emphatic throughout and stresses the offense as the cause of the
curse and of the warfare to follow. The next two lines are
parallel, giving us a constructive treatment of one idea, the
curse. The first of them emphasizes the word "cursed" and gives
us a declaration of the curse. The second emphasizes the words,
"upon your belly" and *"dust"*; thus it portrays the progressive
degradation of the cursed character. The last two lines are
likewise parallel, giving us a constructive treatment of the
defeat. The first emphasizes *"enmity,"* predicting the warfare
that will bring defeat; the second emphasizes *"He"* and *"you,"* the
victor and the vanquished in this coming struggle.

The offense referred to so emphatically is described in
detail at the beginning of the chapter. That description shows
subtlety, falsehood, and malice on the part of the Devil. Thus
it blackens the character of the Devil as that of a personality
malignantly evil in nature.

Subtlety appeared in the Devil's first word to Eve. The
"Yea" at the beginning sounded like a simple question, but it was
not an open, honest request for information. Later words reveal
that he already knew what God had said. His words ". . . in the

day you eat thereof . . ." refer to something not previously
mentioned in this conversation with Eve; so he knew full well
what God had said about the trees. The question was suggestive,
insinuating that what God had said was wrong in some way. It
did not assert anything, but slyly introduced the idea that God's
word should be challenged. It was shrewdly calculated to raise
doubt about the truth, the justice, or the goodness of God's word;
yet it left the way open for Eve to make the first move in the
wrong direction. Out of naive inexperience with devilish ways,
she tried to explain the difference between the trees in the
garden. In doing so she mentioned only one of the trees in the
midst of the garden, the one that was forbidden. Her mind seems
to have been dwelling upon the prohibition. That probably means
that she was inclined to rebel against it. Maybe she would have
gone on to speak of the tree of life, but the Devil did not give
her a chance. She responded in a way he could twist into line
with his insinuation; so he cut her off and plunged onward into
falsehood.

Falsehood appeared in the statement, "You will not surely
die . . . ." Having caught Eve's attention, the Devil no longer
pretended to seek information but assumed the role of one whom
we are in the habit of describing as "he thinks he know everything." He began to talk about what would happen in the day of
eating from the forbidden tree. He cut through the hesitation
and uncertainty of Eve with his sharp contradiction of God's
word, claiming that God had spoken in order to prevent Adam and
Eve from becoming like God. In the light of God's teaching and
benevolence that was a bald and brazen lie.

This falsehood, however, was strangely and ingeniously
persuasive. Any command not to do a certain thing arouses a
stubborn determination in vigorous spirits to rebel. A charge
that the command is given for the benefit of the lawgiver and
contrary to the interests of the governed makes the disobedience
appear yet more highly desirable and important. Thus the first
pair were provoked into thinking that they could possess the
divine prerogative of "knowing good and evil" by simply daring to
do as they pleased.

The appeal of this thought to Eve is described in Genesis
3:6. She observed that the fruit of the tree was "*good* for food."
In other words, disregard for questions of right and wrong would
open quick and easy ways of satisfying human appetite. She
observed that it was "a *delight* to the eyes." Daring to take the
things called evil would give a psychic thrill. She observed
also that it was "*to be desired* in order to make one wise (i.e.,
shrewd or successful)." If moral scruples were not allowed to
restrain one's dealing with others, many ways of gaining a worldly
advantage could be found. Cold, conscienceless reason says that

obedience is unsatisfying labor, dull stupidity, and profitless use of one's faculties. The conclusion to which that kind of reasoning leads is this: "Do unto others what they want to do to you, and do it first."

The appeal to Adam was the same. He listened to the Devil, even as Eve did. He calculated the advantages of disobedience, even as Eve did. He voluntarily and freely decided to do evil, even as Eve did. She was quicker in thought and speech, but he had the opportunity for reflection and a leader's final decision. They were equally guilty.

The subtle temptation presented here is the same as the sophisticated appeal made to the young today. It says that nature must be allowed to express itself. There must be no inhibitions. "Go ahead, do what you want to do" is its advice. "Scrap the Ten Commandments. Throw off restraints. You must try all sides of life in order to know how to choose. Let yourself go."

This argument of the Devil is partly true, and the truth in it is the fancy bait that hides the hook. By doing evil, human beings do become like God in one respect. It is the very point mentioned by the Devil. They become persons who know both good and evil.

But! But! But! The Devil's argument omits another fact, a vital fact, that is decisive in the moral government of life. Man's knowledge of good and evil makes him a slave to evil. God knows good and evil, in the sense of understanding both, because he is omniscient. Man, starting out in innocence but also in ignorance, can know good and evil only by experience. Moreover, experience of evil enslaves him; having tried it, he cannot escape it. In the beginning, the power to make independent judgments, even such as are contrary to God's will, and to act upon them seems to spell freedom. Afterwards it means slavery to a corrupted will. In the beginning, self-centered reason appears to be the most practical approach to life. Such reason turns out to be the most insane practice in all human experience. In the beginning, the satisfaction of selfish desire appears to be the most desirable of all things. In the end, that lustful satisfaction is the gall of bitterness to the soul. What a horrifying lie the Devil led man to believe!

Malice is most clearly seen in the Devil's attitude toward Adam and Eve after the fall. As guilt and shame swept over them, he had nothing more to say. No pity! No comfort! No aid! As God appraised and judged his destiny, there was no evidence of guilt and shame in him. No word of regret! No plea for mercy! Stony silence expressed defiance of God and also malicious satisfaction in the damage he had done. Accordingly, through all the ages since his satanic operations have manifested a desire for nothing better--nothing worse, we may say, looking from God's side--than to see his victims sink in the quicksands of moral degradation.

The worst effects of the Devil's malice are seen in the fall of the entire human race and some of the almost unbelievable psychological contradictions it produces in sinners. The fall is a strange, strange, fact, but all the scriptures and all human experience bear testimony to its existence. As many, caught in the coils of its creeping death, fail to find it in their hearts to believe that God can save, the Devil's malice burns with fiendish contempt for their weakness. Never a word from him except to goad a victim to desperation that makes him sink deeper into the quicksand of death! As the intelligent but unrepentant sinner recognizes his inescapable doom as the fruit of his own folly, he often exults in the things he hates and draws spiritual death to his bosom as a beloved companion. The Devil's delight in such horrors was the motivating drive in all his subtlety and falsehood.

The strange extremes in the Devil's offensive conduct are illustrated by the history of the Hebrew word for "subtle." A primary meaning was "artful," making it fit the craftily conceived appeal the Devil made to the finest faculties of the human soul. Eventually it was used to describe the "circling of trees", the cutting of the bark in order to cut off their sap and make them die. Also it was used to describe "flaying", the stripping of the skin, piece by piece, from a human body in order to torture and to cause a slow but agonizing death. This subtlety and falsehood and malice made the devil's offense a heinous one that merited the declaration of its cursed character.

The curse is described by the passive participle "cursed." This is used frequently to picture a continuous and permanent condition. Passive participles also manifest at times an inherent quality, as in the case of "peaceable" in II Samuel 20:19 and "the faithful" in Psalm 31:23. The judicial atmosphere of this entire passage makes it certain that this participle does manifest an inherent quality here. Thus the curse was the Devil's own nature, and Yahweh's word was merely a declaration of its cursed character. The Devil was doomed because he despised the truth of God, not because he lacked a chance to know the truth, because he hated the love of God, not because the benefits of love were denied him, because he chose the unrighteous ways of evil, not because he was incapable of choosing.

The emphases that are made synonymous with the word "cursed" vividly illustrate the nature of this sentence. *"Upon your belly*

you will go" described the degraded way of life this cursed
character would pursue. "*Dust* you will eat all the days of your
life" expressed the same idea and more. "Dust" stands for what
is low, mean, and worthless. It cannot refer here to the literal
dust of the earth, for even a snake does not eat the dust of the
earth for food. "Dust" does also describe, in one of its strongest metaphorical uses, the remains of bodies once alive but now
dead. Thus usage makes "dust" a symbol of what death leaves
behind after its process of corruption has reached an end. This
is the lifeless, hopeless, pitiless portion of the Devil, the
portion he chose as a satisfaction for his depraved appetite.

The defeat was assured by the warfare Yahweh God promised to
wage. The defeat is a different thing from the curse. His curse
is his own depravity, but his defeat is the prevention of his
malicious purpose to enslave all men in sin. When Yahweh God
said, "And enmity shall I put between you and the woman . . .,"
he promised to initiate this warfare by his own influence upon
the woman. The continuance of the warfare by her seed was likewise assured by his inspiration. Moreover, the prosecution of it
unto a complete victory was implied by his assuming the leadership of this spiritual seed in a supernatural way. He could
have allowed the Devil to go to hell by simply letting nature
takes its course, but the snatching of precious souls from the
snares of sin required the miraculous intervention of Yahweh God
himself.

"Enmity" means "personal antagonism." It signifies a
reaction that produces positive hatred. This warfare against sin
and the Devil is, therefore, a spiritual warfare within one's
self, seeking to cast Satan out of the mind, the heart, and the
will.

The mention of Eve as the one in whose heart Yahweh God
would initiate this fight against the Devil leaves no place for
ignorant prejudice that sometimes excludes her from the company
of the redeemed. An obscure little book entitled *Ladies in Hell*
is an example of such babbling gossip. It assigns Eve to a group
of historically famous but morally infamous women including
Jezebel and Salome. Such contradiction of the Bible is a libel.
In addition to the prophecy in this verse, Eve's naming Cain
(Gen. 4:1) and her naming Seth (Gen. 4:26) reflect her spiritual
perception and give ground for inclusion of her among the Yahweh
worshippers of Genesis 4:26.

The word "seed" usually means descendants or posterity.
Since the Devil's seed are, of course, spiritual seed, a group
spiritually kin to him, it is consistent to understand that Eve's
seed are likewise a group that takes her side in this spiritual
warfare.

This word "seed" can be understood either as a singular or a plural. It was natural for the Yahweh worshippers to think of it at first as a plural including all who took Eve's side in this warfare. Later, as the inability of sinners alone to carry this warfare to complete victory became apparent, the possibility was opened of applying this word to a divine leader who would come from heaven. Little by little their prophets saw that complete victory depended upon that one who would bring supernatural aid and inspiration. Thus Paul, after the coming of Jesus, could write, "He saith not, and to seeds, as of many; but as of one, and to thy seed, which is Christ" (Gal. 3:16). In this verse the seed is Jesus, yet the idea of the seed is again broadened at times to include all believers in Christ. In this final sense, the seed are described as being of one kind, the Christ kind.

The climax of this warfare is indicated by the contrast between the phrases "at the head" and "at the heel." These words illustrate both the manner and the outcome of this fight. As to manner, Satan's seed will strike like a snake in the grass, striking at the heel, while Eve's seed will strike like a conqueror, striking at the head. The one striking in a crafty and underhanded way has murderous intentions but also cringing and paralyzing fears. The one striking openly and directly has confidence and determination to fight until his enemy is destroyed. The victory is guaranteed by the fact that this warfare is the fulfillment of Yahweh God's determination to bring the Devil to utter destruction. As Yahweh God, who intervenes personally in human affairs, he promises to start this warfare. As surely then as he is God, he will finish it and finish it victoriously. He will do so even at the cost of incarnation, crucifixion, and Armageddon.

This mighty declaration was made for the benefit of Adam and Eve. It could not benefit the Devil whose character and destiny were already fixed. It gave to Adam and Eve the matchless assurance of the divine warfare and of their enlistment on God's side It is necessary to understand that this word of hope is carried over into the words of God that follow. To Adam and Eve he said nothing about a curse. He spoke rather of punishment that would be a corrective discipline and make them soldiers prepared to endure hardship in the warfare of God. This declaration, therefore, stands as a Gibraltar of Hope through all ages to follow.

2. Diagnosis of the Effects of Sin on the Woman

In the word to Eve, in Genesis 3:16, Yahweh God gave a diagnosis of the effects of sin in her case. Two main effects are specified, increase of pain in childbirth and subjection to her husband. With the first an increase in pregnancy is linked, and with the second the woman's desire for her husband.

The word "pain" applies to physical and mental grief alike. "Sorrow" is hardly a sufficient translation for it. The word covers all the anguish brought to body and spirit by sin. It is used in Genesis 3:17 to describe the effects of sin on Adam, and it is translated "toil" in his case.

It is increase of pain in childbirth that is emphasized in Eve's case not the mere occurrence of pain in some degree. The increase of pain, therefore, is specified as the result of sin, not normal conception and bearing of children.

The conjunction "and" before "pregnancy" should probably be understood as meaning "and in particular." Thus the increase in pain is not associated with childbirth only, but particularly with it, the time of childbirth being a time when the normal strain upon physique and mind is such as to give unusual occasion for increase of pain. Moreover, the linking of the increase of pain with the increase of pregnancy is made to mean that woman's grief is due in particular to the undue increase of pregnancy caused by sin.

The desire of the woman for her husband may refer to sexual desire only or to that desire as associated with the yearning to be a mother. The meaning here appears to be the normal desire for a husband and children, which leads to acceptance of a dependent estate in order that one may have a home with children. There is, of course, in view of the strife introduced by sin, a declaration of God that the man will be the head of the home, the one to lead in establishing and maintaining order there. According to the Biblical ideal, the headship in that home should be a godly rule and subjection there should be a godly cooperation.

This word to the woman is a word of hope, not a curse. It explains problems to be solved by cooperation and the fear of God.

3. Diagnosis of the Effects of Sin on the Man

God's word to Adam in Genesis 3:17-19 is also a diagnosis of the effects of sin. Two main ones are pointed out, toil and return to the dust. With the toil, there is associated a cursing of the ground. This causes man's effort to make a living to be a grievous struggle. The second makes the toil yet more grievous in that it finally takes the body back to the ground whence it came.

"Toil," as indicated above, represents the same word as "pain." Either translation is an attempt to interpret the grief caused by sin in body and mind. Thus "toil" is something more than the fatigue of hard work. It includes all the anxiety and distress as well as the wear and tear on the human frame involved in the struggle to make a living.

This curse upon the ground is said to be "for man's sake." In Genesis 3:18, thorns and thistles are pointed out as outstanding examples of what that meant. These are undesirable and unprofitable products of the earth, and the statement about them appears to indicate that they were added by God to penalize man's effort to make a living. Moreover, it is said that man will eat bread *"by the sweat* of his brow" (Gen. 3:19), and this appears to be because of such penalties. How then can the curse be "for man's sake?" The clue to the answer appears *in the full meaning* of the original phrase "for your sake." Primarily "for the sake of" means "in order that." This meaning indicates that God had a purpose; he did not merely acquiesce in something that happened by chance. "For the sake of" can also mean "on account of," so it says that the penalties are designed for the benefit of man. The explanation is that the leadership, counsel, and aid of Yahweh God will use man's struggle against physical hardships to produce a spiritual gain. As he used the good earth of the original garden to teach the meaning of the tree of life, so he will use the cursed ground as part of a moral discipline designed to strengthen man for warfare against the Devil.

"Unto dust you will return" declares that the end of all this grief for all mankind is the return of the body to the dust whence it came. It appears, therefore, that this return to the dust is likewise mentioned as a penalty for sin. What would have become of the physical body, if man had not sinned, is not told. We can only guess concerning its possible translation into a glorified body like that of Jesus. However, we may be sure that its transformation, whatever the nature of it, would have been without grief. This grievous end, with all its pain and sadness, became the supreme penalty used of God to keep man dependent upon him and to move the spirit of man to faith in him.

Conclusion: The Son of God Goes Forth to War

The key to the assurance given by Yahweh God is the warfare against the Devil. The promise of his own supernatural aid is the crucial point in this assurance. Upon this promise he challenges sinners to build their hope. Later scriptures associate this first promise of Messiah with other wonderful steps in the plan of salvation.

3. GLIMPSES OF GOD

AS

THE GOD OF PROVIDENTIAL CARE

Genesis 3:20--4:26; Hebrews 11:1-4

Introduction: Turn from Fear to Reverence

One day my father was tearing down an old shed in the yard of our home. It was stoutly built of heavy oak timber. Even the roof was made of oak boards, hewn out and split by hand. The two halves of the roof were finally torn apart at the ridgepole and pushed outward so that they turned over and came to rest leaning against the walls. Their under sides were then outward, and the old cut nails with which the boards had been fastened were sticking up, rusty, rough, and dangerous.

While that part of the work was going on, my father told me to get out of the way and to stay out of the way. He told me more than once, for the intense curiosity of a boy of five or six makes him forget warnings when such a show as that is going on. Finally, my father told me in no uncertain terms what would happen to me if I did not do what he told me to do.

Shortly afterwards, he and the other workmen went into the house to eat their dinner, but I lingered and looked and listened to voices inside me that spoke of the thrill of walking like a billy goat along the top of the walls. The temptation was too great and up I went. Then I slipped, and one of those old nails took a bloody piece of skin out of my bare heal, tough as it was, that was as big as a dime. I hit the ground with a wail.

My yelling brought my daddy back; but lo and behold, it was not my heel he tended to first. He was not in the habit of spanking me often, but when he did, he did a good job of it. That occasion was rather outstanding.

It was not the actual spanking that hurt me most but what I thought was a lack of sympathy. Then, as time went by and I understood my father better, I knew that my father could not have been either truthful or just if he had failed to do to me what he had said he would do. Furthermore, I learned, especially so when I came to bear a father's responsibility for dealing with my own children, that he did it because he loved me. He loved me too much to let the ways of disobedience possess me.

According to Genesis 3:20--4:26, Adam, Eve, Seth, and Enosh learned what Isaiah meant when he wrote:

> *Surely, in the path of thy judgments,* O Yahweh, we
> do wait for thee; / thy name, yea, thy memorial
> (name), is the desire of our soul. /

. . . .

> For *when thy judgments are in the earth,* /
> the inhabitants of the world learn
> righteousness.[1] /

Fear and reverence are strangely close to each other, and
God makes a sinful heart to fear his judgments that he may inspire the faith arising out of reverence and the worship arising
out of prayer. Throughout Genesis 3:20--4:26, this lesson emer-
ges, and we can see it in these seven stages:

(1)   in the provision of clothing (Gen. 3:20,21),
        there is helpful care that provides
        encouragement for the needy;

(2)   in the expulsion from Eden (Gen. 3:22-24),
        there is punishment that is a measure of
        corrective discipline;

(3)   in the acceptance of an offering brought in
        faith (Gen. 4:1-4), there is assurance
        of salvation for the believer;

(4)   in the rejection of an offering not brought
        in faith (Gen. 4:5-7), there is rebuke for
        an unbeliever;

(5)   in the appointment of a sign for Cain
        (Gen. 4:8-15), there is mercy toward an
        unbeliever and continued opportunity for
        him to repent;

(6)   in the fulfillment of Yahweh's predictions
        about Cain (Gen. 4:16-24), there is
        historical demonstration of the results
        of unbelief;

(7)   in the first prayer in Yahweh's name (Gen. 4:25,26),
        there is the providential effect (upon those who
        believed) of all that went before.

----

1.   Isaiah 26:8,9, in the author's translation.

1. Providential Helpfulness: Provision of Clothing

The provision of clothing is stated simply and without interpretation of any kind. It appears, therefore, as a mere act of
kindness that met the need of Adam and Eve. That meaning was so
obvious that it needed no interpretation. It expressed the love
of God in a practical way. God had not forgotten Adam and Eve;
he still cared for them despite their disobedience; he wanted to
help them in every way he could.

There is nothing in the words of this story to indicate that
the use of an animal was intended as a sacrifice. Later,
sacrifice is mentioned, and it is best to let the Bible indicate
the beginning in its own way. God's helpfulness is sufficient
explanation for this incident; therefore, it seems good to rest
the interpretation right there. It is true that the Bible in
various passages that follow mentions the provision of clean
garments as a symbol of imputed righteousness. Those passages,
however, do not refer in any way to this one. It is wise for us
in all cases to avoid running ahead of the Bible and imposing our
suppositions upon it.

2. Providential Discipline: Expulsion from the Garden of Eden

Expulsion from the Garden of Eden was closely associated with
the provision of clothing. Yahweh God tended first to their
physical need, then he dealt with their disobedience by sending
them out to make their own way, suffering the consequences of the
sin they had chosen. In other words, he mixed help and discipline
in a way to teach a lesson that worked two ways. First, it
taught them that the help they needed could be found in God.
Second, it taught them that God's help in dealing with sin would
require punishment for sin. The grievous pain and toil, judiciously described in Genesis 3:14-19, could not be avoided.
Nothing less than acceptance of its stern lessons could open the
door to deliverance from sin.

The meaning of the expulsion is dealt with in three ways:

(1)   as punishment designed to prevent unending continuance
      in sin;

(2)   as punishment executed by God himself;

(3)   as punishment that is universal.

God's purpose to prevent unending continuance in sin appears
in the statement of Genesis 3:22, ". . . and now, in order that
he should not put forth his hand, and take from the tree of life,

and eat, and live forever, ⸺ ."[2] This statement is a rhetorical expression that breaks off suddenly as if the author is unwilling to put into words what he is actually thinking. Grammatically, it is called an aposiopesis. It serves here to draw attention in dramatic fashion to the decision of Yahweh God to leave unstated whatever conclusion he had in mind as a possible means of preventing mankind from continuing in sin forever.

This statement of God's purpose is a complex one that often puzzles us. It can, however, be understood. Evidently it is given as an explanation of the action that followed. The terrible problem of sin, mentioned in the statement, "Behold, the man has become as one of us, to know good and evil" (Gen. 3:22b), is too great for us to understand at first, but this statement as to what God purposed to do about it was evidently meant to be understood. We need, therefore, to distinguish the purpose clause in Genesis 3:22b and its unstated conclusion from the chosen plan of God described in 3:23. They are not the same thing. The purpose clause in Genesis 3:22b begins with a particle meaning "lest" or "in order that . . . not." Thus it evidently was intended to say that sinners could not eat of the tree of life and live forever. The unfinished part leaves unsaid what God might have done to prevent that fulfillment. Since Yahweh God hesitated to utter it, it must have been terrible indeed. It leaves us wondering if it would have involved the extermination of all mankind and the abandonment of all plans to bring men into the glory of a morally tested yet also morally perfected spiritual life. Turning from it as an appalling thing, Yahweh God chose instead to do that which is described in the story that follows.

Yahweh's chosen way, therefore, carried out a purpose to prevent unending continuance in sin, but it included plans for doing so in a redemptive way whenever man's will permits it to be so. The chosen way left the door open for men to return unto God, to be saved, and to eat of the tree of life. This chosen way made it impossible for unrepentant sinners to partake of eternal life, yet left the door open for reconciliation with those who would build their hope upon the promise of Genesis 3:15.

According to Genesis 3:23, Yahweh God executed the expulsion from Eden himself. In other words, this punishment was not the mere working of a moral law, much less the cruel stroke of a blind fate. This was the providential dealing of the fatherly God who helps where he can and punishes where he must in order to accomplish the greatest possible good for his child. Even as he intervened at that time in order to impose penalties for sin, so

---

2. The author's translation.

it was clear to man that he could intervene according to his will to fulfill all points of the declaration in Genesis 3:14-19.

The stationing of the Cherubim eastward of the Garden of Eden appears to mean that sinners would not be allowed to return to the presence of God except as God wills it to be so. The Cherubim are the same order of angels associated with the throne of God in Ezekiel 1:5,22,26, 10:1,15-17,20-22, and in Revelation 4:2-8. In all cases they are associated with the very presence of God. In this instance, the Cherubim are God's representatives in handling the sword. "The flame of the sword that turns itself every way"[3] fittingly symbolizes the intent of the service performed by the Cherubim in this case. Because it is a flaming sword, and because both fire and sword are used to symbolize judgment, the sword stands for universal judgment upon mankind, the expulsion of all men from the presence of God because of sin. Nevertheless, there lay behind this punishment the providential purposes described above.

3. Providential Favor: Acceptance of an Offering Brought in Faith

The story in Genesis 4:1-4 indicates that God did not speak any further word until after Cain and Abel brought their offerings to him. He left them to their own reflections upon the meaning of his previous words and actions. There was no requirement like that of the sacrificial system, which was set up later, to give ground for thinking that Abel brought an animal because a bloody sacrifice was required. There is no evidence of a command given at this time concerning tithes and offerings; therefore, there is no ground for thinking that Cain was condemned because he failed to bring a tithe of his produce. We are told simply that they brought their offerings, and the natural impression is that the bringing of an offering was their own idea. It is added that Abel brought "from the firstlings of his flock, even from the fat parts of them."[4] These features indicate something in Abel's attitude that furnished an explanation for Yahweh's acceptance of his offering. Since we are told immediately afterwards that Yahweh did not accept Cain's offering, we are led to understand that it was rejected because it lacked evidence of an attitude on Cain's part that Yahweh could accept.

The features of the story as it is given to us do give ground for thinking that God's disciplinary judgment upon sin

---

3. Genesis 3:24 in the author's translation.

4. The author's translation.

moved them to seek reconciliation with God. It is possible to
think that one sought escape from its penalties and the other
sought escape from the sin that caused it; nevertheless, both
thought of themselves in the beginning as seeking reconciliation.
Many children, when punished by their parents, offer later a
flower, an apple, or whatever they can lay hands on as a token of
their desire for reconciliation.

This interpretation likewise leads to the conclusion that
Yahweh's response depended upon the attitude of each individual
concerning the sin question. Abel's offering "from the firstlings of his flock" indicates that he put God first in his thinking, providing for himself out of what remained. His offering
"from the fat parts" indicates that he gave to God his best, for
"the fat" was thought of by Hebrew speaking people as that which
was best in all respects. These distinctions warrant the conclusion drawn in Hebrews 11:4 that "by faith Abel offered unto God
a more excellent sacrifice than Cain . . . ."

4. Providential Rebuke: Rejection of an Offering not Brought in
    Faith

In Genesis 4:5-7 every word teaches that Yahweh rejected
Cain's offering for the sole reason that it was not brought in
faith. When he said, "For what reason are you angry . . .?"[5] he
was giving Cain a chance to explain what was in his heart. When
he said, "Is it not true, if you make it right, there is acceptance . . .?"[6] he appears to have meant that the offering would
have been acceptable if made in faith. The preceding explanation
about Abel's faith seems to require this meaning here. Moreover,
teaching about offerings throughout the Bible places supreme
emphasis upon God's desire for the giver rather than the gift.
Even when prescribed offerings are brought by unbelievers, the
offerings are bribes and the offerers are hypocrites. Yahweh God,
seeing in Cain's offering the deadly spiritual poison of hypocrisy, said, "If you do not make it right, *at the very door* sin
is lying in wait."[6] Then he closed with an appeal to Cain to
conquer that deadly sin.

5. Providential Mercy: Appointment of a Sign for Cain

Even as Yahweh closed the former conversation with an appeal
so he continued his efforts to appeal to Cain even after the kill-
ing of Abel. Throughout the events of Genesis 4:8-15 this
effort to win Cain continued.

-----

5. Genesis 4:6 in the author's translation.

6. Genesis 4:7 in the author's translation.

Yahweh's first effort was an unsuccessful attempt to get
Cain to face the facts. Yahweh did not lack knowledge of what
had happened, but he was trying to get Cain to talk so that he
might find a way to help him. Cain, however, tried to hide his
part in the tragedy by lying.

Then Yahweh declared that Cain would be cursed by the ground
that had received his brother's blood and that Cain would become
an unstable man and a wanderer in the earth. The curse "by the
ground" should be distinguished from any curse by Yahweh, like
that upon the Devil. This curse "by the ground," though very
severe, appears to be controlled by the same purpose that controlled the curse upon the ground for Adam's sake recorded in
Genesis 3:17,18. God was making each sinner bear penalties befit-
ting his sin and designed to constrain all who could be influenced
to see the terrible effect of sin and to turn from it. At the
same time, a prediction was added that Cain's reaction would make
him unstable in his ways and constantly unsettled in his life.
This was a very strong warning, but there is no ground in God's
words for taking it as a prediction of an unchangeable, inescapable state like that of the Devil. Yahweh was still trying to
help Cain. Like the efforts of The Angel of Yahweh at a later
time to save Balaam and the efforts of Jesus to save Judas, so
were the efforts of Yahweh God exhausting every possibility of
persuasion.

This effort of Yahweh God to win Cain may be seen more
clearly if certain difficulties about the translation of Genesis
4:13-15 are removed. Translators have differed widely as to
whether Cain said, "My iniquity is too great to forgive," or "My
punishment is too great to bear." Likewise there has been much
uncertainty as to whether God's answer began with the words "Not
so!" or with the words meaning "Therefore."

The first main problem depends upon the translation of a
Hebrew word which sometimes means iniquity, sometimes punishment.
It needs to be remembered that the first and overwhelmingly pre-
dominant meaning is "iniquity" or "guilt of iniquity." The meaning of "punishment" or "punishment for iniquity" is needed only
when there is occasion for thinking that guilt and punishment are
separated in some way, as when one bears the punishment due
another or one bears a punishment out of proportion to his guilt.

The second main problem depends upon a decision as to what
are the words written in the Hebrew text. In the beginning that
text was written without vowels. With one set of vowels the words
mean "Not so!" and with another they mean "Therefore." In other
words, either translation is possible so far as the words alone
are concerned, and our choice must depend upon evidence from the
context. We must draw evidence concerning God's intention in
using these words from other things mentioned in connection with it.

God's intention is bound up with his intention in appointing a sign for Cain. The word "sign" means a "mark," or a "pledge," like a promise pledging aid. In this case, since there is no reference to an external mark on Cain, we are led to believe that the sign was God's pledge of protection for Cain. Therefore, we wonder what was God's intention in giving that pledge. Did God intend it as a warning to others that Cain's destiny was already determined and that the meting out of vengeance should be left in God's hands? Or did God intend it to be a sign to Cain himself and to others that God was protecting him from hasty judgment in order to give him further opportunity to repent?

The trend of thought throughout this passage seems to be the decisive factor in settling all these problems. In all Yahweh's dealing with Cain there is evidence that he never gives up in his search for sinners as long as there is any struggle against sin in the sinner's heart. When Jesus taught that publicans and harlots would go into the Kingdom of God before hardened hypocrites, he was bringing out this same truth. Therefore, it is in keeping with the passage to conclude that Cain misinterpreted Yahweh's efforts to reason with him because he was blind to the necessity for faith in a sinner's plea for exemption from punishment. He became embittered by God's refusal to accept his offering. Then he was so wildly, unreasonably, madly angry that he killed Abel. Then he was sullenly determined to take refuge in lies and his own hateful way. Then he was so spiritually blind that he thought God could not forgive sin like his, and he said, "My iniquity is too great to forgive . . . ." Cain plunged onward in his crooked thinking, adding to God's words, saying that he would be hidden from God's favor, also that anyone finding him would kill him. Yahweh denied all of this when he exclaimed, "Not so!" Then Yahweh, out of merciful longsuffering, went on to assure Cain that his providential protection and willingness to forgive still stood. That was Yahweh's sign for Cain.

6. Providential Predictions: Forecast of Cain's Instability and Wandering

The great wonder about Yahweh's dealing with sinners is that he can be so loving and so just at the same time. With Cain, Yahweh's tender compassion was left standing as an eternal condemnation of the doubt and defiance that gradually dragged Cain into ruin. On the other hand, his warnings and punishments stood as a reminder for all men that all sinners will face God's justice sooner or later. No matter whether they do it willingly or unwillingly, in repentance and renewed life or in rebellion and death, they do face it sooner or later.

The progress of sin and spiritual decay in Cain's line is told without comment in Genesis 4:16-24. The story speaks for

itself. Cain went out into the Land of Nod, which means Land of
Wandering. He built a city. His descendants were industrious and
artful in various instances. There was, however, no respect for
God in their life. In the life of Lamech the son of Methuselah
two dread forms of moral decay appeared, bigamy and murderous
intent. The song which Lamech chanted before his wives was a
defiance of justice. He exulted in his victory over the young
man he had killed, and he dared anyone to punish him. Thus he
voiced the spirit of violence that now threatened all men.

The progress of sinful corruption can be traced in these
terrible words: separation from God, hypocrisy in worship, manslaughter, instability of character, a wandering life, bigamy,
and murder.

7. Providential Effect: Beginning of the Worship of Yahweh

The light of a new dawn breaks through at the end of this
story. The fact that it is made to be the conclusion of the
terrible story of Cain indicates that the threat of violence seen
in Cain and Lamech was part of those influences that provoked the
happy change in others.

Above all other influences that helped to bring about the
change, however, there was the providential care of Yahweh God.
His inspiring grace is reflected in Genesis 4:25,26. Eve saw it
in the birth of her third son; so she named him Seth, The
Appointed One. She meant, of course, that he was appointed of
God as the one through whom the promises of God would be
fulfilled.

Eve's hopes found a bright and beautiful fulfillment in the
days of her grandson Enosh, for "*at that time* the invoking of a
blessing in the name of Yahweh was begun."[7]

The name "Enosh" means Weak (Physically Weak) One or Mortal
One (One Subject to Physical Death). In this case it could hardly mean Weak One, for we are told in Genesis 5:11 that Enosh
lived nine hundred and five years. The foregoing account suggests
that it meant Mortal One, and that it was given because the
threat of violence and death had rolled over the human family
like a stormy cloud. In such circumstances it was natural for
God-fearing souls to think of the ominous fact that men must die
and also turn to their God with a prayer for protection.

"To call upon the name of Yahweh" or "invoke a blessing in
the name of Yahweh" is used in Genesis 12:8 to distinguish the

---

7. Genesis 4:26 in the author's translation.

worship Abram offered to Yahweh. In 1 Kings 18:24, it is used to
distinguish the prayer of Elijah to his God from the prayers of
the priests of Baal to their god. It is used frequently afterwards, as in Jeremiah 10:25, to distinguish the worship of Israel
from the worship of the heathen nations. Thus it stands throughout the Bible as a distinguishing feature of the worship of
Yahweh. This instance in the days of Enosh was the beginning.

This prayer recognized Yahweh as God. The fact that those
praying appealed unto him reflected their thought that he was the
one who had providentially overruled their life from the beginning. Thus he was the one Eve called God when she said, "God has
appointed me another child in the place of Abel, because Cain
slew him."[8] This prayer was worship in the highest sense of the
word. There was no suggestion of dependence upon a mere form of
worship or ritual. There was no dependence upon an image, or a
picture, or any kind of human intermediary. This was worship of
God alone.

This prayer, moreover, recognized Yahweh as a person. From
Genesis 2:4 through Genesis 3:24 "Yahweh Elohim" is used by the
author of Genesis, but in Genesis 4:1 "Yahweh" alone is used by
Eve. "Yahweh God" was used as a title to describe the immanent
God who dealt with Adam and Eve as one person deals with another,
but "Yahweh" was used as a name to distinguish that individual
who cooperated in helping Eve to acquire a child with the divine
image in him. Thus Yahweh became a personal name. In recognition of this fact Yahweh is used alone, as a name, from Genesis
4:1 through Genesis 4:26. All the words and thoughts of Eve, of
Cain, of Abel, of Seth, and of Enosh are related to Yahweh as a
person whom they knew by name.

This use of Yahweh as a name to describe the person of Yahweh
God reflected a personal faith in him on the part of those who
engaged in the worship described by Genesis 4:26. As he had
personally taught and urged Adam and Eve in the beginning to fulfill his purpose for their lives, so they now prayed that he
would enable them to do it. As he judiciously explained the
inevitable consequences of sin and left open a door of hope for
repentant sinners, so they now humbly accepted the hope he
offered. As he providentially distinguished between offerings
brought in faith and those not brought in faith, so they now
clung to him by faith in himself as their personal savior.

Conclusion: Meaning of the Name Yahweh

This story tells of the first use of the name Yahweh on human
lips and also the first use of it in worship. Its application in

---

8. Genesis 4:25 in the author's translation.

these instances to a person furnishes the setting, therefore, in which the study of the original meaning of the name should be made. At the risk of being tedious, an attempt will be made here to consider this evidence thoroughly. The Name is so significantly related to the whole revelation of God to men, to the person of Christ, to the covenant with Israel, and to the plan of salvation that we cannot afford to do less.

The following evidence constitutes an argument in favor of Yahweh as the original form of the Name:

(1) Eve's use of the name was the very first. In Genesis 2:4, and all other passages preceding 4:1, the use of Yahweh is that of the author of Genesis; and his writing, no matter who he was, occurred long after Eve's use of the name. The author was simply saying that the being who dealt with Adam and Eve in the beginning was the one known later as Yahweh; however, neither Yahweh himself nor Adam and Eve are described as using the name prior to the use by Eve at the birth of Cain. Therefore, at the time of Eve's first use, evidence as to what the name meant to her was limited to her circumstances, her words, and her convictions.

(2) Eve made a poetic use of the verb "get" or "acquire" which reflects the nature of the child. The meaning of this verb in ordinary usage is "purchase", but that is obviously impossible here. The verb is used poetically to describe the acquisition of exceedingly precious things. Examples appear in the following:

    (a) in Genesis 14:19,22, where both Abraham and Melchizedek use it of God's creative activity in acquiring "heaven and earth";

    (b) in Proverbs 8:22, where it describes that Wisdom Yahweh possessed and used in his creative work;

    (c) in Psalm 139:13, where the author applies it to God's creating of man's "inward parts", the seat of his emotion and affection, or that spiritual nature concerning which the psalmist exclaims in the next verse:

> I will give thanks unto thee; /
>   for I am fearfully and wonderfully
>   made: /
>
> Wonderful are thy works: /
>   And that my soul knoweth right well. /[9]

---

9. The author's translation.

(d)   in Isaiah 11:1, where the prophet applies it to the
        Lord's redemptive work in recovering a remnant of his
        people;

(e)   in Proverbs 1:5, where it applies to man's acquisi-
        tion of Godly wisdom.

Thus Eve indicated her belief that her child was a being whose
character was exceedingly precious.

(3)   Eve used a noun to describe the child which indicated
the high qualities of manhood. She avoided the noun *adham*, which
was the only other noun used up to this time to describe man, and
which described him as a being made out of the ground. She used
the word introduced by Adam, according to Genesis 2:23. Adam's
use of the word was provoked by the fact that Yahweh God had
sought for a "helpmeet for him" (Gen. 2:18) and failed to find
one. The word "meet" indicated a helper corresponding to him in
character. Not finding one among the animals, Yahweh made one
from "one of his ribs" (Gen. 2:20-22). Then Adam used the new
word to describe himself and the feminine form of it to describe
the helpmeet. The word for man is *ish*, and the word for woman is
ishshah. Therefore, Adam was describing their nature as above
that of the animals. This accords with the author's use of Adam's
words at the end of Chapter II, after he had described the dawn of
man's moral consciousness, after he had recorded Yahweh's solemn
warning concerning the vital issues of moral choices, and at the
end of the story telling about Yahweh's special desire to find a
companion for man whose spiritual capacities would be on an equa-
lity with his own. All this served as an explanation of what it
meant for mankind to be created "in the image of God," as stated
in Genesis 1:27. In Genesis 9:5,6, when *ish* is again used to
describe man, this is the point emphasized.

(4)   Eve described her acquisition of this precious *ish* as
accomplished "with the help of Yahweh." "With the help of" is an
expansion of the Hebrew preposition "with." Because the Hebrew
form of this preposition is exactly like the sign used before a
direct object in Hebrew, some have argued that Eve was making the
name a second object of the verb "gotten," thus equating Yahweh
with *ish*. Thus they would conclude that Eve thought this child
was the promised seed mentioned in Genesis 3:15. That interpretation runs into a fatal objection: namely, if the direct object
sign was to have been used at all, it should have been put before
both objects. On the other hand, the preposition can mean "with
the help of," and this meaning fits this context. This meaning
leads to the conclusion that Eve was thinking of the soul of the
child as brought into being by the creative work of God. She and
Adam were responsible for his body, God and God alone for his
soul. The conclusion, therefore, follows naturally that she used

the name "Yahweh" as meaning "He Who Causes to Be." This meaning
of "Yahweh" fits the causative active form of the verb "to be"
and the spelling given fits this meaning.

The interpretation indicated by Eve's use of the name appears
to be foundational and causative in all Biblical uses of the
name. It furnished occasion for progressive revelations of God's
use of his creative power to bring new life and hope into the
life of fallen men and women who repented of sin and trusted him
for redemption. In Genesis 4:26, we see its first use in
worship; in Genesis 6:4, 8:20, 9:26, the usage which made it to
be the name by which "The God of the Hebrews" was designated in
Exodus 5:1-3; in Genesis 12:1-3; 25:21; 28:13, its relation to
the covenants with Abraham, Isaac, and Jacob; in Exodus 4:15,
6:2-8, 19:5,6, its relation to the covenant with Israel; and in
Exodus 34:6,7, along with the prophets' and psalmists' expositions of that famous passage, its use as a synonym for the moral
attributes of God that furnished a foundation for the plan of
salvation. This salvation is revealed gradually as salvation for
believers, all believers, and believers only. Delineation of
this evidence would require a full commentary. However, in
Genesis 4:1 alone we have sufficient evidence to warrant our use
of Yahweh as a translation.

4. GLIMPSES OF GOD

AS

THE PRESERVER OF WORSHIPPERS OF YAHWEH

Genesis 5--11; Hebrews 11:5-7

Introduction: Enoch's Walk With God

When Enoch and God walked together, as described in Genesis
5:22,24, did God assume a physical form? In case Genesis 2--3 is
interpreted as teaching that God did assume a physical form in
dealing with Adam and Eve, no question arises concerning the
possibility of his doing so in this case. At the same time,
another development in God's relation to men must be considered.
His judgment drove sinners out of his presence and set up the
Cherubim and the sword that turneth itself every way as a barrier
to their return. After the fall, even Adam, Eve, Seth, and Enosh
approached him through prayer rather than talking to him face to
face.

In weighing such questions it is also necessary to remember
that the Biblical interpretations were written long after the
events which were interpreted. The interpretations were explana-

tions of age-old causes accounting for conditions and practices in
the author's day. Thus the interpretations were aetiological,
furnishing explanations of origins. Does this aetiological
character of the literature require that all descriptions of God
as assuming a physical form be taken as mere figures of speech,
not corresponding to any objective reality? A flood of myths and
legends arising from idolatrous sources must be critically evalu-
ated this way. Must these Biblical interpretations be judged as
bearing evidence of the same biased, uncritical, and untrust-
worthy nature?

If the quotations and interpretations of God's will attributed to the patriarchs from Adam on down and recorded in Genesis
are to be taken as fictitious creations of the author of Genesis,
then the aetiological character of these accounts does reflect
seriously upon their objectivity and the trustworthiness of their
teaching.

On the other hand, if the tribute of Adam to Eve in Genesis
2:23 and the interpretation of Yahweh's judgment on sinners handed down through Adam and Eve according to Genesis 3:14-19 are
to be taken as parts of an oral tradition handed down through
worshippers of Yahweh from the earliest days, then the aetiological character of the literature raises no question at all about
its trustworthiness. Such utterances demanded explanation. The
revelations described provided the key to that explanation. The
inspired mind of the author of Genesis provided the literary
dress in which the utterances, the revelations, and many relevant
facts were clothed.

Despite the barrier against sinners' approach to him, it
still remained possible for God to approach men by assuming limited forms. We are not told exactly how it was done, but the
stories indicate that it was done. We are told that he did so
often for the sake of rebuke, exhortation, assurance, and fellowship. He is described as engaging in conversation with Cain.
Believers in later times, like Jacob and Moses, were led to
believe that they could not see the face of God and live; yet
they also believed that The Angel of Yahweh whom they did see was
God. The Shekinah Glory was interpreted by Solomon as possessing
a necessary covering for the Glory of God. In the Holy One, the
Radiance, and the Lord Jesus the same overwhelming mystery and the
same assured revelation appear. A logical deduction, therefore,
is that as long as men are bound within the five senses of the
human body they cannot see through these wonders, yet they can see
them. By their experience with these evidences of God's presence
men in all ages have been led to believe that God did reveal himself to them.

Somewhere within God's means of revelation, his fellowship
with Enoch fitted. The exact mode of this revelation is not so

important as the fact of it. Since the expression "walked with God" (Gen. 5:22,24) is used to describe the habitual nature of that fellowship, and since the statement used "God" instead of "Yahweh", it may be that the author's intent was to describe a purely spiritual fellowship. Even if so, God did give to Enoch evidence of his presence, and we are justified in seeing in it much of the truth conveyed by the imaginative paraphrase which said that God and Enoch walked together one day and walked so far that God said, "Enoch, it is too far for you to go back to your house; come on home with me." As said in Hebrews 11:5, "By faith Enoch was translated that he should not see death . . . ." Thus God took him immediately into his presence. He gave Enoch, as he did Elijah later, to see his glory without waiting for death and resurrection. The impression conveyed by these statements is that men, while yet in this life, cannot see the fullness of God's glory, yet they can see limited forms of it.

Yahweh's use of means in revealing himself to sinners, as judged in the light of the full account, was controlled by his intention to preserve believing sinners. These believers were worshippers of Yahweh. There was at the same time a revelation of his purposes concerning rebellious and incorrigible sinners. This double-edged purpose appears in all chief acts and words of God recorded in Genesis 5--11. All of them take their meaning from God's revelation of himself as Yahweh. He is the God who reveals his supernatural presence in a way to save his own and to destroy his enemies. He is the one who providentially controls history so as to make believers inherit the earth, establishing the kingdom of God on earth. The measures taken are summarized for us as follows:

(1) in Genesis 5:1--6:8, separation of the godly from the ungodly;

(2) in Genesis 6:9--9:29, ordination of human government;

(3) in Genesis 10:1--11:9, frustration of plans for an ungodly kingdom.

1. Separation of the Godly from the Ungodly

Yahweh's separation of the godly from the ungodly takes place in three ways: (1) in divine fellowship, (2) in marriage, and (3) in judgment.

Separation in fellowship is revealed by many circumstances in Genesis 5:1--6:8.

First, comparison of the first verse in this section (Gen. 5:1) and its emphasis upon creation in God's image with the last paragraph in this section (Gen. 6:5-8) with its emphasis upon

Noah as the one out of his generation who found favor with Yahweh
shows that the image of God had been destroyed by violence and
corruption in all who were not worshippers of Yahweh. Therefore,
the corrupt ones were already separated from the fellowship of
Yahweh. Second, the first three persons mentioned in this section
were the ones related to the beginning of the worship of Yahweh
by Genesis 4:26. Third, the names of certain other ones bear
meanings associated with religious experience. Fourth, the mention of other sons and daughters in each family, but without
names, shows that those who were named were selected for some
particular reason. Fifth, there is evidence that Enoch and Noah
made a distinction between The One True God of the worshippers of
Yahweh and the false gods of the heathen. In their cases, "the"
is used with "God" for the first time. Sixth, a distinction is
carefully maintained throughout Genesis 6:1-4 between "the sons
of The One True God" and the earthly, unspiritual men in whom the
Spirit of God could not continue to rule. Seventh, the Nephilim
of Genesis 6:4 are distinguished by a correct translation of the
original text as "the men of the Name."

   The relation of Adam, Seth, and Enosh to the worship of
Yahweh has been carefully discussed in Chapter IV. The specially
significant names used here, in addition to Adam, Seth, and Enosh,
are Mahalalel, Jared, and Enoch. Mahalalel means Praise of God,
and the connection with religious worship is obvious. Jared
means The One Who is Prostrate (or Bowed Down, as in humility or
worship). Enoch is derived from the verb "train up" or "dedicate."
This verb was used of old to describe the rubbing of the palate
of a newborn child by a midwife in order to make it suckle its
mother's breast. It was also used to describe the use of a rope
in a horse's mouth to train it or make it submissive. Either
usage is applicable to the experience of believers as persons
needing both encouragement and training in their efforts to
appropriate the blessings of God.

   The possible significance of the selection of names in other
cases grows out of the fact that Genesis 5:1--6:8 is put under
the heading "Generations of Adam," indicating a unity of some
kind in the account. Since Cain's descendants are not included,
this unity is not that of biological descent. Since there is no
mention of a firstborn in any family, no other reason for this
unity appears except community of faith.

   The thought of Enoch and Noah concerning The One True God
appears in Genesis 5:22,24, 6:2,4,9,11. In each of these six
verses the name "God" appears with a definite article before it.
Though the name appears constantly in the text of Genesis prior
to these passages, its use with "the" occurs for the first time
here. The fact that the experiences interpreted in these verses
parallel the experience of racial corruption described in Genesis

6:2,4, is good ground for thinking that the believers in Yahweh began to use the article with "God" at this time in order to distinguish their God from the false gods of wicked ones. In Genesis 6:2,4, this usage appears in the phrase "the sons of The (One True) God." This leads to the conclusion that "the sons of The (One True) God" were the worshippers of Yahweh who called their God The One True God.

The distinction between "the sons of the God" and the earthly, unspiritual men in whom the Spirit of God could not continue to rule is indicated throughout Genesis 6:1-4 by the use of the word "men." In all cases except the last the word *ha'adham*, the man of the ground, was used. In the last case, where the word "men" appears in "the men of the Name," the word *enoshim* is used. The first is the word used to describe mankind in general (cf. Gen. 2:4-25) and the second is the plural of the word used as a name for Enosh the son of Seth, in whose time worship of Yahweh was begun (cf. Gen. 4:26). This change of words calls attention strongly to the contrast maintained throughout this paragraph between mankind in general and the worshippers of Yahweh. When the author desired to call the worshippers of Yahweh men, he used a different word from the one used to describe ordinary men. Moreover, he used a word very definitely associated with worshippers of Yahweh.

The evidence showing that the Nephilim were called "the men of the Name" will be given below in connection with separation in marriage. It adds weighty evidence to the list of circumstances indicating that the purpose of Genesis 5:1-31 was to list those who were in fellowship with Yahweh.

The use of Noah and his sons to continue Yahweh worship after the flood, as indicated in Genesis 8:20--9:29, gives clear implication of reasons why the author so carefully indicated the origin and the continuance of worship of Yahweh in these early days.

Separation in marriage is described in Genesis 5:32--6:4. The inclusion of Genesis 5:32 as a part of this group of verses is due to the fact that it belongs to the description of Noah's life and to the fact that Noah's life is the key to identification of "the sons of The (One True) God," "the Nephilim," and "the men of the Name". The description of each person mentioned by name in Genesis 5, excepting that of Enoch, ends with the statement "then he died." Enoch's translation was the end of his earthly existence; therefore, the statement "and he was not; for God took him" is a substitute in his case for the statement "then he died." Therefore, the statement "then he died" in Genesis 5:31 marks the turn from the story of Lamech to that of Noah. When we observe that Genesis 5:32 and Genesis 6:1-4 are bound together as a brief description of significant events in Noah's life, we are prepared

to interpret all events and all peoples mentioned in that paragraph in the light of their relation to Noah.

Intermarriage between "the sons of God" and "the daughters
of men" is described in Genesis 6:2. It is indicated that wives
were being chosen merely because they were fair, without regard
for the wickedness in the homes from which they came and which
was bound to influence very deeply the homes into which they were
brought. Even "the sons of God" were making these choices merely
according to their pleasure.

There is no sound basis for saying, as many able interpreters
have done, that the men described here were angels appearing in
human form. The use of the title "The (One True) God" with
Enoch, Noah, and those mentioned here points definitely to men in
this case. If one can believe that the wild tales of mythology
concerning marriage between angels and human beings have crept
into the Bible at this point, he may make out an argument satis-
factory to himself by going on to misuse the word *Nephilim* and
the phrase, "the men of the Name". Without such belief in a
corrupted text and such twisting of words, the argument appears
to be as empty as a heathen idol. The rebuttal of such an argument is found in the unity and consistency appearing in the whole
passage and context when viewed as an account of Noah's life.
When all its words are interpreted in the light of its other words
and ideas, such interpretation becomes quite unreasonable. The
one line of evidence indicating that Noah was one of the "sons of
The (One True) God" seems sufficient to undermine the whole argument.

Genesis 6:3 is easily understood in light of the problem
created by intermarriage of the godly with the ungodly. Yahweh's
statement "my spirit cannot rule in men forever, in that they are
also flesh . . ." was an admission by Yahweh that the spiritual
battle for the hearts of men was going against him. The mixed
marriages were bringing wickedness right into the homes of the
worshippers of Yahweh. Therefore, Yahweh made a decision to set
a limit to the time in which he would bear mercifully with men.
After this limit he would wipe them out. The 120 years were the
period after which he would bring the Flood, as told later to
Noah (cf. Gen. 6:13). This period cannot refer to the life span
of an individual because the word "men" in this passage means
mankind. It describes the whole body of men called *ha'adham*.

The word *Nephilim* has been the main cause of trouble in
interpreting this passage. The translators of the King James
Version jumped to the conclusion that the word meant giants.
They did so because the twelve spies of Israel, according to
Numbers 13:33, said ". . . we saw the Nephilim, the sons of Anak,
who come of the Nephilim." This is the only other place in the

Bible where the word *Nephilim* appears. The verse, however, does
not tell us the meaning of *Nephilim.* The words "come of the
Nephilim" mean "descended from the Nephilim." The men were
giants as indicated by the last half of the verse. The name of
their father, Anak, means a giant. However, the statement that
they were descendants of a people called Nephilim and that they
themselves were called Nephilim makes no suggestion whatever concerning the meaning of the name *Nephilim.* Recognition of that
fact is indicated by the fact that today translators transliter-
ate the word rather than translate it. Transliteration leaves
the question of meaning an open question. Each reader is left to
decide for himself as best he can, using what evidence is available in Genesis, for Numbers does not give any evidence.

Before it is possible to give consideration to the evidence
in Genesis, it is necessary to clear away a list of misinterpre-
tations of words in the context. These have become so prevalent
in the minds of Bible readers that they becloud the issue in many
minds. All of them have been based upon the translation of
Nephilim as "giants." Despite the weakness of the argument for
"giants," that interpretation has persistently affected the
interpretation of other words in the verse. The Nephilim have
been identified with the offspring from the mixed marriages, the
offspring being thought of as giants. "The heroes from ancient
times" have been thought of as men of physical prowess. Moreover,
the phrase "the men of the Name" has been garbled so as to identify these men with the giants who were children of giants.

The error of identifying the Nephilim with the offspring of
the mixed marriages appears in the statement that the Nephilim
"were in the earth during those days and also after that time
during which the sons of The (One True) God married the daughters
of men and children were born to them . . . ."[1] Those days were
the days of corruption before the Flood. If the Nephilim were
there during and after those days, it is obvious that they were
Noah and his sons.

The error of identifying the offspring of the mixed marriages
with the heroes from ancient times" appears in the pronoun "these."
This pronoun is not a relative pronoun, which would refer to the
offspring of the mixed marriages just mentioned. This pronoun
refers emphatically to the Nephilim, the subject of the sentence.
This is in accord with established Hebrew usage in such cases.
It does not refer to the offspring of the mixed marriages.

The error of thinking that "the heroes of ancient times"
were necessarily mighty men of war, giants, offspring of angels,

---

1. Genesis 6:4 in the author's translation.

appears in the fact that the word "heroes" is used of spiritual heroes as well as mighty men of war. Psalm 112:1 says *"Blessed is the man* that fears Yahweh."[2] Psalm 112:2 adds, *"Mighty ones* (heroes) will his seed be in the earth."[3] Then the Psalm goes on to describe their might in terms of righteousness, graciousness, and mercy. It is the identification of the Nephilim with Noah and his sons that rules out the reference to physical prowess and requires this spiritual emphasis in Genesis 6:4.

The error in translating "the men of the Name" as "men of renown"[4] is the worst of these errors. All Hebrew Bibles give it in Hebrew as "the men of the Name". The only reason translators have for changing it is that they think the passage is a mythological interpolation or a corrupt text. Starting with such a supposition, men think it is necessary for them to reconcile the passage with other parts of the Bible in some arbitrary way. If the article "the" were not with the word "name", their translation would be right. "Men of a name" would mean "men of renown". But the article is unquestionably there! Thus all evidence combines to discredit arbitrary change of the text and also to warrant the conclusion that "the Name" in this passage refers to none other than Yahweh.

When we rid our minds of these errors and approach this passage from the viewpoint of its teaching about Noah, about Yahweh, and about worship of Yahweh, we see a unity and meaning in it that reflects Yahweh's efforts to separate his people from the wickedness of the day. Because of mixed marriages, wickedness was overflowing into the homes of worshippers of Yahweh. Therefore, Yahweh wanted separation in marriage as well as separation in spiritual fellowship. The homes of Noah and his sons were examples of such separation. They were the Nephilim. They were "the heroes from ancient times." They were "the men of the Name."

This evidence does not indicate clearly what the meaning of *Nephilim* was, but it does point toward the meaning "Separated Ones." It is quite clear that the Nephilim were associated with the separation from intermarriage with the ungodly. In addition, there are two bare possibilities concerning the root of the word Nephilim which lend strength to this suggestion. One of these

---

2.   The author's translation.

3.   The author's translation.

4.   *King James Version, American Standard Version, American Revised Version,* and others.

possibilities is the Hebrew word *naphal*, fall. The similarity in
spelling suggests a possible connection. The usual meaning "to
fall" does not fit the context; however, in Genesis 25:18 this
verb is used in the following statement concerning Ishmael:
". . . *by reason of opposition to all his brethren* he fell away."[5]
The expression "fell away" unquestionably indicates separation.
This meaning attaches itself to the verb in this case by reason of
of its connection with the preposition "from," or "away from."
This meaning is unusual, but the use of it in connection with
Ishmael shows that it was understood at this early time. The
other possibility is the Hebrew word *palah* which in its passive
form meant "be separated, be distinct." There is no instance in
which *Nephilim* is directly associated with either of these other
words, but similarity in spelling and meaning do make it possible
that *Nephilim* was associated with one or the other of them in the
early stages of the language. It is quite interesting, therefore,
that what possibilities do appear are in accord with the suggestions arising from the context.

Separation in judgment appears in Genesis 6:5-8. This passage states Yahweh's purpose to wipe out all mankind by the
Flood, excepting the little band of worshippers that remained.
The very last word in the passage stresses separation yet more,
saying, "Noah, however, found favor in the eyes of Yahweh."

2. Ordination of Human Government

The ordination of human government involves appointment of
men for the protection of others. Thus men become means in God's
hands of maintaining order even at the cost of eliminating the
stubbornly rebellious by force. This new order on earth is distinguished by the use of force from the fellowship, instruction,
and persuasion Yahweh used hitherto to influence the race of men.
In setting up this new order, three decrees were issued. The
three were not issued at one time like a code of law; they are
found scattered through Genesis 6:9--9:29, each one appearing
with a description of the circumstances that provoked it. They
were measures made necessary by the threat of sin to destroy all
that was good in men and women. They were also measures designed
to preserve the godly. These three decrees were as follows:
(1) the decree of the Flood (Gen. 6:13); (2) the decree of capital punishment for murderers (Gen. 9:6); (3) the decree of a
curse upon Canaan (Gen. 9:25).

The decree of the Flood was preparatory to the setting up of
the new order. While the earth remained corrupt and filled with

----

5. The author's translation.

violence, as described in Genesis 6:11,12, no hope for order and
improvement appeared; so the wiping out of all except the little
band of worshippers was Yahweh's way of opening a new opportunity.

Yahweh himself executed this judgment, but he used Noah as
a prophet. As a "preacher of righteousness" (II Pet. 2:5), he
condemned the corruption and violence around him. As he pleaded
with others to fear Yahweh, he stood for "the longsuffering of
God" (I Pet. 3:20) that shut the unheeding multitude up unto
condemnation. By preparation of "an ark to the saving of his
house" (Heb. 11:7), he was the means of preserving a remnant of
believers. This remnant was to be the nucleus of the new order.

The decree of capital punishment was a crucial step in
accomplishment of the new order. For preservation of human life
three preliminary steps were directed: use of animals for food
(Gen. 9:3); protection against animals of prey (Gen. 9:5a); and
protection against the violence of man (Gen. 9:5b). Then, as a
final, crucial measure in this preservation of human life, man
himself is charged with responsibility of avenging the blood of
one who is slain (Gen. 9:6). Apparently it was recognized that
order could not be maintained in some cases without this extreme
measure. Certainly this scripture declared the sanction of God
upon it at that time.

The reason for this most solemn responsibility is given in
these words, ". . . for *in the image of God* he made mankind."
This explanation follows a significant use of the word *ish*, the
word coined by Adam to express his appreciation of creatures made
in the image of God (cf. Gen. 2:19-23). That word appeared in
this statement, ". . . *at the hand of men* (*ha'adham*), *at the
hand of every man* (*ish*), (one who is) *their brother*, I shall
require the life of man."[6] Thus it is the brotherhood created by
spiritual likeness to God himself that constitutes an obligation
upon all who share it to protect their fellows from murderous
violence by elimination of malicious killers. One cannot appre-
ciate this brotherhood as he should without determination to
eliminate those whose presence would destroy it.

This maintenance of order by use of force has been a corner-
stone of human government ever since. Men of God who uphold it
carry in their hearts continually a prayer that fulfillment of
the ideals of the kingdom of God will make its use unnecessary.
Since those ideals involve only love, persuasion, and godly
fellowship, their fulfillment in society would eliminate it.
Nevertheless, men of God are taught by God to recognize the grim

---

6.   Genesis 9:5 in the author's translation.

necessity for government by force while widespread violence continues in the world. Likewise they are taught to respect the service of those who administer that government. Those who administer it are strictly charged to seek and observe God's direction in doing so. They are also charged to inflict the severest penalty only in cases where the ways of the ungodly are a threat to the lives of their fellowmen.

The curse upon Canaan appears as part of the story running through Genesis 9:20-27. The words of the curse, like all other words in Genesis 9:25-27, are interpreted for us by the account in Genesis 9:20-24.

Noah's conduct is described as the result of his first experience of drunkenness. It is also described as disgraceful. Since the words he uttered afterwards expressed sharp disapproval of what Ham had done to him while he was drunk and deeper appreciation of what Shem and Japheth had done to him, we are warranted in the conclusion that Noah repented of what he had done. We see then that Noah found no pleasure in his sin after he awoke from his drunken stupor. He hated himself for having slipped into disgrace. No matter whether he slipped because of ignorance about the effect of fermented wine or because of weakness in resisting temptation, he did repent. *The words he uttered afterwards* were spoken in the fear of God. They were spoken by a clear mind, aware of the subtle and seductive influence of sin. They arose out of the faith in Yahweh that was the truly characteristic thing in Noah's life. They are not the consequences of confusion arising out of the temporary fall into sin.

These words are in poetic form. Thus we see that they were words Noah prepared with solemn care and that they were passed on to posterity as one of the very important memorials coming down from the past. They were prophetic words. They find fulfillment in the later history of the descendants of Ham, Shem, and Japheth. Later scriptures reflect an acceptance of them by Yahweh's people as prophetic words.

This incident provides occasion for an observation concerning all scriptural accounts of sin in the lives of believers. The Bible never tells about sin so as to reflect any pleasure or profit in it. It does tell very frankly and fully how men like Noah, Abraham, and David fell into sin, but always it tells such stories in a way to show how God saves men from sin.

Noah's experience helps us to understand that of Ham. We are told that "he saw the nakedness of his father and proceeded

to tell his brothers outside."[7] He did nothing to help. He
showed no sense of embarrassment or regret. He did not even
participate in the efforts of his brothers to relieve the situation, to show modesty while doing so, to prevent gossip, shame,
and loss of godly influence. If we judge him by the ways of those
who take pleasure in sin, we suppose that he expressed a sala-
cious attitude. In other words, there was in Ham's heart that
pleasure in sin that could enslave him or his descendants.

The utterance of the curse against Canaan, the son of Ham
rather than Ham himself gives evidence of being due to Noah's
prophetic insight and a revelation that the evil tendency in Ham
would find an unhindered and ruinous response in his son's life.
The so-called "little sin" of the parent works the ruin of the
child in many cases. One of the most tragic effects of sin is the
influence of the parent whose secret delight in the things of
darkness serves to make sin attractive to his child. It can be
first attractive, then possessive, then lecherous, then damnable.
If mere knowledge could turn the hearts of parents back to God's
love and purity, it ought to be a vision of the woe their weakness can work in the ways of their children.

The fulfillment of this curse upon Canaan appears in its
strongest form in the extermination of Canaanites in Palestine.
Four hundred years before Yahweh uttered the command that they
should be destroyed, he said to Abraham, ". . . the iniquity of
the Amorites is not yet full."[8] The Amorites were a part of the
Canaanites (cf. Gen. 10:16). At the time of the command, however,
Yahweh said that their iniquity was full. Not until then did he
direct their destruction. He had been merciful. He had waited
while there was any chance for one like Melchizedek, king of
Salem, to arise among them. Jebus, the city of the Jebusites,
was the Salem of Melchizedek. Thus it is clear that these people
were not condemned to utter destruction until they became reprobate.

To understand the awful necessity for such judgment we need
to bear in mind facts about these people indicated often in the
Bible and verified over and over by the researches of historians
and archaeologists. Their entire life, their entire thought,
became so steeped in the worship of heathen gods that they associated the worst of idolatrous abominations with their worship.
Human sacrifice and "sacred" prostitution were practiced in their
temples. Surely nothing can be more revolting than to realize

---

7.   Genesis 9:22 in the author's translation.

8.   Genesis 15:16 in the *American Standard Version*.

that these peoples called the persons they set aside for participation in these abominations "holy men" and "holy women." These
practices provide evidence of spiritual blindness that called
black white and white black. It was impossible for the light of
God's truth any longer to penetrate the gloom of their night.

To fully understand this curse, one other need should be
seen alongside the necessity for bringing retributive justice
upon them. This is the need of God's children for protection
from the influence of such sinners. As rotten apples, if left in
the barrel, will cause good apples to rot, so will rotten sinners,
unrestrained and uncondemned, corrupt believers. Even as God
himself used the Flood to provide an opportunity for worshippers
of Yahweh to build a new world, so Yahweh charged them to protect
that new order by a system of justice including capital punishment. The destruction of the Midianites, as recorded in Numbers
31:1-8, furnishes an example. These were an immoral and dangerous group, wholly given to the corrupting practices of iniquity;
therefore, they were devoted to destruction. The judicial and
police powers of the state, even when used to take human life in
the fear of God, receive divine sanction from such commands.

Because the attitudes and action of Shem and Japheth were
pure and helpful, Noah saw blessings coming to them and their
descendants. He blessed Yahweh God from whom they learned their
ways of purity and helpfulness. When he called Yahweh "The God
of Shem,"[9] he seems to have recognized Shem as a leader in the
worship of Yahweh. When he prayed that Japheth "should dwell in
the tents (tabernacles) of Shem,"[10] his words indicated continuance in Yahweh worship and continued blessings to flow from it.
The tent dwellers of early days used tents for places of worship,
and the abiding of God among them was thought of as "tenting" or
"tabernacling" among them.

Thus Noah found in his own lapse into sin an occasion for a
prophetic word. Determination to cut off, by the help of God,
one's own members, when they tend to drag one into moral ruin,
became a necessity for believers in Yahweh. Determination to
cut off members of the group who prove to be a threat to the life
of the group became a necessity for believers in Yahweh. It is
not blind hate that does it but love of righteousness. When this
is done, it is not a miscarriage of justice for those eliminated
but a guarantee of justice for all.

---

9.   Genesis 9:26 in the *American Standard Version*.

10.   Genesis 9:27 in the author's translation.

3. Frustration of Plans for an Ungodly Kingdom

The great measure used by Yahweh God for the preservation of
his worshippers was the confusion of tongues at Babel. The entire
section of Genesis entitled "Generations of the Sons of Noah,"
(Gen. 10:1--11:9) leads up to the crisis faced at Babel. The
plans of the men of Babel are carefully stated in Genesis 11:4.
Yahweh God is described in 11:5-7 as personally promoting the
defeat of these plans. And the special attention paid to Shem
and Heber in the arrangement of the story warrants the understanding that Yahweh's desire to preserve these Yahweh worshippers
was as truly a part of his purpose as was the defeat of this
first effort to build an empire around idolatrous and morally
corrupt worship.

Evidence that the whole account is built around the confusion of tongues and consequent division of the nations appears in
Genesis 10:5,13,18,20,26,31,32. Constant reference in these
verses to division, separate families, separate languages, and
separate lands prepares the reader for explanation of the cause
of such serious division. That is given in Genesis 11:1-9.

The purposes of the men of Babel, not the mere building of
a tower, indicate the reason for God's opposition. These purposes, as described in Genesis 11:4, contemplated the building of
a great political union, centered in a state-controlled religious
union, and controlled by dictators for their own fame, power, and
glory. From the viewpoint of God this meant three things directly opposed to Yahweh worship: (1) ungodly political union;
(2) man-made religious union; (3) dictatorial and selfish control
of union.

Ungodly political union was proposed in the word " . . . let
us build for ourselves a city . . . ." The city contemplated was
a city state. There were many examples in later Babylonia. Ur
of the Chaldees was one of them. Nineveh in Assyria (cf. Gen.
10:11) was another. These city-states made themselves the political center of a district or country and sought through control
of trade and military power to extend their rule out and out over
other lands. This means a political union controlled by the
ungodly in ungodly ways.

Man-made religious union was proposed in the words " . . and
a tower with its head in the heavens . . . ." This tower was not
an ordinary tower. The Babylonians called such a tower a
ziggurat. It was a rectangular building with many stories, the
walls of each upper story dropping back some distance from the
outer edge of the story below it. The top story was a heathen
temple, containing an image of the chief god worshipped in its
city. When the *ziggurat* was large and the stories many, the

people thought of its head as being "in the heavens." In their
flat land, this structure was the dominant feature of the city
and the surrounding country. Its builders meant for its influence to dominate the life of the people, their thought, their
culture, their standards of conduct. Therefore, they placed
these temples at the centers of their cities.

To understand this proposal we must remember that the religion involved was to be under control of the state. This *ziggurat* was to be an instrument of the state for the control of its
people. Its religion, therefore, was a man-made religion, made
by men for advancement of their own power.

The influence of such man-made religion can be judged by
another feature of the worship conducted at a *ziggurat*. Round
about these heathen temples were places for the so-called "holy
men" and "holy women" who practiced prostitution as an act of
worship with devotees whose vile passions inclined them to immoral ways. This corruption is the unmistakable evidence that
idolatry has no conception of the moral standards associated with
the worship of Yahweh. This is the rotten fruit by which the
heathen stand condemned in all lands and all times. This is what
Yahweh has sought at all times to eradicate from the life of his
followers.

Dictatorial and selfish control of union was proposed in the
words ". . . and let us make *for ourselves* a name . . . ." That
emphatic phrase *"for ourselves"* never had a more ominous meaning
than here. The men of Babel wanted to use the state and its
religion to build and maintain their dictatorship. They deliberately schemed to make the state powerful and to make its
priesthood pander to human passions in order that their own name
might be great. That would make their ruthless rule and corruption more and more absolute.

Conclusion: God of Vengeance

"Vengeance belongeth unto me; I will recompense, saith the
Lord," is a teaching used by Moses in Deuteronomy 32:35 and by
Paul in Romans 12:19. The truth in their words was based first
upon the events observed in Genesis 5--11. Yahweh's action in
the Flood, in ordination of capital punishment, and in the extermination of those exploiting lechery is ground for this teaching.

The teaching reveals two sides of Yahweh's dealing which
should never be separated in our thinking about vengeance,
Yahweh's longsuffering mercy toward sinners and his indignation
toward their violent or seductive injury of others. The mercy
shows that vengeance is not revenge, that Yahweh's anger is never

unrighteous, and that Yahweh's wrath is never implacable hate. God's wrath upon man is unavoidable only when man's hate of God is implacable. Likewise, his indignation shows that vengeance is inescapable when his mercy is spurned, that his anger burns like consuming fire when his purity and his child's purity is despised, that his wrath inexorably damns man when man's will becomes unchangeably fixed in corruption.

Both sides of God's dealing appear in the Flood. God's witness to Enoch "that before his translation he had been well pleasing to God" (Heb. 11:5) was a lesson to others. Yahweh's appointment through Noah of a period of one hundred and twenty years during which Noah built the Ark and preached righteousness was a merciful means "through which he condemned the world" (Heb. 11:7). Thus Enoch and Noah became men of faith, and those who failed to take sides with them were left without excuse.

Both sides of God's dealing appear in capital punishment. Cain and Lamech were not immediately cut off because they had killed a man. When, however, the spread of sin made violence a threat to the life of all living creatures, God put a sanction upon the ritual slaughter of animals for food but most strongly prohibited slaughter of a being created in the image of God. This word to Noah does not say that the slaughter of animals was begun at this time, but it does put divine controls upon it. Moreover, it magnifies the fact that the divine image in man makes the prohibition of manslaughter a necessity for human society. Man was thereby taught the reason for distinction between animals and men. Law was given both as instruction and warning. It taught that the law-abiding should be protected. At the same time it warned that the man guilty of cold-blooded manslaughter would be without excuse.

Both sides appear again in the curse upon Canaan. Though the prediction of doom in Canaan's case was terrible, the omission of Ham and his other sons showed that it was not a curse upon a family. There is no ground for saying that all Ham's descendants, probably including the Negroes, were included. The entire context leads to the conclusion that the predicted doom would be enslavement of a people by their own depraved nature. In addition, the turning of Rahab unto the God of Israel at the time of Jericho's destruction is a shining example of the forgiveness Yahweh stood ready to show toward individuals, even the Canaanites, when individuals did repent. Moreover, the presence of Tamah, Rahab, Ruth, and Bathsheba (Matthew 1:3-6) in the genealogy of Jesus bears testimony to the fact that any soul out of any race can enter into the glory of Yahweh by faith in Yahweh. The exceptions prove the rule that the masses of the evil ones were left without excuse.

was two hundred and five years old, he died
in Charran.

12:1 Afterwards Yahweh continued to say to Abram:

"Get yourself out from your land, from your
    kinsfolk, and from your father's household, /
Unto the land that I shall show you; /

2   In order that I may make of you a great nation, /
      and in order that I may bless you, / for I am
      determined to make your name great; /
Yea, be thou a blessing; /

3   For I am determined to bless those who bless you,
      and *those cursing you* I shall curse; /
And men shall be blessed through you, /
      even all the families of the earth." /

In this passage Yahweh is presented as the one who inspired Abram's
faith. He did so by means of a call. This description of the
call shows it to have been a *personal* call, persuasion addressed
by Yahweh himself directly to Abram as an individual. The call
is also described as a *persistent* call, presented in various forms
of spiritual persuasion, finally put into words and repeated
until Abram answered. Moreover, this call is described as a *purposeful* call, with purpose expressed first in a great commission,
then in purpose clauses revealing its intention to bless, then in
reason clauses explaining how the divine will and the human will
will be coordinated in fulfillment, making the result to be the
fruitage of mutual determination.

1. By Means of Personal Persuasion

When the telephone operator says, "This is a person-to-
person call," winsome influences are brought to bear upon the
heart of the one called. He says in his heart, "The one calling
knows me already. He wants to talk directly to me. Doubtless he
thinks there is something I can do for him sufficiently important
for him to want to talk about it directly to me. I must answer
if I possibly can."

In Abram's case, as Scripture describes it, the call came
from Yahweh God to Abram son of Terah. Genesis 11:27 identifies
Abram. Genesis 12:1 identifies God, using the personal name
"Yahweh." The force of the personal approach may be felt at each
point in the personal sketch of Abram given in Genesis 11:27-32,
in the use of his name, in the specific explanation of his family
relations, and in the implication of his responsibility for
leadership.

Abram's personal name, if given in full, would be Abram son
of Terah. "Abram his (Terah's) son" in Genesis 12:31 indicates
this. To this day in the lands of the Bible this usage appears,
the given name appearing first and "son of Terah" or the like
appearing in place of a family name.

Abram's personal relations and circumstances are likewise
specific. His brother's names, the death of his brother Haran in
Ur, the marriages of Abram and Nahor, the childlessness of Abram
and Sarai, the movement to Charran, and the death of Terah give a
personal sketch that prepares us for an understanding of vital
family matters involved in the call.

Abram's personal responsibilities are likewise indicated.
We might overlook them if we were not thinking of them in particular, but they are there. His brother Haran died before the
movement to Charran. His brother Nahor was not taken to Charran
along with the others of Terah's immediate family. We are not
told why, but at least he was not there in the beginning of their
stay in Charran. Abram was the only son present to stand next to
Terah in the leadership of the tribe or clan. Though Genesis
24:10,24,27 tell us that Nahor lived with the family group later,
it is clear that Nahor was not in the earlier movement and that
Abram was the second-in-command. Moreover, this responsibility
was a big one. When we are told in Genesis 14:14 that there were
three hundred and eighteen men, "trained men, born in his house
(household)," we are made to realize that the entire household,
fighting men plus all dependents, including children, other kin,
servants, slaves, and others perhaps, probably numbered between
one and two thousand persons. The care of such a group was a
great responsibility. From experience, therefore, Abram already
understood much of the privileges and the privations involved
in his social relations. The call, however, looked to far higher
and greater responsibilities. It involved his yearning for personal purity, for the approval of a righteous God, for a homeland
and a family free of idolatry, and for a son of his own as an
heir. So much of life was bound up in this question! The call
then was touching his heart in all the vital spots.

This personal sketch is framed in exactly such words as are
used in any tongue for historical identification. Any effort to
represent the call as subjective dreaming on the part of Abram
discredits the Biblical account. Any interpretation that makes
it an imaginary description of a legendary hero, clothed by the
author of Genesis in historical language but being in fact what
he or others before him imagined the egotistical ambitions of an
ancestor to have been, substitutes the author's judgment for the
words of the Bible. An example of this appears in the following:
"Thus in vss. 1-4 Abraham is less an individual than a symbol or
personification of the Israelite clans which had moved from the

desert into Palestine and had settled at Hebron."[3]

This personal sketch indicates the possibility of contact during Abram's early years between him and the worshippers of Yahweh who lived after the Flood. These leaders included Noah, Shem, and Eber (or Heber). Each of these could have exercised an important influence on Abram. Perhaps each one did so. Contact with them could have been used of God to prepare Abram for the special call. Antipathy for idolatry and deep sympathy with the ideals of Yahweh worship could have drawn him to them. All that is told of his later life makes it quite natural to suppose that such tendencies existed before the call. Furthermore, Joshua's statement recorded in Joshua 24:2 appears to rule out Terah as a helpful spiritual influence upon Abram while they were in Ur. Joshua gave the following as the word of Yahweh: "Your fathers dwelt of old time beyond the River, even Terah, the father of Abraham, and the father of Nahor: and they served other gods."[4]

Eber was probably the outstanding one in his influence upon Abram. The following facts arising out of Biblical data support this conclusion:

First, Eber was in his prime while Abram was still in Ur, while Noah was very old and Shem well past his prime. The years mentioned between the births of fathers and sons in Genesis 11:10-26 make Eber 235 years old at the time Terah's first child was born. Taking that 235 from his total of 464 (cf. Gen. 11:16), 229 years of Eber's life were left after the birth of Terah's firstborn.

Second, Terah's firstborn could not have been Abram, for the firstborn, being born when Terah was 70, was 135 when Terah died at the age of 205, while Abram who departed after Terah's death (cf. Acts 7:4) was 75 at that time. He is not called the firstborn anywhere in the Bible. We are led to conclude that Abram's name was put first in the story because of his prominence rather than his age.

Third, we can calculate the time of Abram's birth by subtracting his age at Terah's death (75) from the age of Terah's firstborn at that time (135), finding that Abram was born 60

---

3. Cuthbert A. Simpson, *The Book of Genesis* (Introduction and Exegesis) in *The Interpreter's Bible*, Vol. I (New York: Abingdon-Cokesbury Press, 1952), p. 571.

4. Joshua 24:2 in the *American Standard Version*.

years after the firstborn. Eber, therefore, had 169 years to
live after Abram's birth. Certainly he was vigorous and influen-
tial when Abram was still in Ur.

Fourth, according to Genesis 10:21-31, Eber was prominent
among the descendants of Shem. In verse 21 the author of Genesis
went out of his way to mention the children of Eber before the
expected references to him in verse 24 as the son of Shelah and
in verse 25 as the father of Peleg and Joktan. The description
of Shem in 10:21 as "the father of all the children of Eber"
draws special attention to the fact that the line of faithful
ones ran through Shem and Eber to the children of Eber. The message of Genesis 1--11, tracing the line of the faithful from Adam
and Eve through Seth, Enosh, Kenan, Mahallalel, Jared, Enoch,
Methusaleh, Lamech, Noah, Shem, Eber, and the children of Eber,
thus led straight to Abram as one closely related to Eber spiritually.

Fifth, according to Genesis 14:13, Abram was called "the
Hebrew." We are told that an escapee from Sodom, after it was
captured by Eastern invaders and Lot taken captive with the
others, came and told "Abram the Hebrew." Thus he was distinguished from other peoples as a Hebrew. The name is derived from
a verb meaning "to pass over"; so it is often suggested that the
name may describe Abram as one who passed over the River Euphra-
tes when he emigrated from Mesopotamia to the land of Canaan.
However, it is also true that the name "Eber" is the same as
"Heber," the initial "h" being dropped at times. Thus it is
possible that the name "Hebrews" meant descendants of Eber or
Heber. When Pharaoh, a descendant of Ham, said to Moses, "Who is
Yahweh . . .?" Moses answered, "The God of the Hebrews hath met
with us . . ." (Ex. 5:2,3). Thus the descendants of Abraham
emphasized the connection of this racial name "Hebrews" with Yahweh. Seeing that the worship of Yahweh is the central theme in
all the records of Genesis and Exodus and the name of Eber is the
last before that of Abram to be given a place of outstanding importance among worshippers of Yahweh, there is good ground for
thinking that the spiritual influence of Eber upon his life
caused Abram to call himself "a Hebrew" and others to know him as
"the Hebrew."

Florence Marvyne Bauer has given us the following story to
suggest the influence of Eber upon Abram's call:

> His thoughts went back to the days on his farm
> when he and Eber had worked side by side. Perhaps he
> dozed, dreaming of those times of companionship with
> his friend, for he thought he heard the Amorite's
> voice saying, "Abram, son of Terah." He started up,
> his heart swelling with joy. "Here I am!"

But the voice that answered him was not Eber's. It
lacked the gruff qualities he remembered. "Abram, son
of Terah."

Abram opened his eyes and found the tent aglow
with a peculiar radiance . . . .

The voice spoke again. It was warm, compelling,
musical. "Son of Terah, I am your Friend. I am Yah."

Filled with breathless exaltation, Abram heard
himself ask, "Oh Lord Yah, what shall I do?"

"Believe that I am the most high God, Creator of
all things, and I will bless you."

"O Lord most high, I do believe."

"Trust Me, and I will lead you to a land which
your sons shall inherit."

"O Most High, I will trust thee."

"If you will obey my words, I will prosper you and
make your name great among men. Do you believe I am
able to do this?"

Now Abram spoke with assurance. "Is anything too
hard for Him who created all things?" he asked. "O
Lord Yah, . . . I will obey Thy voice."

Gradually the strange light vanished, but the
wondrous peace remained in Abram's heart . . . .[5]

This story is likewise a beautiful illustration of a personal approach by God to one whom he would call. This is a
person-to-person call.

2. By Means of Persistent Persuasion

Expositors of Genesis, even the most diligent searchers for
evidence, have found the time and place of Abram's call a vexa-
tious problem. Their struggle is reflected by the fact that the
King James Version renders Genesis 12:1 this way: "Now the Lord
had said, ..." "Had said" is an unjustifiable rendering of
the Hebrew imperfect. It is probable that the following statement of Robert S. Candlish gives a correct interpretation of the
motive that prompted this rendering: "It is to reconcile the Old
Testament narrative with what Stephen tells us, that our translators have adopted the expression '. . . , 'The Lord had said,

---

5. Florence Marvyne Bauer, "Abram Son of Terah," *The Old
Testament and the Fine Arts* (New York: Harper and Brothers, 1954),
p. 90.

. . . ."[6] The text indicates that the call occurred after
Terah's death. Any effort to solve the problem arbitrarily com-
plicates it. H.C. Leupold, therefore, is moved to describe it
this way:

> . . . Acts 7:4, Stephen, in an inspired address (cf. Acts
> 6:10), tells us that Abraham left, "when his father was
> dead." Yet it appears that Terah lived sixty years after
> Abram's departure from Haran. For his total age was 205
> years, and Abraham was born when Terah was seventy (v. 26)
> and was seventy-five when he left Haran (12:4):
> 205-145 = 60. How can Stephen say, Abram left "when his
> father was dead"? The question is a very difficult one.
> Luther once expressed the thought that he would be
> exceedingly grateful for a man sufficiently clever to
> offer the solution . . . .[7]

In the face of such a problem, we are constrained to move
very cautiously. Nevertheless, we are also constrained by the
importance of the issues to continue as best we can to examine
all evidence. We shall look first at evidence and interpretations
favoring a call in Charran, since the text obviously places it
there, then at evidence and opinions favoring a call in Ur, and
finally at a translation implying a call both at Ur and at
Charran.

Evidence and interpretation favoring Charran appear in Genesis 11:31, 12:1 and in the comments of some outstanding expositors. In using the word "expositors" here, the reference is intended to be to men who have sought to find the meaning of the
Biblical text as it stands. Diligent works of this kind command
respect even when conclusions differ.

The point of conclusive evidence is that Genesis 11:27--12:4
is a narrative with the several steps in the story indicated in
the regular way of a Hebrew narrative. Accordingly, the call is
indicated as occurring after the migration to Charran. All students can agree, therefore, that there was an occurrence of the
call in Charran.

The crux of the problem is in this question, Was there also
an occurrence of the call in Ur?

---

6. Robert S. Candlish, *Commentary on Genesis*, Vol. I, in
Classic Commentary Library (Grand Rapids, Michigan: Zondervan
Publishing Company, reprint (n.d.)), p. 183.

7. H.C. Leupold, *Exposition of Genesis* (Columbus, Ohio: The
Wartburg Press, 1942), p. 401.

C.F. Keil, in a word that represents the conclusion of Franz Delitszch also, said, "It was in Haran that Abram first received the divine call to go to Canaan (xii. 1-4), when he left not only his country and kindred, but also his father's house."[8] Keil's word is positive but also unconvincing. He uses Abram's actual leaving his father's house as evidence concerning the time of his receiving the call to leave it. Abram could have received the call long before he obeyed. It needs to be noted, by the way, that even the call in Charran was not a call "to go to Canaan," but according to Yahweh's word, a call to go "unto the land that I shall show you."

S.R. Driver said concerning Genesis 12:1, "The words state the sequel of xi. 31b, the country which Abram is commanded to leave being not Ur, but Haran."[9] The latter part of this opinion is quite arbitrary, for it carries the implication that inasmuch as the command referred to Charran (Haran, in his spelling) it could not also have referred to Ur. This implication was made without offering proof.

Let it be understood then that no doubt is left concerning a call to Charran. The Biblical text certifies, even as Keil, Delitzsch, and Driver have insisted, that there was a call in Charran. A question does remain, however, concerning Ur.

Evidence and opinions favoring Ur appear in Genesis 12:1-3, 15:7; Nehemiah 9:7, and various Jewish and Christian sources.

"From your land" in Genesis 12:1 uses the word land separately from the word "kindred," which appears in the phrase immediately after this one. The word "land" standing alone can be applied to any land. The word "kindred" standing alone is used to describe things in general which are related to a person by that one's birth. Its most usual application is to one's kin in general. In Genesis 43:7 it is made to include brothers as well as a father. When the two words are tied together in a genitival relation, as in Genesis 11:28, each word restricts the other. The land becomes the land of one's birth or nativity, as in the case of Terah's son Haran. Other instances appear in Genesis 24:7, 31:13; Jeremiah 22:10, 46:16; Ezekiel 23:15; Ruth 2:11. The kin referred to become those who gave one birth in that land, one's forefathers, one's ancestors, rather than kin

---

8. C.F. Keil, *Pentateuch in Commentaries on the Old Testament*, Vol. I (Grand Rapids, Michigan: William B. Eerdmans Publishing Company, reprint in 1949), p. 180.

9. S.R. Driver, *opus citus*, p. 144.

in general. In Biblical usage at least the words are restricted
thus when linked together.

When Abram, according to Genesis 24:4, called Charran "my
land," he used "land" separately, in accord with the usage described. When he, according to Genesis 24:7, referred to the
land of his birth, he used "land" and kindred (forefathers)
together.

Our immediate interest is in the fact that Abram had known
both Ur and Charran as his land before he moved on into Canaan.
Therefore, the words "from your land" could have applied to Ur
at one time and to Charran at another.

"From your kindred" is likewise applicable to the kindred in
Ur and to the kindred in Charran.

"From your father's household" also was applicable in Ur as
well as in Charran.

Concerning Genesis 15:7, C.F. Keil argued thus: ". . . it
is not stated there that God called Abram in Ur, but only that
he brought him out . . . . The simple fact of removing from Ur
might also be called a leading out, as a work of divine superintendence and guidance, without a special call from God."[10] This
must be admitted. Yet it can be said at the same time that this
word by no means denies a call in Ur. Nehemiah 9:7 describes the
experience there in the same way. These and all other references
to the subject indicate that God was certainly dealing with Abram
in Ur in a definitely persuasive way, no matter whether his influence was exercised directly or indirectly. He was at least
preparing Abram for the call while he was yet in Ur, and it remains true that such "divine superintendence and guidance,"
judged merely by the words of Genesis 15:7 and Nehemiah 9:7, could
have included the call. These passages do not settle the question
about a call in Ur one way or the other.

Since all evidence observed thus far leaves the question
open, it is worthwhile to take note of the fact that Jewish tradition has persistently clung to the conviction that there was a
call in Ur. At least it is the oldest tradition. We ought to
hesitate before we conclude there was no ground whatever for it.

Stephen, according to Acts 7:2,3 said, "The God of glory
appeared unto our father Abraham, when he was in Mesopotamia,
before he dwelt in Haran, and said unto him, 'Get thee out of thy

---

10. C.F. Keil, *opus citus*, p. 180.

land . . . .'"[11] Stephen was also dogmatic. He was, however,
preaching at the time he made this dogmatic statement, not writing a commentary with full reason for supporting evidence.
Probably he felt no need before his audience in Jerusalem for
sustaining this statement about Abraham. He seems to have taken
for granted that he was voicing an established conviction about a
well-known matter. Certainly he believed there was evidence to
sustain his statement. He could, of course, have cited what has
been presented here, but his positiveness makes it likely that he
knew more than this.

These scattered and in some cases unsubstantiated bits of
evidence cannot be said to be conclusive. Nevertheless, their
cumulative effect is to create a probability. Accordingly, such
searchers for truth as Martin Luther, John Peter Lange, Robert S.
Candlish, Marcus Dods, and H.C. Leupold have been strongly inclined to accept this probability as the most probable conclusion
indicated by the evidence as a whole. Lange stated his conclusion this way: *"Out of thy country* -- the fatherland. The land
of Mesopotamia as it embraced both Ur of the Chaldees and
Haran."[12] In accord with this conclusion, A. Gosman, who translated Lange's Commentary on Ch. XII-XXXVI,[13] added this note of
his own:

> There is no improbability in the supposition that
> the call was repeated. And this supposition would not
> only reconcile the words of Stephen and Moses, but may
> explain the fifth verse: "And they went forth to go
> into the land of Canaan, and into the land of Canaan
> they came." Abram had left his home in obedience to
> the original call of God, but had not reached the land
> in which he was to dwell. Now, upon the second call,
> he not only sets forth, but continues in his migra-
> tions until he reaches Canaan, to which he was
> directed.[14]

A translation reflecting a repeated call has been offered
by the author for the Biblical text itself. The words that in-

---

11. *American Standard Version.*

12. John Peter Lange, *Genesis in Commentary on the Holy
Scriptures*, Philip Schaff, ed., reprint by Zondervan Publishing
House (n.d.), p. 391.

13. See footnote 12, p. 148.

14. John Peter Lange, *opus citus*, p. 393, footnote by
A. Gosman.

troduce the call are rendered this way: "Afterwards Yahweh continued to say to Abram . . . ." If this translation is correct,
then the evidence for a repeated call is conclusive. The importance of this issue then requires very, very careful examination
of it.

This translation has been made in accord with specific syn-
tactical principles based upon Hebrew usage throughout the Old
Testament and explained in the author's *Survey of Syntax in The
Hebrew Old Testament*, pp. 33-42, 97-100. Anyone disposed to
challenge the translation ought to weigh these principles for himself and also to consider the illustrations which are to follow.

The steps taken in evaluating the force of the verb "say" in
this case are as follows. First, it is observed that this verb
is an indicative imperfect. Second, it is remembered that all indicative imperfects not affected by some unusual influence express
the incompleteness of an act repeated over and over or the incompleteness of a single act in progress. This principle is a summary of things taught by Hebrew grammarians in general. Third,
evidence in the context concerning the number of occurrences is
observed, and the probability of repetition is noted. This was
done above. Fourth, a study is made of this question: Does the
conjunction called *waw consecutive* exercise an unusual influence
upon this verb? This question will be weighed in the discussion
to follow.

Translators, as a rule, have applied to the constructions
considered here a theory which claims that the imperfect is influenced by the conjunction so as to make it a consequence of the
verb that introduced the narrative. Since perfects are used regularly to introduce a narrative, the imperfect is given the force
of a perfect. This interpretation makes the action singular, indicates one occurrence. The construction appears very, very frequently in narrative, almost continually; so the change effected
by this theory appears throughout the Old Testament and greatly
affects its interpretation. The technical aspects of this theory
cannot be studied here, but the practical effects can be considered by anyone through careful observation of the context. To
facilitate such consideration a number of examples will be given.

In the genealogies of Genesis 5:3-32, 11:10-26, words concerning the begetting of sons and daughters occur many times
(cf. 5:4,7,10,13,16,19,22,26,30, 11:16,13,15,17,19,21,23,25). The
first instance, in Genesis 5:3,4, is typical, using imperfects
with *waw consecutive* as all the other verses do. If the imperfect
in 5:3 is handled as an imperfect, the rendering will be: "afterwards (i.e. "after Adam became a hundred and thirty years old") he
proceeded to become the father of a child in his likeness, according to his image . . . " This rendering fits the progressive

force of this imperfect because it refers to one child. If the
same word in 5:4 is handled as an imperfect, the rendering will
be: "and (or meanwhile, i.e. during the eight hundred years Noah
continued to live after he became the father of Seth) he contin-
ed   to become the father of sons and daughters." This rendering
fits the frequentative force of this imperfect because it refers
to more than one child. Throughout these genealogies such distinctions are appropriate. Yet there is not one of our translations, Sep, Syr, OL, Vul, AV, DV, ERV, ASV, JNT, MNT, AAT, or ARV,
that has revealed them.

Repeated action is surely involved in each of these verses:
Genesis 2:20, 5:22,24,32. It is probably involved in each of
these: Genesis 1:5,8,10,12,18,21,25,31, 2:19, 3:9, 7:12.

In Genesis 2:19 an issue of great importance is involved.
S.R. Driver gave concerning this verse an opinion typical of many
used to argue that accounts of Genesis 1:1--2:3 and that of
Genesis 2:4-25 contradict each other. He said: "In ch. i. animals are all created before man; so that it is again apparent
that the writer of ch. ii. 4bff. follows a different conception
of the order of creation."[15] If the imperfect is rendered as a
frequentative, and the verse is translated thus: "And *out of the
ground* Yahweh God continued to form every beast of the field, and
every bird of the heavens . . . ," then this cause for such critical judgment vanishes. In other words, we have produced many
unnecessary causes for criticism by our methods of translation.

In Genesis 3:9 an issue of importance is involved. Genesis
3:8 tells us that Adam and Eve, after their sin, "heard the voice
of Jehovah God walking in the garden in the cool of the day: and
the man and his wife hid themselves . . . ."[16] In similar ways
all other translations recount the first hearing of Yahweh's
voice. How natural it is then to recognize the frequentative
force of the imperfect that follows and translate Genesis 3:9
thus: "But Yahweh God continued to call unto the man, and to say
to him, 'Where are you?'"![17] The initiative of God in searching
for sinners is thus recognized. That initiative is a vital element in all God's efforts to save the lost.

Genesis 12:1, therefore, is not an isolated case by any
means. Recognition of a frequentative force in its first verb
would provide an exceedingly important bit of evidence concerning
Abram's call.

---

15. S.R. Driver, *opus citus*, p. 42, footnote.

16. *American Standard Version*.

17. The author's translation.

The persistent persuasion of Yahweh was a vital element in
the inspiration of Abram's faith. Recognition of the Lord's persistent knocking upon the door of his heart is not dependent upon
recognition of a frequentative imperfect in Genesis 12:1, but it
is made more obvious and forceful by it. The experience of a
call by prophets, preachers, missionaries, and indeed all persons
with a definite sense of call in their souls furnishes many paral-
lels. These parallel experiences are the finest commentary
available for guidance in understanding the call of Abram. How
could his faith or our faith have arisen without the patient, persistent, persuasive pleading of God?

3. By Means of Purposeful Persuasion

The *personal* persuasion and the *persistent* persuasion of
Yahweh paved the way for a detailed declaration of his purposes.
These are set forth in Genesis 12:1b-3. Two imperatives consti-
tuted the great commission that dominated Abram's life from the
day of their acceptance to the end. The first of these imperatives was followed by a purpose clause stating the two great ob-
jectives of his commission. Inasmuch as the final and the spiritually determinative purpose contemplates his being a blessing to
others, the two together may be called the blessed intention of
the call. Connected with each of the imperatives is a reason
clause introduced by "for." These together express assurance of
mutual determination, a union and cooperation of the divine and
human wills in fulfillment of the call.

A great commission is therefore the first means by which
this purposeful persuasion is expressed.

"Get yourself out" (Gen. 12:1) is a strong, urgent, imperi-
ous command. Not too strong, however! The addition of the
phrase "to you" to the imperative "go out," making the whole to
amount to this, "Get yourself going," made a command that
stressed God's call for obedience by Abram no matter what others
might do. Addition of the phases "from your land, from your
kinsfolk, and from your father's household" required obedience
that would sever every earthly tie that could not be made to fit
into the purposes of God.

On the other hand this is not a demand for that kind of implicit obedience that acts without thinking and that obeys without understanding, that yields mechanically and senses nothing of
the willing spirit involved in a faith response. An imperative
like this is a call for an attitude of cooperation that seeks to
understand the purposes behind the command and the expected ob-
jectives to which it leads.

"Yea, be thou a blessing" (12:2b) is a solemn restatement of
the first command with emphasis upon the high point in its objec-

tives. In no sense is it an entirely separate matter. "Yea" is
an asseverative rendering of the conjunction used here because
this command is a repetition of the highest and best of the purposes involved in the first command. Everything else in the call
partakes of an exalted spiritual character because it contributes
to this blessed intention. As the commission is drawn up to the
pinnacle of this blessed intention Abram is challenged to let his
life be the fulfillment of Yahweh's purpose in the first statement of command.

The blessed intention is the second means by which the pur-
posefulness of God's persuasion is expressed. It appears in both
of the clauses introduced by "in order that."

"In order that I may make of you a great nation" expressed
God's intention that Abram's people should be a people determined
by God's providences rather than the mere chances of birth. His
people should be that society to which the author of Hebrews
referred when he said Abraham looked for "the city . . . whose
builder and maker is God."[18]

"And in order that I may bless you" expressed God's intention to make his use of Abram to be not only a blessing to his
people but also the highest possible spiritual development of his
own life. In this way fulfillment of the first intention is to
be a stepping stone to fulfillment of the second. In the experience of any called-out servant of God, the wonder of his call begins to be unveiled in God's declaration of his primary intention,
and the complete revelation will come in the glory of its contribution to the kingdom of God. The purposeful nature of these
clauses is indicated in their grammatical composition by the
following:[19] (1) they follow an imperative; (2) they are introduced by simple conjunctions, not the special ones which always
indicate sequence; (3) they employ imperfects rather than the
perfects that are so common after imperatives; everywhere in the
Old Testament such combinations appear to constitute subordinate
clauses, and such subordinate clauses usually express purpose,
occasionally result. (4) The context here calls for purpose, because Yahweh's use of "I" turns the mind to his purpose in commanding Abram to get out rather than the result, i.e., Abram's
own action in getting out.

The failure of our translations to show purpose here, giving
instead a loosely connected coordinate clause, has been a contin-

---

18. Hebrew 11:10 in the *American Standard Version*.

19. The construction of such clauses is discussed in the
author's *Survey of Syntax in the Hebrew Old Testament*, pp. 96,97.

gent result of the same confusing theory mentioned above in connection with repetition of the call.

The importance of clear statements of purpose here appears in
the insight they give into the proposed interlocking of the divine
and the human wills. In the first place, these are the purposes
prompting the command to get out. Yahweh's plan for Abram could
not be fulfilled until he made himself independent of idolatry and
idolatrous influences, even within his father's household. Yahweh's purpose was to bless him, bless him spiritually, and such a
blessing could not exist in the morally compromising relations of
an idolatrous society. Thus the command was not arbitrary but
essentially reasonable; obedience to it was a crucial step, being
the key to high and holy benefits. In the second place, these
purposes were means of grace whereby Abram would be made a blessing to all men. They showed that Yahweh's favor toward Abram did
not contemplate partiality but rather an absolutely necessary step
in provision of spiritual blessings that may be shared by all who
desire them. Without this gracious 'watch-care' Abram could not
receive the highest blessings, and without the influence of an
example like that of Abram many others could not share them. This
interlocking is in no sense an arbitrary choice on God's part of
a psychological necessity on man's part, but it does put into
effect an eternal design of God and a free election of man.
Accordingly, language that is casual or even ordinary is not sufficient to give it clear and powerful expression. Certainly we
cannot afford to lose anything of the force its author put into it.

Since the thoughts expressed in this call are represented by
the Scriptures as communicated first to Abram and as passed on by
him to spiritual heirs, we are taught that this hope for realization of the promises they contained was the gift of God. His
spiritual aspirations were not presumption because Yahweh had spoken. His conviction that he could be an instrument of universal
blessing in Yahweh's hands was not idle wishing or vain hope, because Yahweh had spoken. These thoughts were inspired by Yahweh,
and he received them by faith.

Assurance of mutual determination is given as the climactic
expression of Yahweh's purposes. Following each purpose clause is
a reason clause introduced by "for." These reason clauses offer
explanations of Yahweh's intentions that tie them to universal and
graciously benevolent ends. Thus they support the bare commands
of the commission with powerfully persuasive logic. "For I am
determined to make your name great" (12:2) supports the demand for
separation, showing that the will to obey will be undergirded by
the purpose of Yahweh to make Abram a great nation and also a
blessing. "For I am determined to bless those who bless you . . ."
(12:3) supports the great command "Be thou a blessing." This is
divine assurance that the will to be a blessing will be empowered

by the partnership of Yahweh. It will be a blessing to all who
bless its owner, and it will be a means of sealing the doom of
those who hate God. The spiritual destinies of others, blessing
or curse, will be determined according to their own appreciation
or condemnation of the means of blessing revealed here. The correlative clause at the end of verse three, "And men shall be
blessed through you . . . ," adds a climactic word to this assurance. It is introduced by a correlative perfect. It gives,
therefore, a restatement of the chief reason Yahweh used to persuade Abram, a plain assertion of God that this supreme purpose
shall find fulfillment in Abram. It is a simple assertion, but
it asserts with an absolute assurance that only the word of God
can give.

The language constructions of these reason clauses express
the coordination of wills with a discriminating understanding that
is beautiful to behold. Their verbs are similar to those in the
purpose clauses except for the addition in each case of the letter "h" at the end. The addition of the letter "h" indicates a
movement or exercise of will power when the speaker is seeking to
influence the relations between himself and another person. When
the speaker is addressing someone who possesses authority over
him, he uses this addition to express a request like that of
Joseph when he said to Pharaoh, "Let me go up, I pray, and let me
bury my father . . . ."[20] The "I Pray" is a polite extension of
the urge voiced by the added "h". When the speaker is the one
who possesses authority, he uses this addition to express his determination to bring a certain thing to pass with the consent,
cooperation, and aid of the one to whom he speaks. In other
words, this construction is the very opposite of an arbitrary
decision or a suggestion of force. It indicates persuasion,
urging, and the coordinated influence of a superior personality
from which the other may gain assurance, instruction, example,
protection, correction, and inspiration. Such inspiration gives
fulfillment to the other's will-to-do without suppressing it,
without destroying its independence and development.

The language used in these reason clauses, like that of the
purpose clauses, is a very important matter. The two sets of
clauses in Abram's call build for us an exalted piece of composition. Any type of translation that fails to break through the
fog of indefiniteness and to give us the vision of Yahweh's call
that Abram received from Yahweh himself is a serious disservice.

Statements of determination, when linked as these are, to
preceding commands and intentions, refer to facts concerning the

---

20. Gen. 50:5 in the author's translation.

will of the speaker that are calculated to strengthen the will of
the one spoken to. Thus they lift the thought of the purpose
clauses, which express mere intention, to yet higher levels.
They express intention plus determination to bring about fulfillment of that intention. When the speaker is one whose intelligence is reasonable in its persuasion, whose love is powerful in
its influence, and whose determination is righteous in its control, then the coordination sought by him guarantees that both
wills will become parties to the call. This kind of determination is the surest ground of ultimate fulfillment that can possibly be found. Eternal destiny is to be determined by it.

Conclusion: The Inspiring Force of the Call is Reflected by
its Poetic Form

The fact that the call was cast in poetic form suggests that
the teaching it expressed was highly significant for Abram and
his descendants. It is possible that its poetry was framed by
Abram himself or that his thought was embodied in poetry by descendants to facilitate the teaching of it by one generation to
another. In any case the poetry bears testimony to the importance of the teaching.

This poetic arrangement makes the coordination of wills in
the call to be its climax. The call of Abram, and all its fulfillment in Abraham, is a key to the character of the man whom
Paul described as the father of the faithful;[21] moreover, the
call becomes a superb illustration of Paul's teaching in Ephesians
2:8, where he says, "By grace have ye been saved through faith;
and that not of yourselves, it is the gift of God." The word
for gift refers to God's plan of salvation. Faith is still a
free and active movement of the human will, voluntarily accept-
ing God's plan of coordination. There is truth then in these
words of the poem "The Water Lily"[22];

> O star on the breast of the river!
> O marvel of bloom and grace!
> Did you fall right down from Heaven
> Out of the sweetest place?
> You are white as the thoughts of an angel,
> Your heart is steeped in the sun;
> Did you grow in the Golden City,
> My pure and radiant one?

---

21. Gal. 3:6-9,29 in the *American Standard Version*.

22. Mary Frances Butts, *Voiceless Lips*, ed., Nell Outlaw,
p. 134.

Nay, nay, I fell not out of Heaven;
None gave me my saintly white;
It slowly grew from the darkness,
Down in the dreary night,
From the ooze of the silent river
I won my glory and grace.
White souls fall not, O my poet,
They rise -- to the sweetest place.

At the same time faith appears as a response to the promises, providences, and the character of God; the water lily must rise, but it rises in response to the light of the sun; the water lily rises from a bulb with a living seed therein, but the sun brings the warmth that awakens that seed; the water lily grows and blooms and is glorious, but the sun sends the light that draws its tender growth upward out of the night into the light of day and the glory of a flower. Thus was the faith of Abraham drawn by the inspiration of Yahweh.

6. GLIMPSES OF GOD

AS

THE GROUND OF ABRAM'S FAITH

Genesis 15:6; Hebrews 11:1

Introduction: Faith *In* Yahweh

Looking back at Abraham across the years, we are prone to stress the man of unshakable faith that finally emerged out of struggle. Thus Lola F. Echard has written:

God's chosen Child of Faith across the years
He fathered nations, dauntless, unafraid--
And each command was but to be obeyed.
His trusting heart that knew no fears
Arose above all agony and tears,
And thus his sacrifice supreme he made,
And little Isaac on God's altar laid, [1]
Abiding in a Faith that calms and clears.

The preceding struggle in which there were many fears and many failures but also much sustaining grace, also holds for us some great lessons. Even as the inspiring grace of Abram's

1. Lola F. Echard, "Father Abraham" in *The Old Testament and the Fine Arts* (New York: Harper and Brothers, 1954), p. 80.

early faith, so the sustaining grace of Yahweh surrounded the
slender seedling with a supporting frame of revealed truth about
God. When the gusty winds of stress and strain pulled the young
tree from its support, the intervention of Yahweh prevented it
from being uprooted. His refreshing forgiveness replaced its
protecting frame. His instruction brought to it strength that
increased with every lesson taught by experience. These lessons
are reflected in the names Abram used for God.

The names for God associated with intermediate stages of
Abram's spiritual development were as follows: (1) Yahweh, in
which name Abram worshipped at all the altars he built in the
Promised Land; (2) God Most High and Lord Yahweh, both of which
are associated with the vision of Genesis 15; also (3) The Angel
of Yahweh and El Shaddai, both of which are associated with the
vision of Genesis 17. All of these reflect a growth in Abram's
understanding that is aptly described by these words of Genesis
15:6, ". . . he believed in Yahweh . . . ." In other words, his
faith became something greater than mere acceptance of God's word
or God's promises; his faith became faith in God himself.

Never was there a more momentous meaning in a little word
than there was in the preposition "in" when "he (Abram) believed
in Yahweh, and he (Yahweh) reckoned it to him for righteousness"
(Gen. 15:6). Hebrews 11 amounts to a commentary upon the phrase
"in Yahweh." Hebrews 11:1 puts the heart of the message in
these words: "Now faith is the assurance (the confirmation, the
title deed) of the things (we) hope for, being the proof of
things (we) do not see and the conviction of their reality --
faith perceiving as real fact what is not revealed to the senses."[2]
The entire chapter illustrates this word in terms of the faith of
Old Testament saints including Abraham.

1. As Yahweh, the One Overruling Abram himself in Fulfillment of
the Promises

The record of Abram's altars provides evidence concerning
Abram's understanding of God at the time they were built. The
references to these altars appear in Genesis 12:7,8 13:4,18.
They show first that Abram used the name Yahweh at this time and
thought of God as Yahweh the maker of the promises. They show
also that he recognized Yahweh as the one who selected Canaan as
the land to be given to his descendants. They show furthermore
that he learned in connection with these altars the necessity for
Yahweh's overruling of himself in order to keep his faith in the
fulfillment of this promise steadfast.

---

2. Translation of the *Amplified New Testament*.

Use of the name "Yahweh" is mentioned in connection with each instance of worship at these altars. Each is said to have been built "to Yahweh," i.e., in the name of Yahweh. In two instances mention is made of the fact that Abram "called upon the name of Yahweh," i.e., "invoked a blessing in the name of Yahweh" (Gen. 12:8, 13:4). Remembering that it was Yahweh who uttered the call and the promises, we know that Abram thought of Yahweh as maker of the promises. Naturally the one concerning the land received the main stress in the beginning. All of Genesis 12:4--13:18 deals with it.

Yahweh as the one who selected Canaan to be the Promised Land was worshipped at the first altar near Shechem and likewise at the other. When Abram came to Shechem, "Yahweh revealed himself unto Abram and said, *'To your descendants* I shall give this land.'"[3] The original text emphasized the word "there," i.e., at the place of Yahweh's appearance and Yahweh's promise. In addition Yahweh is described as "Yahweh who appeared unto him." This appearance unto him in the land of the Canaanites was assurance of Yahweh's presence with him there. Moreover, the appearance for the specific purpose of designating this land as the Promised Land was assurance that Yahweh could fulfill the promise by dispossessing the Canaanites. When the author of Genesis said immediately before telling of this appearance, "And the Canaanite was then in the land," he was probably intending to prepare the reader to grasp the force of this promise concerning the land. In building the altar, therefore, Abram expressed his faith that Yahweh could and would deal with the problems involved in dispossession of the Canaanites. This same faith was expressed in worship at the other altars, for they were in the Promised Land and they too were erected for worship of Yahweh after his selection of this land as the Promised Land.

Yahweh's overruling of Abram himself appeared in the encouragement already described and also in the rescue of Abram from trouble in Egypt.

The occasion for his going to Egypt was a severe famine in Canaan. There is no evidence he sought guidance in this matter, and the very fact that it meant leaving the Promised Land was enough to raise questions about the wisdom of it. We need to recognize, however, that there had been no instruction concerning the matter.

Yahweh used his own experiences to teach him the dangers of a sojourn in Egypt. The statements made by Abram and Sarai that

---

3. The author's translation.

she was his sister led to serious trouble, and it was largely
their fault. The statement was based upon a half-truth, for she
was his half-sister (cf. Gen. 20:12). At the same time, the
statements were consciously intended to deceive others concerning
the fact that she was also his wife. They evidently thought it
unavoidable and necessary. It was their planning, however, that
led them into this compromising and shameful situation. Failure
to seek guidance started their backsliding. Failure to build
altars in Egypt left them without spiritual supports of regular,
open, and courageous confession of their faith before the lecherous idolators who surrounded them. The results of their man-
made strategy were exactly the opposite of what they desired.
When Pharaoh took Sarai into his harem with the expectation of
making her his wife, the consequences were approaching disaster.
Abram and Sarai were snatched out of this dreadful predicament by
the miraculous intervention of Yahweh, but not without serious
'loss of face' and correction at the hand of Yahweh that was implicit in his deliverance. When Pharaoh's men "proceeded to
escort him on his way with his wife and everything belonging to
him,"[4] it meant that Pharaoh sent him across the border in pro-
tective custody. He was put out, diplomatically but with the
understanding that he was not to return. Thus the intervention
of Yahweh effected his deliverance but also corrected him very
sternly.

     This lesson was taken to heart. Abram returned to the land
never again to leave it. Also he renewed his worship and re-
freshed his faith at the altar near Bethel (cf. Gen. 13:4). When
he and Lot separated (cf. Gen. 13:5-13), Yahweh appeared again to
strengthen his faith that the promise concerning the land still
stood. Accordingly, when Abram moved to Hebron, he built another
altar to Yahweh. From that time forward there was no evidence of
uncertainty concerning the land.

2.   God Most High and Lord Yahweh, the One Able to Overrule
     Historical Developments in Fulfillment of the Promises.

     Genesis 14 and 15 deal with a series of events very closely
related. At the heart of all lies Abram's struggle over the
promise concerning an heir. The names "God Most High" and "Lord
Yahweh" are both related to this struggle because both describe
the sovereignty of Yahweh and are related to his sovereign control over the question of an heir. Certain circumstances in
Genesis 14 call for the use there of "God Most High," and other
circumstances in Genesis 15 call for the use of "Lord Yahweh"
there, but in Abram's struggle for understanding concerning the
heir there is a thread that ties together his use of these names.

---

     4.   The author's translation of Genesis 12:20.

This use of other names in no sense indicates that Abram was thinking of another god than Yahweh. They indicate instead his recognition of various characteristics of Yahweh. The other names were names for Yahweh.

Abram's use of "God Most High" arose out of his relations with Melchizedek, king of Salem, and the king of Sodom. According to Genesis 14, both of these kings met him as he journeyed toward his camp near Hebron after delivering Lot and the other people of Sodom from the hand of Eastern invaders. Apparently they were together when the statements recorded in verses 17-23 were made. It is natural, therefore, to understand that each was influenced by the presence of the others during this exchange.

Melchizedek, priest of God Most High, blessed Abram in the name of "God Most High."

Abram accepted the blessing and gave to Melchizedek a tithe of all the goods.

The king of Sodom offered to take the people and to leave the remainder of the goods for Abram as spoil.

Abram's use of "God Most High" was affected apparently by a desire to assert his conviction about God in the hearing of both of the other men; however, the reasons for his wanting to make this assertion evidently differed according to the character of the others.

When Melchizedek blessed Abram, he described God as "God Most High, the one possessing heaven and earth." When Abram answered the proposition of the king of Sodom about the people and goods Abram had captured, he used both the name and the description used by Melchizedek, putting them in apposition with "Yahweh." Thus Abram did these three things: (1) he accepted "God Most High" as a fitting description of the one sovereign God; (2) he asserted that the one sovereign God is Yahweh; (3) he asserted the sovereignty of Yahweh as a supreme moral obligation which forbade his receiving any favor from an idolator like the king of Sodom.

The whole account indicates that Abram's use of "God Most High" was due to the character of Melchizedek. He was called by the author of Genesis "a priest of God Most High" (Gen. 14:18). His name meant King of Righteousness, and there is nothing to deny its fitness. Abram accepted Melchizedek's blessing, though he rejected favors from the king of Sodom. Accordingly, Ps. 110:4 cites Melchizedek as a type of the coming messiah, and Hebrews 7 explains the eternal priesthood of Christ in the light of this example. It was fitting, therefore, that Abram should

agree that both he and Melchizedek worshipped the one sovereign
God, that he should accept Melchizedek's blessing in the name of
their God, and that he should pay the tithe which the priestly
ministry of Melchizedek justified. The following words of
H.C. Leupold concerning Melchizedek appear to be warranted:

> Since this man is a priest of 'El 'Elyon, i.e.,
> "God Most High," and this is a name of Yahweh,
> found indeed not only in Ps. 78:35 but in many
> similar combinations quite frequently, we are
> compelled to regard this venerable king-priest
> as a worshipper and publicly an adherent of the
> true religion of Yahweh as handed down from the
> sounder tradition of the times of the Flood.
> That this was the actual course of development
> of religion, and that monotheism definitely
> preceded polytheism may now be regarded as fully
> demonstrated by works such as Samuel Zwemer's
> *The Origin of Religion*.[5]

The Genesis account gives us no reason for thinking that
this name was new to Abram but rather that he used it to emphasize the stress which both he and Melchizedek placed upon the
sovereignty of God. The name alone did not assert that there was
only one true God, but the connection with the earlier records in
Genesis gives strong ground for thinking that the implication
concerning gods of lesser rank pointed to idols. In the thinking
of the peoples, idols were gods; but in the thinking of Melchizedek and Abram, they were merely called gods, being in no sense
really God. These men of God were asserting, in a way even their
idolatrous neighbors could understand, that God Most High exercised supremacy over all so-called gods. To them all idol gods
were earthly, local, and limited. To them God Most High was the
one possessing heaven and earth. He was of the earth but of all
the earth. Also he was of the heaven and of all the heaven. It
is not stated precisely but it certainly appears that to them
God Most High was not the highest among other divine powers but
The One True God.

When the king of Sodom said, "Give me the persons, but *as
for the goods*, take them for yourself," Abram made no objection
to his taking the persons. Evidently he acknowledged the king's
right to take the persons involved back to Sodom. Lot was one of
them; however, Lot had chosen to go to Sodom, and Abram could not
do more for him than to leave him now to his choices. The offer

---

5. H.C. Leupold, *opus citus*, p. 463.

of reward to Abram involved something else. Various explanations for Abram's refusal of the goods have been suggested by expositors, such as mere magnanimity or disdainful pride. The story, however, appears to give its own explanation in Abram's use of the names for God. He took an oath in the name of God Most High, using the same description of him which Melchizedek had used. Thus he asserted, apparently for the benefit of the king of Sodom and all others present, that his decision was made in the fear of the one sovereign God worshipped by himself and Melchizedek. He was saying that his God, and likewise he, could not accept favors tainted by the rotten immorality of Sodom. Furthermore, he put Yahweh in apposition with God Most High. Thus he asserted that they were the same. Thus he also asserted that this one sovereign God was the one who gave to him the promises. This probably meant to him that the promise of the land depended solely upon the sovereign right and power of Yahweh, not upon idolatrous kings and peoples living in it. When he added, ". . . that you may not say, 'I made Abram rich,'" his words described a look into future possibilities which may have reached beyond the benefits involved in the captured goods, which may have included the increases necessary to a possession of the land eventually. The verb "may not say" is an imperfect whose frequentative action can cover any number of repetitions. At least Abram is asserting that his increases will be untainted by any aid from idolators and their gods.

Abram's bold assertion of dependence upon Yahweh only brings into focus another point in his faith, a higher hope than possession of the land. After these things, when Yahweh appeared again to assure him of protection from dangers arising out of his daring raid against the eastern invaders, his first word of response was this: "O Lord Yahweh, what will you give me, seeing that I am going on and on without a child, and my heir is from Damascus, even Eliezer (Gen. 15:2)."[6] This problem of the heir was weighing upon his mind continually. Naturally this problem was upon his mind as he dealt with the king of Sodom concerning the people of Sodom, including Lot.

Lot was the only kinsman who had chosen to accompany Abram when he came to Canaan.

Lot had shared something of his experiences at Shechem and Bethel. He at least had had the opportunity to know what the faith of Abram was.

Lot was a believer in Yahweh. Despite the shocking lack of good judgment shown by his move to Sodom, he "vexed his righteous

---

6. The author's translation.

soul from day to day" (cf. II Peter 2:7) with the lawless deeds
of the Sodomites. There was in him that which caused God to
spare Lot for Abraham's sake when he overthrew Sodom and
Gomorrah (cf. Gen. 19:29).

Lot caused a deep, deep concern to come to Abram's heart
when he allowed the strife between herdsmen to become a cause for
separation between him and Abram. The appearance of Yahweh to
Abram after the separation to assure him that the promise concerning the land stood as it was when first made shows how deep
Abram's concern was. It is probable that thought about Lot as a
possible heir was part of this concern, for no mention was made
of Eliezer as the heir until Lot went back to Sodom after the
rescue by Abram. If so, the motive that moved Abram in the
daring rescue was very clear and strong.

Lot, however, sat there, said nothing, and did nothing when
the king of Sodom offered to let Abram keep the spoil while he
took the people. At least he could have made a plea if he had
desired to give up Sodom. This incident, therefore, was sufficient to prove to Abram that there was no longer ground for hope
that Lot might return to him and be his heir. This nephew had
separated from him willingly. He was now so associated with
Sodom that the king of Sodom could claim him with the remainder
of his people. Moreover, Lot himself had not shown any desire to
return to Abram. He was now out of the picture.

As Abram was grimly but faithfully pondering the question of
an heir, his bold assertion of dependence upon Yahweh, right in
face of a final separation from Lot, meant that he trusted "in
Yahweh" for solution of this problem also.

Abram's use of "Lord Yahweh" appears in Genesis 15. The
experiences recounted there are closely associated with those of
Genesis 14, for *"after these things"* in verse one links them emphatically. This shows that Yahweh said, "Have no fear," because
Abram needed assurance at that time. Accordingly, the words "I
am your shield" gave him assurance of protection against reprisals
by the Eastern invaders. However, the words "your reward will be
exceedingly great" looked forward to greater things than that.
Since Lot was gone, the question of the heir was a poignant one
for Abram. The question of reward brought his thoughts to a focus at this point; so he implored Yahweh for an explanation. In
doing so, according to Genesis 15:2, he addressed Yahweh as "Lord
Yahweh." According to Genesis 15:4, Yahweh answered by telling
him that his heir would be a child of his own. Yahweh added a
thrilling prophecy that his descendants would be like the stars
in number. At this point, according to Genesis 15:6, the author
tells us that "he believed in Yahweh"; so his faith did not
stagger. However, as Yahweh continued speaking about possession

of the land by his descendants, he did implore him again for an explanation. In doing so, according to Genesis 15:8, he again addressed him as "Lord Yahweh." Thus twice during this communion with Yahweh he used "Lord Yahweh" when imploring explanation concerning fulfillment of the promise of posterity.

This application of the title "Lord Yahweh" to God is the first in the Bible; so Abram led the way here. This fact emphasizes yet more the connection between this title and the problem of the inheritance. Why did he link the two? What reasons did he have for originating the title in this connection?

The fact that the use of "Lord" with "Yahweh" acknowledged Yahweh's lordship or sovereignty offers a partial answer. Abram expected the heir to be a gift of Yahweh, as shown by his question in Genesis 15:2, a dispensation of his sovereign power. "Lord," therefore, fitted as part of his appeal for an explanation.

If Abram desired to acknowledge the sovereignty of Yahweh, why did he not put "Yahweh" in apposition with "God Most High," as he did when talking with Melchizedek and the king of Sodom? The combination of "Lord" with "Yahweh" offers an answer here. "God Most High" described God as transcendent, while "Yahweh" described God as the one intervening in human affairs, making himself seen and heard, his influence felt, in order to assure fulfillment of the promises. This God of the promises was the one Abram chose to call "Lord," the sovereign of his heart and life.

If Abram desired to acknowledge the presence of Yahweh, why did he not use the name "Yahweh" alone? The tremendous power involved in the provision of an heir, especially a child of his own, probably prompted the addition of "Lord." Time had already removed the prospect of his having a child by Sarai in a natural way. Eliezer would be his heir legally unless he could have a child (cf. Gen. 15:3). How then could he have a child of his own? In facing this it was fitting indeed to use "Lord" to emphasize the sovereignty of Yahweh. To do so meant to acknowledge Yahweh as his own Lord and master and to do so in an appealing way.

When Yahweh said there would be a child of his own and his descendants would be as the stars (cf. Gen. 15:4,5), his faith did not waver. Concerning this experience in particular the author of Genesis recorded the comment "he believed in Yahweh."

When Yahweh went on to remind him that he had brought him from Ur to Canaan in order that he might inherit it, he asked for evidence that he would inherit it (cf. Gen. 15:8). Did this re-

quest express uncertainty or skepticism? Again the author's comment "he believed in Yahweh" provides the answer.

In the affirmation ". . . he believed in Yahweh . . ." both
the verb and the adverbial phrase bear a peculiar importance.
Together they glorify the believer's ground of assurance.

The verb "believe" means "confirm or support." The form of
the verb in this case is causative; so it means "cause to be firm
or sure." Thus, when one sincerely believes, his own faith makes
the word of promise to be sure for him. There cannot be in the
believer any misgiving, any fear of change on the part of the one
promising. The very opposite of misgiving, uncertainty, or skepticism is expressed by the verb "believe." The preposition "in"
describes motion into and abiding within. Thus Yahweh is pointed
out as the ground of faith. This ground is all of Yahweh, not
one word or part of him. The whole of the character represented
by his name, all its sovereign power and all its person-to-person
application of influence is involved. To believe upon Yahweh,
therefore, means to depend upon him and him alone for all the aid
that wondrous name implies. Belief *in* Yahweh, therefore, was as
high above self-assurance and possible loss of it as the heaven
is above the earth.

The fact that the author of Genesis turns aside from telling
the story to make a comment is remarkable. It was his established
custom to let the stories speak for themselves. Evidently then
he felt the point of his comment to be a matter of great importance. We can understand when we observe how his comment ruled
out any form of doubt on Abram's part and showed that the questions he asked were prayers for a guided understanding of the implicit faith he already had. He was begging for answers to questions concerning the ways in which Yahweh's sovereign control
would work.

The vision and covenant that followed (cf. Gen. 15:9-21)
furnished the great answer by explaining Yahweh's expected con--
trol of history, overruling it and guiding it unto fulfillment of
the promises.

The question concerning the immediate heir was only the
first of many questions to be answered. The question of time required for possession of the land by his descendants was a second.
The vision indicated four hundred years, according to Genesis 15:
13, and four generations, according to Genesis 15:16. According
to the span of life among the people involved, a generation was
approximately one hundred years. This sojourn in a land not
theirs before the time of possessing Canaan was to be the answer.

The question of increase, development, discipline, and material gain required for possessing Canaan was another great ques-

tion. Development within the land while cherishing hopes of possessing it would probably have precipitated conflict while his descendants were still weak and their enemies still strong. The sojourn and also the slavery in a land where they would learn industry, organization, and art, followed by Yahweh's deliverance, furnished the answer.

The question of justice due the inhabitants of Canaan was a great moral problem. When Yahweh, according to Genesis 15:16, said, ". . . for the iniquity of the Amorite is not yet full," he showed that all claims of these peoples upon divine justice would expire before the edict of dispossession would be executed.

This assurance that Yahweh would overrule historical developments so as to fulfill his covenant with Abraham is magnified throughout the Old Testament and the New. The forecast given here is exceedingly important to the understanding of later passages.

The rise of this faith "in Yahweh" furnished occasion for extensive explanations of the covenant under very solemn circumstances. The dividing of the animals and the passing of "a smoking furnace and a flaming torch" (cf. Gen. 15:9-11,17) appear to have been intended to furnish the symbols of a blood covenant on Abram's part sanctioned by miraculous evidences of Yahweh's presence and Yahweh's approval of the terms.

Faith *in* Yahweh meant confidence that Yahweh would handle all situations so as to fulfill the promises yet not be unreasonable or unjust with anyone concerned. While Abram was yet limited in his understanding, he believed that the reasonableness, the righteousness, and the goodness of Yahweh's sovereign control could be revealed and understood. He recognized the necessity for Yahweh's protection, discipline, encouragement, instruction, guidance, and gradual impartation of his wisdom. This faith warranted the added statement that Yahweh "accounted it to him for righteousness." Paul, therefore, used his righteousness in Galatians and in Romans as an example of the righteousness that comes by faith and faith alone. Accordingly, the phrase "in Yahweh" became a fore-runner of the New Testament phrase "in Christ."

3. The Angel of Yahweh and *El Shaddai*, the One Able to Overrule the Laws of Nature in Fulfillment of the Promises

Genesis 16 and 17 also deal with events very closely related. As in Genesis 14 and 15, the promise concerning an heir is central. The birth of Ishmael was a human plan to secure the promised heir. Evidently Sarai and Abram came to the conclusion that circumstances required it. By it Abram secured a child of his own. The child, however, lacked the spiritual qualifications

needed in the heir to the promises. Yahweh made this clear when
he revealed to Hagar what the future character of her child would
be. According to Genesis 16:12, he would be "a wild ass of a
man," not a friend of God and a friend to man as Abram was; he
would dwell "in defiance of all his brothers,"[7] not in relations
that would bring blessings to all men. In the face of this dis-
couragement, Yahweh intervened again to tell Abram that the promised heir would be his child and also Sarai's child.

The events of each chapter gave rise to a new name for Yahweh. That in Genesis 16 is "The Angel of Yahweh." That in Genesis 17 is "*El Shaddai*." The meaning of each is revealed by the
circumstances that gave rise to it. In turn each name marks progress in the consciousness of Abram concerning the ways of Yahweh
in revelation of himself and in exercising his sovereign control.
In both cases these ways involved control of the laws of nature
in a supernatural manner.

"*The Angel of Yahweh*" was used to describe Yahweh as he
appeared to Hagar, but the meaning of her experience to Abram is
the point of special concern to us. According to Genesis 24:7,
Abram taught the servant he sent to find a wife for Isaac concerning the character of this angel. Therefore, Abram's interpretation of Hagar's experience becomes quite interesting and
quite important. Was it Hagar's experience that furnished ground
for his understanding concerning this angel?

Abram's marriage to Hagar meant that he again drifted into a
distressing situation. He hearkened, as recorded in Genesis 16:2,
to the proposition of Sarai that they seek the long-desired heir
by letting Sarai give Hagar, her slave, to Abram as a concubine.
The laws their people had long known and respected, the laws of
Hammurabi, permitted a childless wife to give her slave this way.
If the concubine should bear a child, the child would belong
legally to the wife. This human effort to manage God's plans for
him, to run ahead of him, led to trouble for all concerned, pride
and insubordination in Hagar, harshness in Sarai, and sorrow in
Abram's heart. He allowed Sarai to have a free hand in dealing
with Hagar, she dealt harshly, and Hagar ran away. All this led
to another intervention of Yahweh, overruling all concerned to
restore order, and giving Abram another lesson in divine discipline.

The new and remarkable fact embedded in this story of Genesis
16 is the first use of "The Angel of Yahweh" to describe Yahweh.
Its use in 16:7 is the first instance in the entire Bible. In

---

7. The author's translation.

rapid succession it recurs in 16:9,10,11,13. In these verses the author seems to take care to repeat this name in full. He could have referred to this wonderful being by a relative pronoun, as he did in 16:8, but he apparently desired to impress this new name upon the consciousness of readers.

When we observe that it was the author of Genesis that introduced the new name, not Hagar, and not Abram, we are provoked to ask this question, What gave the author cause for this new interpretation of the character of God? Search for an answer requires a sifting of the relations of each person who may have had anything to do with this use of the new name.

Hagar's relation was first because it was her experience with which the new name was associated. She, however, did not use "Yahweh" or "The Angel of Yahweh." She used "God-of-Seeing," a name devised by her. She was amazed at the fact that God actually appeared to her, as indicated in 16:13 by her suggestive question, "Is it also true that *here* I have seen the back of the one seeing me?"[8] Her question referred both to the fact that God saw her and that she believed she had seen some form of God. The important fact to her was that he had actually appeared to her in order to give a treasured promise concerning the child she was to bear.

The report of this experience came to Abram, of course through Hagar. Her return to Abram's household, submitting herself to Sarai's authority as God directed, gave Hagar opportunity to tell her story. She had a great story to tell. Abram, better than any other, would understand it. Abram, more than all others, would rejoice in it. Abram, probably, had taught her to believe in God, the one sovereign God, recognized by some like Melchizedek who were not Hebrews, as well as by himself. The Philistine Abimelech, according to Genesis 20:22, did so, and like Hagar he used the name "God." Moreover, the history of Ishmaelites bears testimony to their deep regard for Abram as their father, and this bears testimony to spiritual understanding between Hagar and Abraham.

Abram's relation, as already indicated, may have been the crucial one in giving this new interpretation. He heard the story. He was the only one at that time prepared to interpret it. His mind was already quite active in efforts to interpret the character and describe the ways of Yahweh. It is quite probable that he tried to show Hagar that the God who appeared to her was his God, Yahweh. It could be that by reason of efforts on his

---

8. The author's translation.

part to explain God's limitation of himself when appearing to
human eyes he used the new name "The Angel of Yahweh (The Messenger of Yahweh)." It is certain, as shown by Genesis 24:7,12,21,
27,40,42,48, that Abram taught Eliezer at a later day to use this
name. Thus the evidence points strongly toward Abram as its original user.

The relation of the author of Genesis involves nothing to
deny this theory concerning the new name. Since he may naturally
be credited with writing both Genesis 16 and Genesis 24 in their
present form, it needs to be observed that he did not indicate
himself or any other than Abram as the possible author of the
name. Furthermore, it needs to be observed that he passed on the
message of the angel to Hagar in poetic form and linked the new
name with that poetic message. Even if Abram's descendants
framed the poetry to preserve all points of a tradition handed
down from Abram, the original author of the name would be Abram.

Stephen's use of this name, as recorded in Acts 7:30-35,
summarized in a startling way the insights indicated in Genesis
16, Exodus 3:1--4:17, and many other passages recounting the
activities of The Angel of Yahweh.

The words of Stephen give us the New Testament view of the
angel who said, "I am . . . The God of Abraham . . . , Isaac,
and . . . Jacob." Stephen repeated in his own way the account
given in Exodus 3:1--4:17 of Moses' experience at the burning
bush. He said, ". . . an angel appeared . . . in a flame of fire
in a bush." In Exodus 3:2 this angel is called "The Angel of
Yahweh," identifying him with Jacob as seen in Genesis 12--50.
Accordingly Stephen added this word, ". . . there came a voice of
the Lord, I am the God of Thy fathers, the God of Abraham, and of
Isaac, and of Jacob." Thus Stephen identified the Lord with The
Angel of Yahweh and with God.

The mystery involved in these words is described by John
Macartney Wilson in this way:

> The question still remains, Who is the theophanic
> angel? To this many answers have been given, of
> which the following may be mentioned: (1) This
> angel is simply an angel with a special commission;
> (2) He may be a momentary descent of God into
> visibility; (3) He may be the Logos, a kind of
> temporary preincarnation of the second person of
> the Trinity. Each has its difficulties, but the
> last is certainly the most tempting to the mind.
> Yet it must be remembered that at best these are
> only conjectures that touch upon a great mystery.
> It is certain that from the beginning God used

> angels in human form, with human voices, to
> communicate with man; and the appearances of
> the angel of the Lord, with his special re-
> demptive relation to God's people, show the
> working of that Divine mode of self-revelation
> which culminated in the coming of the Saviour,
> and thus a foreshadowing of, and a prepara-
> tion for, the full revelation of God in Jesus
> Christ. Further than this it is not safe
> to go.[9]

It is true that this mystery is not fully unveiled in the
Bible, yet the main point involved, i.e., the identification of
The Angel of Yahweh and of the Lord Jesus Christ with God, is
bound in Biblical teaching with that concerning the existence of
the Trinity. While human beings remain bound in human limita-
tions, we cannot escape the mystery of miracles, especially the
mystery of God's revelation of himself in physical forms, but we
should not pass by these mysterious revelations without realizing
that there is in them an inescapable implication of the full
deity of The Angel of Yahweh and of Jesus. Even as "God was in
Christ reconciling the world unto himself" (II Cor. 5:19), so God
was in Yahweh God who appeared in the Garden of Eden to build a
redemptive hope for Adam and Eve and in The Angel of Yahweh who
dealt in redemptive ways with Abraham, Isaac, and Jacob.

In order to see clearly the exact accord between Stephen's
faith and that of Moses, we may observe Stephen's words yet further. Stephen attributed to the Lord these words of Yahweh God
to Moses, ". . . the place whereon thou standest is holy ground."
Thus Stephen indicated his conviction that the Lord himself was
actually present in that spot. Furthermore, he reported the Lord
as saying, "I am come down to deliver them (the Israelites): and
now come, I will send thee into Egypt"; then he went on to speak
of "the hand of the angel that appeared to him in the bush" as
the power that worked with Moses in the deliverance of Israel.
Thus he thought of this angel as speaking for God, as acting for
God, and as being the voice of God or God in sensible form.

No other being anywhere in the Bible, except Jesus, is described as The Angel of Yahweh is in these passages. Therefore,

---

9. James Macartney Wilson, "Angels" (II Angels in OT-3.
The Angel of The Theophany) in *International Standard Bible Encyclopedia*, Vol. I, p. 134. (References to "The Angel of Jehovah"
pointed out in this article include Gen. 16:7ff., 22:11f., 24:7,40,
31:11ff., 32:24ff., 48:15f.; Ex. 3 (cf. Acts 7:30ff.); 13:21,
14:19 (cf. Num. 20:16, 23:20ff., 32:34--33:17 (cf. Isa. 63:9);
Josh. 5:13--6:2; Jgs. 2:1-5, 6:11ff.).

we see this angel as a unique being, above all other angels, and
his name used as another name for God. When the word "angel" is
joined with the name "Yahweh" in this name, it is capitalized to
show that the name is a name for God.

Behind this faith of Stephen and Moses, there lay the experiences and the faith of Abram. One thing that makes the connection of Abram with this faith so highly interesting is the fact
that use of the term "angel" to describe visible or audible or
otherwise sensible forms of Yahweh is made explicit in the
accounts of Abraham. Moreover, this usage appears in such a way
as to give reason for thinking that it represents a crucial stage
in Abram's efforts to understand the character and the ways of
his God. He used many names for God, and they stand in the
record like milestones marking his spiritual progress. This one
apparently was his way of saying that God himself did assume this
mode of being from time to time in order to deliver his messages
to the hearts of human beings. In doing so he did not cease to
be God, but he did so overrule the laws of nature as to reveal
himself in and through the natural forms that man could see and
hear. He thus became his own messenger, The Angel of Yahweh.

This name in particular ties the thinking of Abram about God
with descriptions of The Angel of Yahweh as the Fear of Isaac
(Gen. 31:42,53), as The Angel who redeemed Jacob from all evil
(Gen. 48:16), and as The One True God of Joseph and Judah (Gen.
44:16, 45:8).

"*El Shaddai*" was applied by Yahweh to himself as the ground
for assurance that Yahweh would fulfill the promise of an heir
despite the rejection of Ishmael (Gen. 17:1,2). Yahweh linked
with this description of his character a restatement of his commands to Abram and a restatement of his determination to make, to
cause, to assure the success of the covenant, including the increase of his descendants. His declaration of intention was explained and analyzed in the prolonged conversation that followed.
It gives us the most detailed statement of the promises made to
Abraham. This importance is indicated by poetic form.

The poetic form of this statement is worthy of critical observation. It is further evidence that important revelations of
this kind were put by Abraham or his spiritual successors into
memorable form and handed down through the centuries. This evidence of its importance is likewise a suggestion to all who read
it to take note of its main points. These are marked by a series
of correlative perfects, and they can be easily located by observation of the marks for correlative perfects as given in the
author's translation that follows. These marks are little
circles (o) put after and above the English equivalent of these
correlative perfects. This series is an excellent example of the

use of correlative perfects, because of the clarity with which they tie their several points to the introductory statement "my covenant is with you." They are so stated as to show that they are fixed and permanent parts of that main statement, as certain of fulfillment as it is.

> *As for me*, behold, my covenant is with you,[10] /
> And you shall be° the father of a multitude of nations. /
> Also your name will no longer be called Abram;[11] /
> Yea, your name shall be° Abraham.[12] /
> Indeed *the father of a multitude of nations will I*
>   *make you;* /
> Yea, I will make° you exceedingly fruitful. /
> Also I will make° nations of you, /
> And *kings from you* will go forth. /
> Also I will establish° my covenant between myself and you /
>   and with your descendants after you throughout their
>   generations as an everlasting covenant, /
> To be to you God and to your descendants after you. /
> Also I will give° *to you and to your descendants after you*
>   the land of your sojournings, / all the land of Canaan, /
> Also I will be° *to them* God. /
>
>   (Gen. 17:4-8)

All seven of the covenant provisions stated by the correlatives have a common ground in the fatherhood of Abraham. The following restatement of them will make this obvious:

(1) A father of "a multitude of nations" (Genesis 17:4b);
(2) A father bearing the name Abraham "Father of a Multitude"
        (Genesis 17:5);
(3) The father of a large, "exceedingly fruitful," nation
        (Genesis 17:6a);
(4) The father of independent nations with "kings"
        descended from Abraham (Genesis 17:6b);
(5) The father of descendants with whom Yahweh will continue
        to establish the Abrahamic covenant as an "everlasting
        covenant" (Genesis 17:7);
(6) The father of descendants who will inherit the land of
        Abraham's sojournings (Genesis 17:8a);
(7) The father of descendants to whom Yahweh will be God
        (Genesis 17:8b).

---

10. A series of seven cor. pfs. is linked with the antecedent "My covenant is with you."

11. Exalted Father.

12. Father of a Multitude.

The tremendous emphasis given here to Abraham's fatherhood, especially to his spiritual fatherhood in the last three points, and to those receiving its benefits, links Yahweh's great promises to the name he gave himself. It asserts a crucial point in the ground for this wonderful assurance.

"El Shaddai" has been interpreted in many and various ways. The differences arise from the word "Shaddai," for there is no doubt that "El" is a short form for God carrying the same force as "Elohim," no matter whether from the same root or not. Ancient Jewish rabbis explained the name "Shaddai" as a compound word made up of the following words: (1) the relative particle, meaning "who"; (2) the verb "to be," having the meaning "is" in this case; and (3) the word "sufficient." Some moderns think "Shaddai" is derived from a verb meaning "to deal violently." These would make the name equivalent to "almighty." The violence signified by this root, however, is never associated in the Bible with "El Shaddai." Others think the word to be the late form of a word which is equivalent to "lord" or "master." This word, however, is associated in Dt. 32:17 with heathen gods and thus discredited. Others associate "Shaddai" with a root meaning "to pour," as rain is poured forth, or with a noun meaning "mountain," but evidence from the Bible has not been found for either of these. Others make the name to be the plural of the word "breast" with the possessive pronoun for the first person added, but this receives no definite support from the Bible.

No conclusive evidence has been produced by anyone, but the trend of thought we have observed in Abram's thinking about God favors the old interpretation of the rabbis, "he who is sufficient."

When Abram believed the promises made by Yahweh, he believed Yahweh had the sovereign power to fulfill them. He was prepared, therefore, to call Yahweh "God Most High" and "Lord Yahweh." Still he had no definite understanding of the way in which Yahweh's sovereign power would work to fulfill the promises. When he realized that the God who revealed himself to Hagar was Yahweh in a form so limited that Hagar could see him yet also know that he was God, he identified that limited form with the sovereign Yahweh and began to use the name "The Angel of Yahweh" to distinguish the limited form from the infinite. He knew then that in either mode of being it was Yahweh who was at work in their lives. No matter whether he was the infinite spirit who rules all things or the limited human-like person necessary to arrest the attention of a distraught human being, it was Yahweh who was working, now to challenge, now to correct, now to test, now to aid and deliver, doing what was necessary to fulfill his promises. When Yahweh revealed himself again to Abram, Abram was ninety-nine years old and his wife was past the age for bearing children.

Ages and conditions were then so obvious as to make the message concerning a child of their own unbelievable at first. Yahweh started the conversation by saying, "I am *El Shaddai*," and he concluded it by insisting that Ishmael could not be the heir but that within that year he would give Abraham a child by Sarah. New names he gave to them then, and these names were to memorialize this promise. Though Abraham "fell upon his face and laughed" (cf. Gen. 17:17)—a laugh of incredulity, of course—Yahweh repeatedly assured him that the heir would be Sarah's child and commanded him to call the promised son Isaac, which means "Laughter." In other words, God was drilling into Abraham the conviction that the necessity for overruling the laws of nature to fulfill the promise was no barrier to his power or his purpose. He not only possessed the power but he intended to use it. He was quite sufficient for these things. Not only was his will supreme in its control of nature but his ways could be adapted so as to intervene in a personal way in human affairs and to exercise the personal influence on human hearts necessary to fulfill his will in them. Though he deals with free human hearts, still, when they are the hearts of his spiritual children, he can correct them. When they lack knowledge, he can teach them. When they are weak, he can strengthen them. In dealing with his own, he is able to meet any situation that may arise in their experience. He is sufficient; therefore his name may well be "He Who Is Sufficient." The faith of Abraham that had previously been anchored "in Yahweh" was really swept by a storm at this time, but its anchor still held because Yahweh was able to make it hold.

Conclusion: Higher Ground

These assurances were indeed a call to higher ground, for Abram and for all believers.

Abram gave evidence immediately that his faith ascended to this higher ground. In the midst of this long conversation about the covenant, Yahweh had commanded Abram to observe circumcision as a symbol of it (Gen. 17:9-14). When Yahweh ceased speaking and went up from him, he proceeded with this memorial rite. Yahweh had also directed him to call Sarai Sarah (Princess) from that time on (Gen. 17:15-21). The declaration of the covenant had already given his name as Abraham (Father of a Multitude) rather than Abram. Within these verses the names are changed. Thus was their faith expressed that *El Shaddai* was sufficient for fulfillment of all the wonders he had promised.

We in turn may show our faith by letting these accounts stir within our breast a desire to sing with passionate feeling these familiar words:

Lord lift me up and let me stand
By faith on heaven's tableland,
A higher plane than I have found:
Lord, plant my feet on higher ground.[13]

7. GLIMPSES OF GOD

AS

THE PERFECTER OF ABRAHAM'S FAITH

Genesis 22:1-19; Hebrews 11:17-19

Introduction: The Wonder of Biblical Paradoxes

     God's command that Abraham offer Isaac as a burnt offering,
like a sacrificial animal, strikes a reader's reason like an unbelievable word, like a denial of all Abraham's former faith,
like a fatal misunderstanding, like a thing of evil. Yet, it is
made to appear at the end like a blessing.

     In 1882 George Matheson wrote the hymn "O Love That Will Not
Let Me Go." Its last two verses are as follows:

O Joy that seekest me through pain,
I cannot close my heart to thee;
I trace the rainbow thro' the rain,
And feel the promise is not vain
That morn shall tearless be.

O Cross that liftest up my head,
I dare not ask to fly from thee;
I lay in dust life's glory dead,
And from the ground there blossoms red
Life that shall endless be.[1]

The immortal paradoxes of this hymn have moved the hearts of believers to see more clearly the amazing experiences of Christ on
Mount Calvary and of Abraham on Mount Moriah. The truths involved are mysteries that stagger our reason. That is why we

------

     13. Johnson Oatman, Jr., "Higher Ground," in *Baptist Hymnal*,
Walter Hines Simms, editor, (Nashville, Tennessee: Broadman
Press, 1926), No. 319.

     1. George Matheson, "O Love That Will Not Let Me Go," in
New Baptist Hymnal (Nashville, Tennessee: Broadman Press, 1926),
No. 232.

call them paradoxes. Nevertheless, an utterly devoted soul can
sense in them assurance that reconciliation of our conflicting
human emotions is provided in the providential control of that
wondrous being who was The Angel of Yahweh on Mount Moriah and
Jesus of Nazareth on Mount Calvary.

In the light of this faith, it is becoming for a believer to
search the Scriptures for all evidence that harmonizes with the
redemptive work of Christ. Accordingly, we find in Genesis 22:
1-19 much evidence that God was perfecting Abraham's faith by
these several tests: (1) a test which proved Abraham's utter devotion to Yahweh; (2) a test which proved Abraham's abhorrence
of idolatry; (3) a test which proved Abraham's complete reliance
upon Yahweh's providential control.

1. The One Who Proved Abraham's Utter Devotion to Yahweh

God is called "The (One True) God" several times in Genesis
22:1-19. This occurs in verses one, three, and nine. He is
called "God," without the definite article, in verses eight and
twelve, "The Angel of Yahweh" in verses eleven and fifteen, and
"Yahweh" in verses fourteen and sixteen. In the beginning, however, and twice afterwards, in words related each time to the
revelation of the place where Abraham was to offer Isaac, the
author took care to make it unmistakably clear that this direction came from The One True God, not from a god associated with
idolatry. Throughout Genesis the definite article with the name
"God" distinguishes Yahweh in an unmistakable way from the idols
of the heathen.

The test of Abraham is described accordingly as a test of
his faith which proved its perfection rather than a temptation
which was a lure unto evil. The One True God never tempts men
into evil. Rather, as James teaches, every sinner is "drawn away
by his own lust and enticed"(1 James 1:14). The translation of
the *King James Version* at this point which used the word "tempted"
is therefore unfortunate. The Hebrew verb means "put to the
test." Theophile Meek in *An American Translation*, James Moffatt
in his *New Translation*, H.C. Leupold in his *Commentary on Genesis*, and the *Revised Standard Version* use this meaning. The
American Standard Version, however, gave the best rendering of
the verb in this context, using the word "proved." The evidence
out of the context *that required "proved"* is the evidence we are
presenting as the basis of this entire message.

The One True God took great care in referring to Isaac to
make it clear to Abraham that in commanding the sacrifice of him
God was not forgetting that he was Abraham's son, Abraham's only
son, the one Abraham loved very dearly. He said, "Take now your
son, your only son, whom you love, even Isaac, ..." The use

of the word "*only*" here is an exceedingly significant expression. It is repeated in verse twelve and in verse sixteen *as the final and emphatic description*. Any thought that Ishmael was overlooked for the moment cannot furnish a reasonable explanation for this emphasis. Instead this word forces us back to *the primary meaning* of its root, which is "*be united*." This son was the only son so united with his father by the promise of God, by the miraculous birth, and by his own personal faith in Yahweh that he was a son in the spiritual sense. In other words, this word is used as a similar Greek word is used in the New Testament to describe the unique sonship of Jesus. When Jesus is called "*The only begotten son of God*," there is no possible reference to physical generation, as Jehovah's Witnesses claim. It refers to *that spiritual relation* between Jesus and his Heavenly Father *that is absolutely unique, so definitely one of a kind that there is no other*. This same description is given of Isaac in Hebrews 11:17.

When The One True God commanded that this "only son" be made a burnt offering, he did indeed demand of Abraham an offering that required utter devotion. Concerning the burnt offering which was a sacrifice completely consumed by fire Alfred Edersheim said:

> The derivation of the term Olah (the Hebrew word for burnt offering), as wholly "ascending" unto God, indicates alike the mode of the sacrifice and its meaning. It symbolised the entire surrender unto God . . . and His acceptance thereof.[2]

In Abraham's case it meant that a priceless and irreplacable possession should be surrendered unto God.

One other feature of the burnt offering needs to be remembered. The burnt offering represented the one making the offering, even the whole of him. *The surrender of the offering* by the one offering it rather than consumption by fire of the offering itself was *uppermost in the concern of God*. This fact offers an explanation of Yahweh's willingness to provide a substitute for Isaac once the surrender by Abraham was thoroughly demonstrated. So long as Abraham felt that Isaac was his possession rather than God's, there was an obstacle to the perfection of his faith. *Once surrendered, utterly devoted, God could use a substitute to remind him continually of the necessity of that surrender in a perfect faith.*

---

2. Alfred Edersheim, *The Temple, Its Ministry and Its Services* (London: The Religious Tract Society, 1874), p. 99.

Certain silent spots in the story bear witness to an agony in Abraham's heart as he prepared to obey. He did not tell Sarah where he was taking their son or why. He did not tell Isaac, not then.

But he obeyed! With staccato effect the steps of his response are recited. "Therefore, Abraham got up early, saddled his ass, took with him two of his young men, also Isaac his son, split wood for the burnt offering, arose, and went toward the place of which The (One True) God had spoken to him."[3] Perhaps his only way for controlling pent-up emotion that threatened to break out in an uncontrollable flood was rapid preparation for his journey. Without hesitation he set out. By that action he made known to God his devotion of himself and his son. Despite the struggle, despite the lack of understanding, he would obey.

2. The One Who Proved Abraham's Abhorrence of Idolatry

At the beginning of verse four there is an emphasis upon the words "On the third day." This emphasis breaks a long silence that covered more than two days. At the end of it Abraham "lifted up his eyes and saw the place some distance away." Yes, the place of which he had thought day and night without saying anything! As soon as God assured him of the very place, he became articulate, positive, strong. But how was his heart during those many long silent hours?

Commentators have tried hard to read between the lines and to explain Abraham's attitudes. In doing so several of the ablest and best, not to mention the school of destructive critics, have advanced one interpretation that must be rejected. S.R. Driver said, "The command would not . . . shock the moral standard to which Abraham was accustomed, as it would shock ourselves."[4] Marcus Dods said, ". . . Abraham did not think it wrong to sacrifice his son. His own conscience did not clash with God's command.[5] Even Alexander Maclaren said, ". . . it was not wrong in Abraham's eyes for a father to slay his son."[6]

---

3. The author's translation.

4. S.R. Driver, *opus citus*, p. 222.

5. Marcus Dods, "The Book of Genesis," *The Expositor's Bible* (London: Hodder and Stoughton, 1893), p. 199.

6. Alexander Maclaren, *Expositions of Holy Scripture*, Vol. I (New York: George H. Doran Company, n.d.), p. 154.

There was occasion for a debate in Abraham's heard over this command to offer Isaac as a burnt offering. The command used the very word the idolaters round about used to describe their human sacrifices. *How then could the thing God required be distinguished from heathen practice?*

It is true that the written text does not fill the gap for us at this point, but it does provide for an understanding of it in terms of the characterizations of Abraham given previously. Not the guesses quoted above!

That paralyzing inner struggle of Abraham that held him in the grip of silence for two days or more can be fittingly understood as burning into his very soul a debate of this kind:

> O Lord Yahweh that spoke to me long ago in Ur, is it possible that you can ask for a sacrifice such as the heathen offer to gods of their own making?
>
> In Ur I knew what their vile offerings meant. Here, in sight of Sodom, their abominations are known to have brought down fires of judgment from Yahweh's own hand. By sacred prostitution, devoting maidens to satisfy their own lusts, they call that which is unspeakably corrupt a sacred or devoted thing. By human sacrifice, devoting innocent children to inhuman torture, they seek to escape the guilt of their own sins by devoting those dearest to them to appease gods cunningly devised by their own blind and distorted consciences.
>
> O Yahweh my God, The One True God, you brought me out of Ur to deliver me from idolatry. You separated me from my kin, even from my father's household, to deliver me from idolatry. After the rescue of Lot you moved me to refuse any profit from the goods of Sodom that I might avoid any appearance of sanction upon blasphemous claims of Sodom's sordid, utterly selfish, and horribly cruel worship. Cursed degradation is brought by idolatry upon all who participate.
>
> Even as I ask, so I know the answer; your way, O Yahweh is as different as light is from darkness. Forgive me for asking! Now I know Yahweh can never ask one to selfishly sacrifice another for his sake, only to sacrifice himself lovingly for another's sake.[7]

---

7. An interpretation of Abraham's thoughts by the author.

When Abraham broke his silence, he was able to speak confidently of the outcome of this test. He told the servants to wait, "for," said he, "I and the lad purpose to go yonder that we may worship, then to return unto you."[8] He was not lying, covering fear with falsehood. He used another cohortative of determination; so his intention was not one of these weak-minded intentions depending for fulfillment upon the way the wind blows. His intentions were grounded in the intentions of his God, and he spoke with unwavering assurance. He expected *to worship and to return* in peace. He spoke both of *himself and of Isaac,* with respect to *going together* to worship *and* with respect to *returning together*. The only son was to be united with him all the way. Just how Yahweh would manage he did not know, but the corruptions of idolatry could not enter here.

3. The One who Proved the Complete Reliance of Abraham Upon the Providential Control of Yahweh

Abraham put the wood on Isaac's back, but "he took *in his hand* the fire and the knife."[9] The words "in his hand" are placed emphatically. His hand could now handle these symbols of death without fear, for Yahweh would control his hands.

Isaac asked a natural question, " . . . where is the lamb . . . .?" But his father did not falter as he replied, "God himself will provide the lamb . . . ."[10] The words *"God himself"* are placed emphatically. Moreover, the word "himself" is added to emphasize the fact that this providential control would be exercised by God, directly and independently, not depending upon Abraham's understanding of the way it would be done. *Abraham was confident but moved by faith alone.* Is it any wonder that the sublime confidence expressed by this word of wisdom, was caught up into a proverb even before the Scriptures were written saying, *"In the mountain of Yahweh it will be provided"*[11] (Gen. 22:14)?

The building and preparation of the altar, the binding of Isaac without resistance on his part, the laying of him on the altar, and the actual lifting of the sacrificial knife seem to say that *Isaac* was so instructed on the spot in the meaning of

---

8. The author's translation.

9. The author's translation of Genesis 22:6.

10. The author's translation of Genesis 22:8.

11. The author's translation.

the command that he *yielded because he shared his father's faith.*
Be that as it may, the steadfast calm with which Abraham did
everything at this time prepares us for this explanation by the
author of Hebrews:

> By faith Abraham, being tried, offered up
> Isaac; yea, he that had gladly received the
> promises was offering up his only begotten son;
> even he to whom it was said, In Isaac shall thy
> seed be called; accounting that God is able to
> raise up, even from the dead; from which he did
> also in a figure receive him back. (Heb. 11:17-19)

The providential control was never more in control than
here. Thus was *proof provided that Abraham's faith had reached
a pinnacle of perfection.*

Expositors generally have recognized the outcome of this
exceedingly severe test as the most rewarding experience of
Abraham's life. S. R. Driver said, ". . . Abraham's faith is
triumphantly established in the face of the most severe test of
all."[12]   Marcus Dods said, "The faith which had been schooled
. . . by so many minor trials was here perfected and exhibited
as perfect."[13] Alexander Maclaren put this truth this way,
"Sharp trial means increased possession of God. So his last
terrible experience turned to his crowning glory."[14] H. C.
Leupold's word is this, "With this chapter we reach the climax
of the faith life of Abraham."[15]

Genesis 18-24 makes the third promise to Abraham, the
promise that he would be a blessing to all men, its central
theme. Thus his experience in the offering of Isaac is the climax
of all. Chapters 18-19 dealt with the deliverance of Lot from
Sodom, and in 19:29 it is said that Yahweh did it for the sake of
Abraham. Chapter 20 deals with the rescue of Sarah from Abimelech's household. Despite a wrong done to Abimelech by Abraham
(20:4, 5), God was able to reveal Abraham to Abimelech as a
prophet and one who would pray for him (20:7). According to
Genesis 21:13, God said to Abraham that he would make Ishmael a
nation because he was Abraham's child. According to Genesis 21:

---

12. S. R. Driver, *opus citus*, p. 216.

13. Marcus Dods, *opus citus*, p. 198.

14. Alexander Maclaren, *opus citus*, p. 152.

15. H. C. Leupold, *opus citus*, p. 616.

22-34, Abimelech the philistine sought a treaty of peace between them and between their people because he realized that God was with Abraham. All these experiences broadened and strengthened Abraham's influence. Then, after the offering of Isaac, Yahweh said, " . . . *in thy seed* shall all the nations of the earth be blessed . . ." (Gen. 22:18).

Conclusion: From Paradox to Prophecy

Abraham's trust that God could and if need be would bring Isaac back from the dead was a magnificent exercise of faith, but the ground for it was indeed a paradox. Belief in the possibility of a resurrection flew in the face of reason.

At that very moment, however, The Angel of Yahweh stayed the uplifted hand of Abraham. He provided the sacrificial ram, a substitute to die in Isaac's stead. Then he proceeded to explain the ground for fulfillment of Abraham's faith. In this he brought into clear view the great stream of Messianic prophecy that runs through Israel's history straight to its fulfillment in the death and resurrection of Jesus Christ.

To understand the exceedingly significant relation between Abraham's faith and Messianic prophecy, careful consideration must be given to the substitute offered for Isaac. As a burnt offering accepted by the Lord it was ground for assurance that the complete consecration of the believer would be brought about under the providence of Yahweh and that the extension of the believer's influence to the full extent of the promises would likewise be brought about under the providence of Yahweh. Not only was Abraham's faith perfected at this time but the ground of assurance contained in the burnt offering was perfected at this time. By acceptance of the offering from Abraham's hand, Yahweh accepted responsibility for bringing to perfection the things promised in Abraham's life, Isaac's life, and the life of their spiritual seed. In that responsibility of Yahweh was the foundation of prophecy.

The crucial point in it all appeared in these words of Yahweh: *"'By myself* I have sworn,' is the very word of Yahweh, 'that *by reason of the fact that you have done this thing, and you have not withheld your son, your only son.* I shall surely bless you, . . . your descendants . . ., and all the nations of the earth . . . .'"* There were two great emphases in this statement. The last was a final recounting of the evidence of Abraham's faith. The first was new, totally new, startlingly new, wonderfully, wonderfully new. It had the wondrous good news of Messianic prophecy in its. Yea, the theophanic angel, The Angel of Yahweh, very solemnly affirmed that *"by himself"* he had sworn to fulfill the promises. That meant, to start with,

fulfilling in himself the assurances of atonement symbolized by
the burnt offering. That meant, moreover, fulfilling by means of
his own perfecting discipline the crowning symbolism of the burnt
offering, even the chastening necessary to procure perfect peace
with God for the one making the offering.

This matchless assurance of the Lord Yahweh comes only to a
believer whose all is laid on the altar. The hymn "Is Your All
on the Altar?" states the lesson beautifully in these words:

You have longed for sweet peace, and for faith to increase,
And you have earnestly, fervently prayed;
But you cannot have rest or be perfectly blest
Until all on the altar is laid.

Is your all on the altar of sacrifice laid?
Your heart, does the Spirit control?
You can only be blest and have peace and sweet rest,
As you yield Him your body and soul.[16]

8. GLIMPSES OF GOD

AS

THE HEAVENLY MATCHMAKER

Genesis 24; Psalms 37:3-5; II Corinthians 6:14

Introduction: Are Marriages Made in Heaven?

Nothing is said in Genesis 24 about the season in which
Abraham sent his servant to seek a bride for Isaac. That season,
however, was quite probably spring. In the lands of the Bible
spring is conducive to travel. In all lands spring is conducive
to courting, matchmaking, and marriage.

The season that brings out the grass and a multitude of
multi-colored anemones on the hills of Galilee is indeed a wonderful season. It is possible that those anemones are the lilies
of the field of which Jesus spoke, saying, "Even Solomon in all

---

16. Elisha A. Hoffman, "Is Your All on the Altar," in
Baptist Hymnal, Walter Hines Simms, editor (Nashville, Tennessee:
Convention Press, 1956), No. 350.

his glory was not arrayed like one of these" (Luke 12:27).

The season that makes a hyacinth thrust its tender head
through the clay of the flower beds is a season that stirs human
hearts. A hyacinth -- how very, very beautiful it is! Its bell-
shaped blooms are so perfectly symmetrical that one may think in
fancy that Santa Claus dropped a string of his bells at Christmas
time. Their whiteness is so perfectly white that one may dream
of them as cut from the robe of an angel attending the heavenly
throne. Their beauty in any color is so exquisite that, if one
is looking with the eyes of his soul, it will take his breath
away. At that time we know that spring is coming in, and any day
may bring fulfillment of the old saying, "In the springtime a
young man's fancy lightly turns to thoughts of love." And that
is all right, quite all right, if only the matter is not treated
too lightly.

For every child of God, every believer, marriage is an
important matter. Every one contemplating it may well pray with
Abraham, "O Lord, let it be a marriage made in heaven."

Is it really true that marriages are made in heaven? Well!
At least Abraham thought they could be. That faith of Abraham
makes the story of Genesis 24 to be one of the most charming and
instructive ever written. In it we find the teaching that there
is a heavenly matchmaker. We find it taught moreover that, for
those who seek his guidance, he renders many important services:
(1) he guides a faithful parent in giving counsel; (2) he
guides a faithful child in receiving counsel; (3) he guides a
faithful friend in giving aid; (4) he accepts a test of providential control; (5) he satisfies the prospective in-laws;
(6) he persuades the bride-to-be; (7) he makes a love-match.

1. He Guides a Faithful Parent in Giving Counsel

Abraham was old. In all things he had thus far been
blessed, as we are told in Genesis 24:1. The future, however,
depended largely upon the finding of a wife, the right wife,
for Isaac. Sarah was dead, Isaac was more than old enough to
be married, all the neighbors were Canaanites, peoples of low
standards religiously and morally, and the finding of a girl who
would help to establish a home in the fear of The One True God
was a great big problem. It weighed heavily upon Abraham. He
decided that the time had come for him to do something about it.

Not entirely alone, however! Abraham had to face the decision alone so far as human advice was concerned, but the over-
shadowing 'watch-care' of The Angel of Yahweh was expected by him
now in all things. His directions to his servant about this
matter later reflected this expectation. He expected this

'watch-care' over his own thinking and planning as well as over
his servant's assistance.

The one point that was absolutely fixed in Abraham's thinking was that Isaac's wife must be found in his land and among his
kin. This meant that she must be a worshipper of Yahweh, under
no circumstances an idolater, an ungodly and unprincipled person.
About this he was very positive. In taking an oath of his servant
that he would make the journey in search of her, he emphasized the
words "unto my land and unto my kindred." Furthermore, to the
command "you will go," he added the correlative statement "and
you shall take a wife for my son" (Gen. 24:4). This meant more
than a mere command or mere expectation. It expressed Abraham's
absolute assurance concerning the successful outcome of the servant's efforts. Further on in the conversation he explained to
the servant his faith about this matter (cf. Gen. 24:7). He
referred emphatically to Yahweh who called him out of Ur. He
referred also to the revelation that emphatically designated
Canaan as the land promised to his descendants. He added then
this word, "he will send his angel before you," seeing this development as the means ordained for fulfillment of the former
providences. Finally he repeated the correlative statement, the
one with "shall" in it, which he added to the command to go.
This reveals the characteristic force of a correlative perfect.
Thus Abraham expressed his unshakable assurance that The Angel
of Yahweh would guarantee the success of this matchmaking effort.

We are not told in a direct way that Abraham counselled with
Isaac, but a direct statement was unnecessary. The spiritual harmony existing between Abraham and Isaac testifies concerning that.
The harmony that led to Isaac's voluntary submission when he was
offered on Mt. Moriah was a continuing harmony. Yahweh worship
did not permit arbitrary dealing in such matters. Moreover,
Isaac's happy cooperation in receiving Rebekah when she came
reveals his harmonious participation in the plan from its beginning. Thus we know that Abraham's planning was godly and fatherly counsel to a beloved son and a spiritual heir. It certainly
was not the autocratic, inconsiderate, selfishly greedy bargaining
so often carried on by heads of families in the Bible lands of
today in arranging marriage contracts.

2. He Guides a Faithful Child in Receiving Counsel

The exercise of faith in Yahweh on the part of Isaac is
assured by the entire spiritual history of those reckoned in the
Scriptures as inheriting the blessing promised to Abraham. This
blessing was the third of the great promises included in the call.
It was the purely personal, spiritual, and universal one. Inheritance of it placed one in the line of chosen ones, those with whom
and through whom God established his covenants.

In the families, tribes, and nations surrounding Abraham, the regular custom concerning inheritance of leadership was to determine it by birth. The rights of inheritance ran through first-born sons. Archeology is telling us today that the situation at Salem, where Melchizedek was priest of God Most High, was an exception, but this law was almost universal.

In the family of Abraham, a prospect concerning the succession different from all others was set up by the promises. There was to be a succession among Abraham's heirs spiritually determined and yet unbroken. The promises assured an unbroken succession of heirs and the spiritual principles of the character of Yahweh required that each heir be a believer. This combination of promises made the Abrahamic succession to be a supremely significant fact.

In accord with this twofold assurance, the blessing went first to Isaac rather than Ishmael. Afterwards it went to Jacob rather than Esau, to Judah rather than Rueben, to David rather than any older brother or to Saul, and to the Second David who was the child of a virgin daughter of David rather than the reprobate King Ahaz who represented the line of David through Solomon.

Thus history gives affirmation to the conclusion that Isaac both heard and received the counsel of the Heavenly Matchmaker.

3. He Guides a Faithful Friend in Giving Aid

The servant upon whom Abraham depended in this effort was much more than an ordinary servant. He was the oldest in Abraham's household. He enjoyed, therefore, the benefits of long experience. He was "the one managing all his (Abraham's) possessions."[1] He had, therefore, proved his ability and trustworthiness as a manager of money and men. He feared God, because he took an oath in the name of "Yahweh, the God of the heavens and the God of the earth."[2] He could, therefore, be depended upon to accept this responsibility most conscientiously.

This steward or general manager of all Abraham's household was shrewd enough to say, "Perhaps the woman will not be willing to come after me unto this land. Shall I indeed carry back your

---

1. Genesis 24:2, in the author's translation.

2. Genesis 24:3, in the author's translation.

son unto the land from which you went out?"[3] Abraham warned him
sharply not to carry Isaac back, guarding strictly against the
possibility that a courtship developing in Mesopotamia should
tempt Isaac or the girl to forget the Promised Land. Then
Abraham explained his faith concerning the 'watch-care' to be
expected from The Angel of Yahweh. The steward accepted this
explanation by taking the oath; so he confessed his own faith in
this Heavenly Matchmaker.

Later, according to Genesis 24:27, the steward said, " . . .
and *as for me, in the way* hath Yahweh led me, even to the house
of my lord's brothers."[4] Thus he testified that the faith
Abraham and he had shared had been realized.

4. He Accepts a Test of his Providential Control

When the servant reached the city of Nahor in Mesopotamia,
he prayed to Yahweh for the help he needed (Gen. 24:12-14). In
doing so he proposed a test of the Lord's providential control of
his quest. The test involved both the control of Yahweh in many
ways and the yielding of the servant to his guidance in many ways.
Observation of the circumstances on both sides may be quite
instructive.

The servant's role included the strategic move he had already made in halting his caravan by the well of water, at evening
time, when the women were accustomed to go to the well with large
water jars on their heads or their shoulders and to replenish the
household supply of water. The well was the common source of supply for all families. The young women were the ones expected to
perform this household chore. The evening time was the time when
they gathered to chat as well as to get water. That place and
that time, therefore, provided a series of opportunities each of
which was very important to the business in hand.

First, there was opportunity for the servant to observe the
young women apart from their families. Any approach to a father
or brother before there was opportunity to observe the young lady
herself and to know the Lord's will would have complicated the
situation before there was opportunity for Yahweh to reveal his
choice.

Second, opportunity was provided for the young women to express themselves naturally and reveal personal characteristics

----

3. Genesis 24:5, in the author's translation.

4. The author's translation.

without realizing that they were being observed. Evidences of
maturity, healthy vigor, intelligence, beauty, vivacity, sociabil-
ity, kindness, and the like appear very quickly in lively conversation.

Third, opportunity was provided for the servant to open a
conversation naturally by asking for a drink of water. The
presence of his camels, his age, and his leadership of the caravan would make it appear to be an approach without any ulterior
motive.

Fourth, there would be opportunity for the young women to
respond naturally. No embarrassment or ulterior motive on her
part need inhibit her responding in her natural way, politely,
graciously, generously, or any other manner, revealing her real
self.

The role of The Angel of Yahweh is revealed by the servant's
prayer.

First, he is Yahweh's means of answering a believer's prayer.
There is no theophany in this case, but the spiritual guidance,
the influence of spirit on spirit, exercises the same vital influence it does in the experience of all God's children who seek
his guidance.

Second, he controls circumstances so as to make them an
evidence of his will. As the godly often say to one another,
"he closes some doors and opens others." In this case many doors
had been closed to Abraham in the years past, especially Canaanite
doors, also doors in Lot's family, and the like. Now, in accord
with Abraham's plan and in response to the servant's prayer,
Rebekah comes to the well.

Third, he uses the judgment, action, and influence of a peti-
tioner who holds himself available circumstantially and fit
spiritually. The servant, having placed himself in the midst of
the busy scene by the well, continued to observe and doubtless
continued to pray. Doubtless he said to himself, "Not this one!
Not that one!" Then there was Rebekah! Her name, her family he
could not know, but her beauty he could certainly see. According
to Genesis 24:16, "the maiden was very beautiful." Evidences of
character were in her face. Her way with people showed itself
as she exchanged greetings here and there. No sign of haughtiness
or wantonness appeared. He continued to watch as she went down
the steps, put the pitcher on her shoulder, and came up again.
The vitality of her mind and body was evident in the springiness
of her step, the poise, ease, and grace of her bearing. There was
kindness in her eyes. He was impressed. He was so eager that he

ran to meet her (cf. Gen. 24:17). She responded to his request
for a drink of water most readily and helpfully. She even did
more than he asked and proceeded to draw water for his camels.
There were ten of them (cf. Gen. 24:10), at the end of a long
journey, but she was not above or afraid of work. He, of course,
was very favorably inclined.

Fourth, The Angel gives clear assurance finally to the peti-
tioner who is patient, perceptive, and yielding. In Genesis
24:21 we are told that "the man was looking steadfastly upon her,
while remaining silent, in order to know whether Yahweh had
really made his way to prosper or not."[5]   He was waiting for that
final assurance. Her preoccupation with the camels gave him a
free time for spiritual waiting and listening. Before she finished he was sure in his own heart that he knew the will of the Lord.
Accordingly, he brought forth gifts, inquired concerning her name
and family, and prepared to make known his intentions to all of
them. Immediately, however, he paused to worship and give thanks
for the blessed guidance of the Heavenly Matchmaker.

The certainty felt by the servant was due to faith in the
guidance of The Angel of Yahweh. He expressed it in his first
prayer at the well, in the test of The Angel's control which he
proposed at that time. He did it as faithfully as Abraham could
have done it. He used the same kind of language Abraham used in
expressing his assurance concerning the outcome of the plan as a
whole. That language was a correlative statement. It is found
in Genesis 24:14 in these words, "and it shall be." The verb is
a Hebrew correlative perfect. It did not describe a future event
as merely expected, giving no stronger grounds for hope than
human confidence, saying simply, "it will happen." It was cor-
related with the prayer he put into these words: "O Yahweh, cause
it to happen, I pray, . . ." (Gen. 24:12). It said that as surely
as the Lord would answer that prayer he would answer it in the way
requested. His assurance, therefore, was based upon alignment
with the promises, a surrendered will, and faithful prayer for
divine control. It expressed absolute assurance of a God-given
answer. This assurance is expressed in English by the auxiliary
"shall." In the words of George O. Curme, ". . .it indicates
the will of someone other than its subject, representing its subject as standing under the will of another who commands him,
promises or assures him something . . . . It represents the
speaker as proclaiming the will of God or destiny in a prophetic

---

5.   The author's translation.

or oracular announcement of something that shall take place."[6]

Confirmation of the servant's certainty is described with a charm that can give an ecstatic thrill to a believer. He had just said, *"By this* I shall know . . ." (Gen. 24:14).[7] Then, "while *he* had *not yet* finished speaking, Rebekah was coming out . . . " (Gen. 24:15).[8]

5. He Satisfies the Prospective In-Laws

Rebekah also did some running (cf. Gen. 24:28). And some talking! She had quite a story to tell to her family. It is said that she told it "to the household of her mother"; so all the servants and connections were gathered together to hear. The reference here to the household of her mother rather than the household of her father may mean that he was no longer physically active in management of the household. He was, however, included in the family decision concerning this startling news (cf. Gen. 24:50). The whole family was agog. Laban, Rebekah's brother, ran to bring the servant with his camels and attendants inside and to provide for their needs.

When the time to eat was announced, the servant said, "I shall not eat, until I have told my business" (Gen. 24:33). The business was too important to wait. While the impression of what had just happened at the well was clear, thrilling, and convincing to him and Rebekah, before someone partially informed or skeptical could put doubts in her mind, he would tell the whole story and call for an answer. So he told it and said, "Now, therefore, if you will be dealing loyally and faithfully with my lord, tell me; and if not, tell me, that I may turn to the right hand or the left" (Gen. 24:49).[9]

Then Laban and Bethuel, the heads of the household, gave the answer that must have been obvious in all eyes in that household circle, *"From Yahweh* the matter has come forth."[10] That emphasis of theirs was a real tribute to the Heavenly Matchmaker.

---

6. George O. Curme, *A Grammar of the English Language,* III (New York: D. C. Heath and Company, 1931), pp. 364, 365.

7. The author's translation.

8. The author's translation.

9. The author's translation.

10. The author's translation.

6. He Persuades the Bride-To-Be

Rebekah was obviously a party to this family council. The
freedom with which she talked to the old servant at the well is
evidence that she knew no such subjection as women experience in
Mohammedan harems today. It is mentioned in verse 55 that her
mother, along with her brother, proposed that she stay with the
family at least ten days before her departure; so the women had a
voice in these things. Moreover, the decision concerning time
for leaving was left to Rebekah alone.

Hasty judges sometimes accuse Rebekah of being influenced
chiefly by the gifts and the prospect of riches. Such things are
not without influence in any case, of course, but balanced judgment should give her credit for being a faithful believer as well.
She manifested strong faith in later life. Moreover, leaving
home to marry a man she had never seen and to live in a foreign
land among foreign peoples was surely a challenge to real faith.
Mere selfish advantage and vain glory were doubtless not enough
to explain her decision.

There was no evidence of hesitation on Rebekah's part even
from the beginning. When the family asked concerning the question
of immediate departure, "Will you go with this man?" she answered
quickly and decisively, saying, "I shall go" (Gen. 24:58). It is
not too much then to say that the bride-to-be was happily per-
suaded by the guidance of the Heavenly Matchmaker.

7. He Makes a Love Match

Against this background, the meeting of Isaac and Rebekah
makes the end of a perfect chapter in their lives.

Isaac, according to Genesis 24:63a, had gone out from his
camp "to meditate in the field at the approach of evening time."[11]
It is easy to imagine some of the thoughts that filled his heart.
Perhaps enough time had elapsed for the servant's return. What if
this were the day? What would she be like? "Then he lifted up
his eyes and looked, and behold, camels were coming" (Gen. 24:63b).

"Likewise Rebekah lifted up her eyes and saw Isaac" (Gen.
24:64a). She did not know that the man she saw was Isaac, for she
asked the servant who he was. She had, however, been asking over
and over, "When shall we get there?" Perhaps they had camped the
night before at Bethlehem, where the servant would naturally go

---

11. The author's translation.

to seek information about Abraham and Isaac. He had heard that
Isaac, after a movement toward *Beer-Lahai-Roi* near the Mediter-
ranean coast, had returned to the *Negev,* perhaps that part due
south of Bethlehem. All this day they had been coming nearer and
nearer to his camp. Rebekah was watching and ready. She had
"the veil," the wedding veil, ready to be put on quickly. She
saw the man she thought might be Isaac before anyone told her
it was he. And "she fell off" that camel. Translations have
to say "she got down hastily" or something like that, for the
verb describes deliberate haste in this context, certainly not
an accidental fall. But she fell all right. The way she got off
that camel meant that she fell as any girl with a faith like hers
and an energy like hers falls for the man of her choice.

The crowning touch to this story is given at the end when we
are told that Isaac "proceeded to take Rebekah, she to become his
wife, and he to love her." Thus reliance upon the Heavenly Matchmaker makes a love match.

Conclusion

The Angel of Yahweh is as available for matchmaking today as
he was in the long ago. While he helps as best he can in any
case, only those who answer God's call as Abraham did, and as
Isaac was expected to do, receive the fullness of his services.
The matches he controls fully must serve God's purposes, in a
land of his choosing, among a people of his choosing, with a
family of his choosing. How foolish it would have been if Isaac
had said, "I must see her first, I must go back to Mesopotamia,
May be I must stay there."! How foolish it would have been for
Rebekah to say, "I'm willing but I can't; I can't leave Mama; I
can serve here but not there; I can be a deacon's wife but never
a preacher's wife; I can serve at home but never in a foreign
land."!

One fall day in 1919, Dr. Eugene Sallee, a missionary to
China, came to The Southern Baptist Seminary in Louisville,
Kentucky for a special service. Southern Baptists had arranged
for special services at that season throughout the Southern Baptist Convention. These servies were for the purpose of "calling
out the called."

In the congregation that day sat two young people who were
engaged to be married. These were seated, however, on opposite
sides of the chapel. In those days girls from the Woman's
Missionary Union Training School and Seminary students were very
strictly separated.

In special prayer meetings that continued through many days
preceding this service, each of these young persons had come face

to face with a challenge to surrender for service as foreign
missionaries. Each was deeply concerned but uncertain. In a
very brief conversation a few days before, each had confessed a
deep struggle over the question. There was, however, no opportunity at all for further consideration of the great and urgent
questions which it raised. Should the call of one be determined
by the call of the other? If one was called and the other was
not, was the engagement broken? Could the conviction they had
shared that their engagement was guided be wrong? No special
arrangements could be made in those days for opportunity "to
talk things out," "to pray it through." There was no personnel
secretary in those days to give advice and to be a mediator. Each
had come into that meeting, despite intense inward struggle, without another word. And that meeting was a meeting for decision.

As the message unfolded through explanation, challenge, and
appeal, the struggle in each heart was much the same and more
intense than ever. Little by little each recognized that each
must put its destiny in the Lord's hands, no matter what the consequences. Finally, the invitation was being given for volunteers
to come to the front. In the midst of his struggle the young man
had asked the Lord for a sign. It was not unusual in those days
at the Seminary to make appeals for volunteers to make their first
declaration under any kind of emotional stress. The quiet, pri-
vate judiciously made declaration was preferred, and students were
not prepared to expect an invitation for public declaration in
this service. The young man, greatly concerned about opportunity
for consultation later with his fiancee and with parents, told the
Lord that he would go if there was an invitation, otherwise he
would wait. Now it was being given; so he went, still wondering
what was happening on the other side.

Little by little two lines of volunteers converged upon the
speaker. Because the crowd filled the chapel to capacity, there
was not much room at the front. Those coming from one side could
not see those coming from the other till they met in front of the
speaker. In the end, there they were, even these two, side by
side.

Theirs too was a marriage made in heaven!

9. GLIMPSES OF GOD

AS

THE FEAR OF ISAAC

Genesis 27:1-40, 31:42,53; Hebrews 12:1-13

Introduction: Words Hard To Handle

The name "Isaac" means Laughter. When his mother was told,
after she had passed the time of childbearing, that she would have
a child of her own, she laughed (Gen. 18:15) - a laugh of incredulity, of unbelief. When that child was born, she laughed in a
different way indeed, a great big burst of laughter (Gen. 26:6) -
laughter that was sheer exultation, spontaneous joy in the fear of
Yahweh.

Moreover, we are constrained to believe that Isaac shared
with his father the profound faith in Yahweh God seen in the offering of Isaac on Mt. Moriah (Gen. 22:5).

According to Genesis 26:24, Yahweh God appeared to Isaac
personally and made with him the same covenant made with Abraham.

Each of these experiences is described by words that are wonderful. They can be laid hold upon by faith, faith born of a
spiritual transformation in one's self, but they do speak of
miracles.

In the words of Jacob, we find a word used to describe
Isaac's faith that perplexes us yet more. As Jacob returned from
Paddan-aran, and was providentially aided by Yahweh to make a
treaty of peace with Laban, he sanctioned it twice (Gen. 31:42,53)
by an oath in the name of "Yahweh God of Abraham, and the Fear of
Isaac."

The word "fear (dread)" used by Jacob at this point is not
the word ordinarily used in the Bible to describe the fear of God.
The ordinary word appears in this statement of Proverbs 1:7, "The
fear of Yahweh is the beginning of wisdom." That words appears
in the Bible very frequently, and it means profound reverential
respect. This word used by Jacob, when standing alone, describes
the terrifying dread of disaster. It is used in other connections
than that with God to describe what a snake is to a bird, what a
trap is to an animal, what the savagery of vengeance is to a

victim, what the pit of destruction is to the damned.

This word, therefore, is hard to handle when used to describe
the discipline of God to a chastened child in the hour of reproof
and correction. Where is the line of distinction between the
threat of utter destruction and the recognized means of saving
grace?

Jacob looking back twenty years upon his own experiences in
receiving the blessing from Isaac, remembers something in that
experience that had not merely surprised him but staggered him,
even as it staggers us. He remembers how Isaac "trembled a great
trembling" (Gen. 27:33) when Esau appeared and he realized that
he had pronounced the blessing on Jacob. Moreover he remembers
that Isaac believed that God had overruled all concerned and indeed guided him unexpectedly, yea, contrary to his own intentions
and effort in this blessing. Accordingly, his father had said to
Esau, " . . . I have blessed him; also blessed will he be" (Gen.
27:33). Despite Esau's bitter complaint, that was the way Isaac
had left it. Now looking back, with Yahweh's providential protection as he also concluded a treaty of peace with Laban, Jacob
invoked God's sanction upon it with a new name for Yahweh, "The
Fear (Dread) of Isaac."

The use of this word as a name for God occurs *only* at this
point. It was used *by Jacob only*, and both times it was related
to Jacob's encounter with Laban on Mt. Gilead as told in Genesis
31:22-55. This restriction to Jacob's words at this particular
time leaves no opening for a search for comparisons or contrasts
in the experience of others. It limits us to what Jacob already
knew about his father, even before he left home. It concentrates
upon those experiences which forced him to leave. He had probably
told the story to Laban over and over; so he could expect Laban
to know why he used it. The climax of the story brings us to a
juncture in Isaac's experience and thought where two great tides
of emotion meet. The relation of this word to the crisscross
currents of those two emotional tides does indeed make it hard
to handle.

Nevertheless, this little word, this four-letter word in
Hebrew or English, exercises a fascinating attraction that makes
it nigh to impossible for the mind to turn it loose once the
facts already noted have been really grasped. Like the word
"chastening" in Hebrews 12:1-13, it holds a 'secret' concerning
the Lord's dealing with his children that is irresistably attractive.

Once upon a time in his boyhood this author found a bull calf
very attractive. Trying to be friendly and to hold on to him, he
caught hold of the calf's tail. Then the calf ran away with him.

The faster the calf ran, the tighter he held on to that tail.
Faster and faster they went, till he was terrified, but he simply
could not turn loose. He was scared out of his wits. Finally,
he began to yell, "Daddy! D-ad-d-y! Come help me turn this calf
loose." Then, when his daddy had roped that calf and stopped him,
he sat down to teach his boy which end of a bull calf to take hold
of *first*.

Let us ask, in the midst of our wrestling with this particular word for "fear," that the Lord will use the distress of Isaac
as well as our own spiritual complexes to teach us how to take
hold of the causes of "fear." Certainly he shows us in the story
of Isaac that he brought this "fear" upon Isaac and did it for his
own good. This chastening influence is, therefore, the end of the
problem to be laid hold of first. Then there are three glimpses
of God to be seen in his chastening of Isaac, each glimpse helping
us to see the next. These are as follows: (1) as the one who
made Isaac to tremble; (2) as the one who convicted Isaac of misjudgment concerning his sons; (3) as the one who used a shocking
fear to make Isaac's blessings fit.

1. The One Who Made Isaac to Tremble

In Genesis 27:33 this is written, "Then Isaac was seized by
an exceedingly great trembling (literally, he trembled an exceedingly great trembling) and said, 'Who then was he who hunted game
and brought it to me? As a result I ate from all of it before
you (Esau) came and blessed him (Jacob). *Moreover, blessed* will
he be.'"[1]

Why did Isaac tremble so?

This trembling was quite different from the trembling caused
by age or illness. Feeble he was, but he was not trembling this
way when he pronounced the blessing on Jacob a few minutes before.

This great trembling came upon him suddenly, at the very
moment he realized that the one he had blessed was not Esau.

The immediate reason was Yahweh's condemnation of Isaac's
plan to bless Esau. Isaac had made that plan without guidance
from Yahweh and without effort to obtain guidance. Seemingly he
proceeded upon the assumption that his position as head of the
household gave him the right to work this matter out according to
his own opinion, his own selfish and unguided judgment. When
Yahweh allowed it to happen contrary to his purposes, he knew

---

1. The author's translation.

that he had been overruled. This was reproof, rebuke, correction for the one who was supposed to instruct other members of the household in the will of the Lord. It was condemnation of a plan that involved many other things in the family situation. No wonder then that this sudden turn of events upset him very badly!

Isaac recognized the fact that Yahweh had allowed it to happen this way, for he said without hesitation and with emphasis, *"Moreover blessed* will he be." Despite the fact that Jacob and his mother had acted deceitfully, Yahweh had taken sides and declared his will. His will, whether fully understood or not, was to be accepted. Esau complained about it bitterly, but Isaac made it clear that what was done was done, because Yahweh ruled it that way.

A contributory reason was Yahweh's condemnation of Isaac's part in the family strife that precipitated this distressing conflict. Instead of using his headship of the household to root out misunderstandings and wrongs, Isaac had become a party to them. Probably his quick submission to the Lord's rebuke meant that his conscience had been hurting him all along. In any case he knew now that he bore a major portion of the blame because he had been in position to do most to remedy the situation and he had not.

Another contributory reason was Yahweh's condemnation of his part in magnifying children's personal differences. Isaac cultivated his contacts with Esau, to the exclusion of Jacob, because Esau brought him game that he liked (Gen. 25:27,28). Though Rebekah did something of the same sort with Jacob, still the primary responsibility was his, simply because he was the head of the household.

Another contributory reason appears at the same point as the preceding. This was Yahweh's condemnation of his part in the parental favoritism that had been practiced. He loved Esau, and Rebekah loved Jacob. They let their favoritism show, and the children both knew and felt their partiality. While it is doubtless expecting the impossible to think that a parent can avoid special appreciation for certain personality traits in a child, one is not naturally compelled to allow appreciation to make a distinction in attention, fellowship, and instruction. Isaac's misuse of opportunity at this point was also condemned.

A basic reason was Yahweh's strong disapproval of Isaac's failure to recognize Yahweh's revelation to Rebekah concerning the character and destiny of the twins (Gen. 25:22,23). Yahweh's word to her was as follows:

> Two nations are in your womb; / and *two peoples*
> *from the time of their birth* will be hostile
> to each other; /
> Also *one people* will be stronger *than the other*; /
> and *the elder* will serve the younger./[2]

The poetic form again reflects the importance attached by succeeding generations to such revelations as this. Emphasis upon the
ascendency of the younger son can help us to understand Esau's
rebellion against it. But why did Isaac refuse to accept it? Was
he inclined to put his own reasoning about Esau's fitness for
leadership above that of 'so-called revelation'? Was there some
sort of doubt in Isaac's mind about this being actually a revelation from the Lord?

Some sort of doubt about Rebekah's experience appears to be
the only sufficient explanation of Isaac's attitude in this case.
Since there was no charge during the twenty years that intervened
against his sincerity in reporting her experience, that thought
must be dismissed. He could, however, that thought that her condition at the time, her pregnancy and the struggling of the babies
in her womb, (Gen. 25:22) had unduly affected her interpretation
of her experience. In other words, he could have thought that her
belief that she received a revelation from Yahweh was a subjective
judgment, not really true though she thought it was.

In any case Isaac could have sought an indication of Yahweh's
will, and he did not. There was not even an effort to teach these
boys the error of their way when Jacob tried to buy the birthright
and when Esau obviously despised it (cf. Gen. 25:29-34). The
result was that the spiritual harmony between Isaac and Rebekah
that existed before the birth of the children (cf. Gen. 25:21)
had been disrupted. The love they had for each other in the beginning was in eclipse. There was no longer a family altar, no
real prayer life, no sympathetic effort at understanding. There
was instead selfish and unscrupulous grabbing for advantage by
each member of the family. Not merely partiality had crept in
but obstinacy, arbitrariness, distruct, trickery, deceit, and
lies.

The failure of Isaac to accept the revelation to Rebekah was
a basic cause of this very bad situation in a supposedly God-
fearing family. His trembling, therefore, revealed a realization
on his part that he had been wrong. When Yahweh allowed his self-
willed plans to be upset, even by trickery, it was his deliberate

---

2. The author's translation.

defiance of Yahweh's will that was put to shame.

The "fear," i.e., confusion, embarrassment, and terror, that
threw Isaac into panic did him good. The effect appeared when he
emphatically declared, ". . . *blessed* will he be." In this he
made a complete surrender after a long, hard struggle.

2. The One Who Convicted Isaac of Misjudgment Concerning
   His Sons

At the time of surrender Isaac could not possibly see all
that was involved in the foresight of God concerning Esau and
Jacob. As we are told in I Peter 1:1,2, "the elect" are elected
"according to the foreknowledge of God the Father . . ." Doubtless Isaac was convicted in heart later concerning many of the
characteristic traits of the boys and the destinies to which they
pointed. He lived to see much of the results of Esau's marriage
with ungodly women (cf. Gen. 26:34,35, 28:8,9). Esau was gradually estranged from the worship of Yahweh altogether and became the
leader of the Edomites (cf. Gen. 36). Isaac lived to see Jacob
after his return from Paddan-aram (cf. Gen. 35:29) and to know
his devotion to the Promised Land (cf. Gen. 37:1) with all that
inheritance of the promise implied. There are no recorded comments made by him, but his convictions are surely reflected in
Scriptural teaching concerning Esau and Jacob, supported by facts
that are implicit in these early accounts. These convictions
arose out of recognition of the worldliness of Esau and the
spiritual hunger of Jacob.

Recognition of the inherent worldliness of Esau was forced
upon Isaac by his experience at the time of blessing.

First of all, Esau was inordinately sportive, "sporty" as
we say today. In Genesis 25:27, he is called "a skillful hunter,
a man of the field."[3] He liked the outdoor life. He enjoyed
the prowess that brought in the meat, the venison that won favor
for him in his father's eyes. This in itself was not bad. Only
when enjoyed in excess, to the point of crowding God out, does it
characterize a life as worldly. In Esau's life it did that very
thing. How strange then that Isaac should allow his love of venison -- a fleshly appetite -- to blind his eyes to his son's lack
of spiritual understanding. From childhood his first-born was
spiritually blind, and he had not hitherto allowed himself to
admit that tragedy of tragedies.

---

3. *American Standard Version.*

In the second place, Esau was spiritually reckless. Coming
in from hunting, thoroughly worn out, even to the point of feeling
faint, he smelled Jacob's pottage, and suddenly there was nothing
else in life so desirable to him. That pottage was lentil soup.
Now lentil soup can really smell good. Oh my! But the smelling
was only the beginning. With appetite possessing him, he made
this exaggerated statement, "I am about to die." He followed that
with the reckless insinuation that the birthright could not profit
him. He thought about the birthright as a right that could be
sold for money or goods or food. So did Jacob at the time, but
Jacob learned better, while he did not. After the blessing was
given to Jacob, his bitter complaint implied that the birthright
and the blessing could be separate things (cf. Gen. 27:36). How
little he understood the call of Abram! How little he understood
the conditions under which his father was declared by Yahweh the
heir to the promises! In the words of the text (Gen. 25:34), he
"despised his birthright." Such privileges and responsibilities
as family leadership and being a blessing to other peoples were
worthless in his eyes. His was a devil-may-care attitude. If we
dare to use the words of reckless men of the world today, we must
say, "He didn't give a 'damn.'"

Moreover, Esau was dangerous. When he heard his father's explanation about the blessing, he was not prepared to submit as his
father did. Having had no personal experience with Yahweh, he was
incapable of understanding the belief of Isaac that Yahweh had
overruled all of them and had settled the matter of the blessing.
He attributed his loss solely to Jacob's guile. He hated Jacob
for it, and he purposed to kill him. Thus the heated passions of
a man of the world swept over him, wave after wave.

Finally, Esau was a profane man. The use of this word "profane" in Hebrews 12:16 to characterize Esau was a fitting summary
of all we see in the Genesis accounts. He loved the things of
this world. This does not say that there was no good in him.
Doubtless he was attractive and likable in many ways. But, his
heart was set on the things of this world. He was so far from
understanding the faith that moved his parents to "bitterness of
spirit" when he married Hittite women (Gen. 26:34,35) that he
married another who was a daughter of Ishmael (Gen. 28:6-9) as a
move calculated to appease them. He was blind to the real meaning
of their faith.

Recognition of the spiritual hunger of Jacob was likewise
forced upon Isaac by his experience with the blessing.

For one thing, Jacob was self-possessed. The description of
him in Genesis 25:27 as "a quiet man," according to some translations, "a plain man" in others, and "a calm man" elsewhere, may be

better rendered in this case as "self-possessed." He was not
easily agitated, angered, or distracted, as Esau was, but calmly
self-possessed even under pressure. This was one reason why he
was a very shrewd trader. Furthermore, he remained at home,
"dwelling in tents"; he stuck to his business, not letting sports
or pleasure interfere with it. In this trait, he was like his
mother, having inherited her thrifty nature. Thrown with her more
and more by the favoritism practiced by both parents, he learned
habits that depended upon diligence, quick wits, and hard bargaining.

Jacob was also unscrupulous in his early days. Being quick
to see opportunity for profit, he did not hesitate to take advantage of it because questions of right and wrong were involved.
Because he subscribed to the philosophy that the end justifies
the means, he was able to cooperate with his mother in deceiving
Isaac in order to get Isaac's blessing. Seemingly his only hesitation arose from fear that their trickery might be discovered
before the blessing should be pronounced.

Moreover, Jacob was ambitious. The very fact that he was so
ready to bargain with Esau for the birthright bore testimony to
the longing in his heart to inherit the land promised to Abraham.
The trouble about this was not that he was ambitious but that he
tried to satisfy his ambition by shrewdness and deceit. His ambition was different from Esau's ambition because his was set upon
the things of God while Esau's was set upon the things of this
world. Jacob, though very ignorant of spiritual principles as
yet, was indeed hungry for the things of God. Yahweh can deal
with an appetite like that, setting better food before it, cultivating a taste for spiritual likeness to God, and satisfying it
finally with righteousness. These words of Jesus apply in such a
case: "Blessed are they that hunger and thirst after righteousness for they shall be filled."[4]

Basically Jacob was God-fearing. His mother saw that characteristic and cultivated it, not wisely but zealously. Isaac
failed to see it until Yahweh shocked him with this experience
and awakened him to many things hitherto unappreciated. He had
failed to get close enough to the boy to know the real hunger of
his heart. He was missing, therefore, the highest privilege
Yahweh could give him, that of preparing the next heir to the
promises for the exalted privilege of cultivating his children
and his household after him that they in turn should keep the way
of Yahweh (cf. Gen. 18:19).

---

4. Matthew 5:6 in *American Standard Version*.

3. The One Who Used a Shocking Fear to Make Isaac's
   Blessings Fit

If Yahweh had not interfered with Isaac's plans for blessing
Esau, Isaac's blessing of him would have been a misfit and a false
prophecy. The new one he was forced to make did fit and has found
fulfillment in the history of Esau and his descendants. Careful
comparison of these blessings can be instructive.

The blessing of Jacob, the one planned by Isaac for Esau but
given to Jacob, was stated thus:

> See, the smell of my son / is as the smell of the
>   field / which Yahweh has blessed; /
> Now let The (One True) God give *to you* of the dew of
>   heaven, / and of the fatness of the earth, / even
>   plenty of grain and new wine. /
> Let peoples serve *you;* / yea, let nations bow down *to
>   you;* / be master of your brothers; / yea, let the
>   sons of your mother bow down *to you.* /
> Let *those cursing you* be cursed, / and *those blessing
>   you* be blessed. /[5]

The special features in this blessing which did not fit Esau but
did fit Jacob are as follows:

(1) Invocation of material blessings from "The (One True)
God." Esau had not recognized The One True God, Jacob had done
so.

(2) Petition that The One True God should make him master
of peoples, including his own brothers, even his mother's sons.
That last point, when spoken of Esau, was a direct contradiction
of the revelation given earlier to their mother.

(3) Emphatic expression of hope that those cursing him would
be cursed (by The One True God, of course) and those blessing him
would be blessed. This high point of promise among the promises
to Abraham could be fulfilled only in a believer in Yahweh.

The blessing of Esau, the new one, the one made in the light
of "the fear" Yahweh brought upon Isaac, was expressed this way:

> Behold, *away from the fatness of the earth* will be
>   your dwelling, / and away from the dew of the
>   heavens above. /

---

5. Genesis 27:27-29 in the author's translation.

> *By your sword** will you live, / and *your brother*
>   you will serve; /
> And it shall be,° *even as you become restless,* / that
>   you shall break off° his yoke from your neck. /[6]

The features of this blessing which fitted Esau and have found
fulfillment are as follows:

(1) No reverence at all to God. As both Scripture and
history have proved, he was a profane person. Any implication of
association with God would have been out of keeping with his
character.

(2) Prediction of association with the desert. The words
"away from the dew of the heavens above" fit the land of Edom to
the southeast of the Dead Sea.

(3) Prediction that he would live by his sword. History
again, both sacred and profane, has recorded that Edom lived by
the sword and perished by the sword.

(4) Submission *to Jacob*, even though temporary. The fulfillment of this point occupies many passages in the Bible.

Jacob's reflections upon Isaac's experiences, as shown in his
use of the name "The Fear of Isaac" as a name for Yahweh, not only
magnified the fact that Yahweh used that experience to set the
blessings straight but also made his father a channel of blessing
to all his descendants.

As Jacob looked back after years in the school of hard knocks
after years in which he too had experienced the chastening discipline of The Angel of Yahweh, he could understand his father's
struggle far better than he could at the time it occurred. With a
warmth of sympathy, touching both the weaknesses of human judgment
and the powers of influence even in a chastened life, he introduced a rare discrimination and a marvelous balance into his use
of "shocking fear" or "terror" as a name for God. It discrimi-
nates between that fear of the Lord that is an awesome thrill producing reverential worship and that fear of the Lord that is a
shocking terror, producing an agonizing purge of obstinacy from
the will of a saint. It balances the Lord's love with his chastening severity. It makes his rectifying justice, his unending
faithfulness to every promise, and his unfailing love toward any
believer to work together. By the balance of these he accomplishes

---

6. Genesis 27:39,40 in the author's translation.

the fulfillment of his high purposes despite the willfulness and wayward ways of his children.

The blessing Isaac planned for Esau could never have fitted him, for it invoked material blessings in the name of "The (One True) God" (Gen. 27:27). It made petition for him to be ruler over Jacob, contrary to the revelation received by their mother before their birth. Contrary to the blessing given Abraham, every point in it had to be subject to the will of The One True God. This could not be true in Esau.

Conclusion: "The Author and Perfecter of Our Faith"

When the author of Hebrews, in Hebrews 12:2, described Jesus as "the author and perfecter of our faith," he identified Jesus with Yahweh, The Fear of Isaac. In the last two verses of Hebrews 11 he teaches that Old Testament believers are not made perfect apart from New Testament believers in Christ. As he then proceeds immediately in Hebrews 12:1-13 with a discussion of chastisement, he is teaching that God carried on his perfecting work in Old Testament believers as The Angel of Yahweh and in New Testament believers as Jesus Christ. As "God was in Christ" (II Cor. 5:19), so was God in The Angel of Yahweh. This author and perfecter of the faith of believers is The One True God.

Cynthia Pearl Maus, as editor of *The Old Testament and the Fine Arts*, appears to be responsible for the interpretation given in that volume[7] of the famous picture by Jan Victoors entitled "Isaac Blesses Jacob." In the interpretation this is written: "After Isaac had eaten, he gave Jacob the blessing that right-fully belonged to Esau." Likewise, in the same volume,[8] in the interpretation of another great picture, painted by Giulio Romano and entitled "Esau Back From the Hunt Asks the Benediction," this is written: "But Jacob . . . tricked him (Esau) out of the blessing due by rights to the eldest son."

These interpretations of Esau's rights persist in the ways of this world rather than the ways of God. The heathen families round about Abraham, Isaac, and Jacob reckoned the rights of inheritance that way. The laws of many peoples, even till today, especially in the law of primogeniture, have reckoned leadership in families and in kingdoms that way. In this case there was far more than property rights involved. The blessing, which included spiritual leadership of God's chosen ones, depended upon an

---

7. P. 68.

8. P. 70.

exercise of faith in Yahweh himself. When Yahweh showed Abraham
that his heir would be Isaac rather than Ishmael, when he taught
Isaac that his heir would be Jacob rather than Esau, when he later
revealed to Jacob that the leadership among his sons would pass
through Judah on to Messiah, he substituted a higher law, the law
of inheritance of the Abrahamic promises by faith and faith alone.
This reckoning of the heirs according to their faith counted Esau
out. He had no faith in Yahweh. This reckoning according to
faith made it possible for John the Baptist to say to Jews:
"Bring forth therefore fruit worthy of repentance: and think not
to say within yourselves, we have Abraham to our father: for I
say unto you, that God is able of these stones to raise up children unto Abraham"(Mt. 3:8,9). This reckoning according to faith
made it possible for Paul to say to the Galatians: "And if ye
are Christ's, then are ye Abraham's seed, heirs according to
promise" (Gal. 3:29).

Other words appearing in the interpretation of Romano's picture in *The Old Testament and the Fine Arts*[9] furnish a clue to
the author's failure to discern the law of God concerning inheritance of the blessing. The words are "an angel" in this statement: "Just before his reunion with his brother an angel changed
Jacob's name to 'Israel' . . ." Failure to recognize The Angel
of Yahweh as a unique being, not *an* angel but God himself, in a
mode of being fitted to deal with faltering saints, God of the
Patriarchs and God of Christians, leads to many sad misinterpreta-
tions of Scripture. In this case it prevents realization that the
God who makes "all things work together for good" to them that
love God, even to them that are called according to his purpose
(cf. Romans 8:28), is the same God in both testaments. Those who
miss this teaching in the Genesis stories miss their essence.

The Fear of Isaac, the author and perfecter of our faith,
prepares us to sing with William Cowper, as he did in the gloom
of mental distress, these words of his hymn "God Moves in a
Mysterious Way":

> Ye fearful saints, fresh courage take;
> The clouds ye so much dread
> Are big with mercy, and shall break
> With blessing on your head.
>
> Judge not the Lord by feeble sense;
> But trust him for his grace;

---

9. P. 70.

Behind a frowning providence
He hides a smiling face.[10]

10. GLIMPSES OF GOD

AS

THE REDEEMER OF JACOB

Genesis 48:15,16;   Psalms 103:4

Introduction: The Kinsman Redeemer of Believers

The outstanding glimpse of God in Abraham's experience was memorialized in the name *El Shaddai.*   That in Isaac's experience is recorded for us in the name "The Fear of Isaac."   That in Jacob's experience appears in the blessing upon Joseph's sons, recorded in poetic form in Genesis 48:15-16 in these words:

> *The* (One True) *God,* before whom my fathers
>   Abraham and Isaac walked, /
> *The* (One True) *God,* the one shepherding me /
>   all my life long to this day. /
> *The Angel,* the one redeeming me from all
>   evil, / bless the lads . . . .[1]

The grammatical construction of this invocation indicates that the being called The Angel is the same as the being called The One True God.   The three names for God are placed in apposition, there being no conjunction to indicate reference to more than one being.   The verb "bless" follows its subject, in which case the Hebrew language calls for agreement between subject and predicate in person, number, and gender.   This verb is in the third person, singular number, and masculine gender; so it does agree with "The Angel."   It agrees likewise with "The (One True) God," making this another name for the same person.   Moreover, each name is placed emphatically, the climactic emphasis coming

---

10.   William Cowper, "God Moves in a Mysterious Way," in *New Baptist Hymnal* (Nashville, Tennessee: Broadman Press, 1926), No.55.

1.   The author's translation.

upon the last, "The Angel." Thus the invocation magnifies greatly
the conviction of Jacob that this unique angel is God himself.

The logical justification of this appeal to The Angel as God
lies in the redemptive work credited to him. Jacob in this
passage was the first to use it. This redemptive work identifies
him with God and with Christ. The word "redemption" is given an
exalted place in the Old Testament and the New Testament. It
describes deliverance from loss, wrong, or injustice. It is
accomplished by the payment of one's debts by another, the substitution of one person for another, or the avenging of one's
wrongs by another. It is made to cover deliverance by a near
kinsman from such losses as these: (1) loss of freedom, (2) loss
of the God-allotted family homestead, (3) loss of one's hope for
a son to carry on the family name, (4) loss of life. Such responsibility is laid upon a near kinsman as a sacred duty he owes
to God. In human affairs the near kinsman is a blood relation.
Thus the Book of Ruth illustrates application of the law in the
affairs of Ruth and Boaz. This obligation of a near kinsman is
also applied to God, and it implies a very close personal rela-
tionship between God and his spiritual children. The teaching
is pressed to the point of assuring those in covenant relations
with Yahweh that he will take personal responsibility for redeeming them from the hands of the enemies of their soul. That was
the responsibility assumed by The Angel of Yahweh when he said to
Abraham after his offering of Isaac, *"By myself* I have sworn, is
the express utterance of Yahweh, . . . that I shall indeed bless
you . . ." (Gen. 22:15,17). The Angel's faithful discharge of
this responsibility was described by David as he called upon his
own soul to bless Yahweh, saying of him, "Who redeemeth your life
from destruction" (Ps. 103:4). Peter was describing his redemptive work at a later time when he said ". . . pass the time of
your sojourning in fear (reverential fear), knowing that ye were
redeemed, . . . with precious blood . . . even the blood of Christ
. . . ." (I Peter 1:17-21).

The word "redeemer" or "the one redeeming" in Genesis 48:16
is a participle; thus the redemptive work of The Angel is
described as continuous. This is a parallel to many other
descriptions in the Bible, especially that of Jesus when he said,
" . . . I am with you always . . . ."(Mt. 28:20). In this redemptive work, therefore, there are innumerable incidents of which the
child is unaware, as was Isaac before The Angel cast dread into
him. This is true of the divine 'watchcare' over a believer as it
is of the parental 'watchcare' over a child. There are some experiences, however, that leave an indelible impression upon the
child. Accordingly, we search the story of Jacob's life for crucial incidents which led him to be the first to use this word
"Redeemer" as a name for God.

Jacob's full description of Yahweh as "the one redeeming me
from all evil" fits the crucial experiences of his life in a remarkable way. Each of these illustrates vividly the personal
responsibility and the redemptive action of Yahweh on Jacob's
behalf. The first was at Bethel, where the one calling himself
"Yahweh, the God of Abraham thy father, and the God of Isaac"
redeemed him from the hate of Esau. Another occurred in Mt.
Gilead, where the one who had said, "I am the God of Bethel,"
redeemed him from the deceit of Laban. Another occurred at
Peniel, where the one who changed Jacob's name to Israel redeemed
him from vain self-confidence. Yet another outstanding one occurred at Beersheba, when the one identifying himself as "The God,
the God of thy father," redeemed him from fear, a paralyzing fear
of going down into Egypt.

1.   The One Who Redeemed Him From the Hate of Esau

The hate with which Esau hated Jacob after Isaac blessed him
is described in Genesis 27:41 by a word even stronger than the
ordinary verb "to hate." The ordinary one may express no more
than strong disfavor like that Jacob had for Leah later (cf. Gen.
29:31). To the intense dislike expressed by the ordinary verb
this one adds the cherished bitterness of malice. Its ominous
meaning appears in these words of Esau: "Let come the days of
mourning for my father, for I am determined to kill Jacob my
brother" (Gen. 27:41).

Redemption of Jacob from the dangers involved in Esau's
threat included much more than saving his life. The plan of his
parents for him to go to the home of his uncle Laban in search of
a wife removed the immediate threat to his life. Still there was
inevitably a great fear in his heart concerning possible loss of
the promises, the land, the chosen posterity, and the spiritual
blessing. Redemption from the threat and from the fear came as
Yahweh revealed himself to him at Bethel. In that revelation were
three distinct experiences that were new to Jacob and directly
related to his need for personal assurance. These were a personal
vision of God, a personal covenant with God, and assurance of the
personal 'watchcare' of God over him. These expressions of
Yahweh's unwavering intention to take responsibility for him gave
courage for struggles ahead and preparation of heart for a reconciliation with Esau upon his return.

The personal vision is described in Genesis 28:13a. Yahweh
not only revealed himself but identified himself, saying, "I am
Yahweh, the God of Abraham your father and the God of Isaac." By
this direct approach to Jacob, Yahweh gave the same ground of personal assurance he gave earlier to Abraham and to Isaac.

The personal covenant is described in Genesis 28:13b,14. It refers, as did the covenants with Abraham and Isaac, to the land, the posterity, and the blessing. These were involved in the revelation to Jacob's mother. These were specified in the blessing of his father. They were summarized as "the blessing of Abraham" in the invocation spoken by his father at the time of his leaving home (Gen. 28:3,4). Here, however, they were put into a covenant made directly with Jacob. The strengthening of spirit this gave to the young wayfarer, leaving the land for the first time, can hardly be overestimated.

The personal 'watchcare' promised him is described in Genesis 28:15. He was made to understand that this included Yahweh's presence with him, Yahweh's keeping of him, and Yahweh's restoration of him to the Land of Promise.

"I am with you" is the simplest and most appealing affirmation of a close personal relation that can be made. It carries assurance of a supporting presence under all conditions and at all times.

"I will keep you wherever you go" is given as a correlative statement of the assurance given by Yahweh's presence. Because he is with him, *both beside him and for him*, he will be a guardian of him in all places and under all circumstances.

"I will bring you back to this land" is an assertion of Yahweh's responsibility for fulfillment of the promises. The promise concerning the land is the primary means for fulfillment of the others. This assertion concerning return utilizes Jacob's steadfast interest in the land to promote his preparation for inheritance of it. Thus the personal redeemer develops his personal fitness to be the heir.

". . . for I shall not leave you until I have accomplished that concerning which I have spoken to you" is a reason clause restating the ground for the three assurances just given. Yahweh is that ground for all believers. However, the crux of his problem is to plant the faith of a child on that ground. His words in this case are a superb example of his planting a believer on sure ground.

The response of Jacob to this vision is excellent evidence that his faith was firmly planted at this time. He acknowledged the shortsightedness of his spiritual vision hitherto, saying next morning, "Surely Yahweh is in this place, and *as for me*, I did not know it" (Gen. 28:17). His own emphasis is the key to his confession. Then he expressed the reverential awe he felt in that place by setting up the stone which had been used as a pillow for a pillar to mark the place, by consecrating it with oil, and by calling it Bethel or House of God (Gen. 28:18, 19). Next he made a vow which expressed his acceptance of the covenant.

Jacob has been charged often with bargaining in his dealing with the Lord at this point. The "if" ordinarily used in translations of his vow is the first of the alleged reasons for this charge. The promise to tithe, given at the end, is the other main point in the alleged reasons. On the other hand, everything in this charge depends upon the translation of the first word of the vow, for tithing can be evidence of obedience, gratitude, and acknowledgement of Yahweh's lordship. The participle used to introduce the condition indicates in some cases, even as the English "if" does, that *the author assumes the certainty of the condition's fulfillment* (cf. Num. 36:4; Isa. 4:4). Inasmuch as Yahweh had just said, "I am with you," and this vow expressed Jacob's acceptance of the covenant, making his acceptance begin with a restatement of Yahweh's assurance about being with him, it is not reasonable to make his restatement indicate uncertainty. He was making God's assurance the foundation of everything in his vow. Accordingly, he added three correlatives which were restatements of God's additional assurances. Then he added a fourth correlative in these words, ". . . and Yahweh shall be my God." No matter whether this fourth correlative be considered a part of his conditions, being therefore an assumption that his faith in Yahweh existed already, or a part of his conclusions, being therefore an avowal of his future faith, it is an assertion of faith. This being true, *his pledge of worship* and *his pledge of tithing* (Gen. 28:22) must be considered *fruits of genuine faith*.

In the making of this personal covenant, therefore, Yahweh redeemed him from the hate of Esau and all the fears it stirred up.

2. The One Who Redeemed Him From the Deceit of Laban

While Jacob was with Laban in Paddan-aran, the deceit constantly practiced by Laban posed a serious threat to his faith, his material prosperity, and his return. Pointed reference to Laban's deceitfulness is made in Genesis 29:25, 31:7,41. The first of these three verses refers to Laban's fraud in substituting Leah for Rachel after promising to give Rachel; the second to Laban's frequent and utterly arbitrary change of Jacob's wages after having made a firm agreement; and the third to the threat of interference with Jacob's return to Canaan. In each case, according to the Biblical account, the redemptive work of The Angel of Yahweh delivered Jacob. The means he used were as follows: in the first case, the inspiration of the assurance he had given at Bethel; in the second, providential control of the

increase of Jacob's flock; in the third, a revelation to Laban
that warned him to let Jacob alone.

A widespread tendency on the part of readers of the Bible to
estimate Jacob in this period as merely a keen witted sharper,
i.e., a swindler or cheating gamester, needs to be checked. As
compared with Laban, Jacob's conduct was honorable. Laban was
basely selfish, made no pretense of keeping his word, and was
obviously hypocritical. H. C. Leupold calls him "an eminently
selfish man."[2] John Peter Lange said that his consent to Jacob's
proposal concerning the new agreement about wages "breathes in the
very expression the joy of selfishness."[3] Walter Russell Bowie
reflected his opinion in this remark, "Anybody would have said
that if Laban could now be cheated in his turn, it would be what
he thoroughly deserved."[4] Jacob was not above criticism by any
means, but he did reveal conscientious and very zealous effort
to fulfill all agreement. Moreover, Jacob revealed a faith in
Yahweh that grew stronger and surer the further he went. Above
all else Yahweh's acceptance of him as Abraham's spiritual heir
must be reckoned always as the decisive point in his favor.
Yahweh can see the gem concealed by the rough strata of a man's
character, and he will work unceasingly to uncover it and to
polish it.

Laban's substitution of Leah for Rachel placed Jacob in an
exceedingly aggravating position, but it did not drive him to
despair or rebellion. He charged Laban with serious damage to
his rights, perpetrated by deceit, but he proceeded to agree to
terms whereby he could deal honorably with Leah, with Rachel, and
with Laban. He submitted rather meekly to the wrong already done
him by Laban. He agreed to harsh terms for further service as
Laban took advantage of his ardent love for Rachel. The only
sufficient explanation in either case is that he believed Yahweh
would have him discharge his obligations this way.

With respect to Leah an obligation arose out of the fact
that he was already married to her. Though he had taken her
while thinking she was Rachel, the marriage had been consummated.
Though the festivities of the wedding ceremonies had left him
without opportunity to talk with her normally because others were

---

2. H. C. Leupold, *opus citus*, p. 818.

3. John Peter Lange, *opus citus*, p. 536.

4. Walter Russell Bowie, "Genesis" (Exposition) in *The
Interpreter's Bible*, Vol. I (New York: Abingdon-Cokesbury Press,
1952), p. 707.

continually singing or making speeches to the bride, and without opportunity to see her normally because she doubtless wore the bridal veil, still the men of the city had been there to witness his acceptance of her. Though Laban had violated the solemn agreement concerning Rachel, there had been nothing to arouse his suspicion until the light of morning revealed his bride as Leah. Though Leah herself had doubtless participated deliberately in the fraud, thinking probably that there might not be any other way for her to get a husband, at least one as good as Jacob, she was now his wife. Though he did not love her, the marriage vows had been taken.

With respect to Rachel the obligation was simply one of love. Rightfully he had already paid her dowry. Laban's demand of another seven years of service was a flagrantly selfish imposition, for the marriage of Leah had already relieved him of an embarrassing responsibility. Nevertheless, Jacob could secure in this way an amicable agreement on the part of all that would give him Rachel, and for the sake of Rachel he acquiesced.

With respect to Laban the only obligation arose out of Jacob's agreement. Since Jacob wanted to conclude the agreement for Rachel's sake, he assumed this obligation too.

It seems to be useless to raise questions here about Jacob's falling short because he participated in polygamy. Though it is obvious that the patriarchs as a group fell short of the ideal set up by Yahweh in the beginning, it is also true that Yahweh did not demand perfection of them at this time. The legal code under which their people had lived for a long time, which defined and protected the rights of women and slaves in many ways, was far above the way of the peoples round about them. Yahweh allowed them for the time being to strive for the fulfillment of this lower goal. He took them where he found them and lifted them gradually. There was, therefore, no reproach for Jacob on this score.

Jacob did have a sense of honor about fulfillment of his agreements, and that lifted him far above Laban.

The foundation of Jacob's sense of responsibility was faith in Yahweh. Yahweh, who was with him at Bethel despite the sore troubles in his father's home at Beersheba, was still with him despite these troubles in Paddan-aram. To have run away would have meant despair as to his faith in Yahweh. To have demanded Rachel without Leah would have meant rebellion against a situation Yahweh had allowed to happen. Instead he stayed, he submitted, and he labored to fulfill all agreements. He believed Yahweh would enable him to fulfill all of them.

The changing of wages by Laban was also intensely and continually aggravating, yet it furnished occasion for Yahweh's
vindication of Jacob and Yahweh's abundant blessing of him
materially. Laban was frustrated more and more. Jacob was led
to depend more and more upon Yahweh. In the end even Rachel and
Leah had lost confidence in their father and were ready to go
with Jacob to Canaan. They too believed that Yahweh had brought
about this turn of events.

The new agreement concerning wages, made after the fourteen
years of service for Leah and Rachel, was made at Laban's request
(Gen. 30:27,28). He knew that he had prospered because of Jacob's
management. He asked Jacob to name his wages, and he eagerly
accepted Jacob's suggestion. His reversal of the terms, over and
over, shows therefore how unexpected the results were to him and
how shameless was his effort to grab the advantage away from
Jacob. Only the providential control of Yahweh could have kept
that advantage on Jacob's side.

Laban's response, as given in Genesis 30:34, clearly expressed surprise, eagerness to accept, and immediate acceptance
on Jacob's terms. The word "behold!" revealed his surprise,
thinking that Jacob's terms were amazingly favorable to him.
Ordinarily the black lambs and the vari-colored kids were few
in number in their flocks. "Would that (it were so)!" revealed
Laban's eagerness to close the deal before Jacob could change
his statement of terms. "Let it be according to your word"
revealed acceptance with a reminder to Jacob that he had set the
terms. Laban had no objection, no hesitation, no reservation.

Jacob's devices for prenatal control of the color of his
animals are commented upon by H. C. Leupold in these words, "The
observations of the ancients, backed by the experience of many
moderns, seems to confirm the practicability of the device here
described."[5] The observations of the ancients referred to by
Leupold are cited in a note by S. R. Driver, as follows:

> The physiological principle involved is well
> established, and, as Bochart showed (Hieroz.
> II. c. 49; I. p. 619ff., ed Rosemn.), was
> known to the ancients, and was applied, for
> instance, for the purpose of obtaining par-
> ticular colours in horses and dogs (Oppian,
> *Kynegetica,* I. 327ff., 353-6). According to
> an authority quoted by Delitzsch, cattle

---

5. H. C. Leupold, *opus citus,* p. 824.

breeders now, in order to secure white
lambs, surround the drinking troughs with
white objects."[6]

The use of these devices was certainly not forbidden by the
terms of the agreement. It may be that in the use of them Jacob
tended to depend upon his own ingenuity and meet cunning with
cunning. In the comments of Keil and Delitzsch this is written,
" . . . the fact that God defended him from Laban's revenge did
not prove it to be right."[7] Nevertheless, we can agree with
Lange in this comment: ". . .Jacob did not act against his conscience, but thought that he might anticipate and assist by human
means the fulfillment of those visions in which rewards of this
kind were promised to him."[8]

Yahweh's control of the results is declared in no uncertain
terms. According to Genesis 31:6, Jacob said to Rachel and Leah,
after describing the deceitful dealing of their father as a
matter they knew full well, ". . . yet God did not permit him to
do me harm." According to Genesis 31:9, Jacob added, after
describing how the flock increased so as to benefit him despite
all the desperate efforts of Laban to turn things his way, "Thus
God took away the cattle of your father and gave them to me." In
Genesis 31:10-12 Jacob attributed his plans and their success to
guidance by "The Angel of The (One True) God." Rachel and Leah
accepted all this. While some commentators, even Keil and
Delitzsch, have not accepted this vision of Jacob as a real revelation, Lange, Driver, Leupold, and others have done so. Even
Cuthbert Simpson says, "God, however, intervened to protect Jacob
from being victimized (31:7b)."[9] At least it is definitely assured that Jacob believed his vision to be a revelation of "The
Angel who redeems him from all evil." All agree that the results
were due to control of the situation by The Angel.

Laban's threat to prevent Jacob's return to Canaan provoked
another intervention by Yahweh. Laban pursued him as far as Mt.
Gilead, but there God stopped him. He continued to bluster, even
after failing to find the household images stolen by Rachel,
which he called "my gods" (Gen. 31:30), but he whittled down his
claims to a request for a non-aggression pact (Gen. 31:44-53).

---

6. S. R. Driver, *opus citus*, p. 279.

7. C. F. Keil, and F. Delitasch, *opus citus*, p. 299.

8. John Peter Lange, *opus citus*, p. 538.

9. Cuthbert A. Simpson, *opus citus*, p. 709.

Laban took his kinsmen along in the pursuit of Jacob (Gen. 31:23), as intending to deal with Jacob by force. His intention posed a very serious threat. As he said, according to Genesis 31:29, it was in the power of his hand to do Jacob harm. As before, however, Yahweh intervened where it was necessary to intervene. Laban himself reported that God spoke to him in a way to prohibit his saying anything to Jacob so far as the return was concerned. He complained about his gods, he asked for a covenant, but not one thing did he do or say to prevent Jacob's return.

Whatever Laban said to imply previous willingness to let Jacob return was hypocritical face-saving. Who believed him when he said, ". . . that I might send you away with mirth and songs, tabret, and harp" (Gen. 31:27)? What did Rachel and Leah think when he tried to make it appear that he loved his daughters and their children so much (Gen. 31:28,43)?

The decision of Jacob to slip away secretly may not have been wise. His failure to declare complete dependence upon the Lord at that time certainly did not make his faith fully known. On the other hand, when Yahweh's intervention gave him the upper hand, he described the honesty and diligence of his service to Laban through twenty years in terms that Laban could not deny (Gen. 31:28-41). Moreover, he boldly confessed his faith in these words: *"If the God of my father, the God of Abraham, and The Fear of Isaac had not been with me, indeed now empty-handed had you sent me away"* (Gen. 31:42).[10]

3.   The One Who Redeemed Him From His Own Self-Confidence

At Peniel The Angel of Yahweh met Jacob again. This time he dealt with him in opposition up to a certain point, then he sent him on to the greatest spiritual triumph of his career. The opposition of The Angel was forcibly revealed by the wrestling in which Jacob's hip was thrown out of joint, leaving him to go forward to the meeting with Esau limping upon his thigh. The wonderful change accomplished in Jacob's spiritual nature and the mighty spiritual preparation for dealing with Esau were revealed in the change of name from Jacob to Israel. These made the experience at Peniel an experience worthy to be memorialized permanently by the children of Israel in refraining from eating "the sinew of the hip which is upon the hollow of the thigh" (Gen. 32:32).

----

10.   The author's translation.

The redemption accomplished in this experience was deliverance from self-confidence which threatened at this time to confirm Jacob's tendencies toward three very serious spiritual evils
as follows: (1) trust in luck, (2) trust in bribery, (3) trust
in trickery.

Trust in luck made Jacob divide his company into two camps,
saying, ". . . if Esau comes to one camp and shall destroy it,
still the remaining camp shall escape" (Gen. 32:8). He had sent
messengers to tell Esau of his return. The messengers' report
had indicated that Esau was coming to meet him and that he would
have four hundred men with him. In the twenty years Jacob had
been gone Esau had become the chieftain of desert tribes to the
southeast of the Dead Sea. During later centuries these were the
people who built almost impregnable fortresses like Petra or Sela
in their rocky mountain region. From these inaccessible fast-
nesses their raiding parties controlled caravan routes passing
through their land. In all probability Esau's band was such a
party, one bent on pillage, living by robbery, murder, and spoil.
No wonder then that "Jacob was very much afraid, yea, terrified"
(Gen. 32:8)![11] The danger and his terror were quite understand-
able. Nevertheless, plans reflecting nothing more than trust in
luck were not worthy reflections of the faith he had professed
when facing Laban.

Trust in bribery made Jacob prepare a very, very handsome
present for Esau, one fit for a desert king (Gen. 32:13-21). He
had, in the meantime, prayed very earnestly that Yahweh would
deliver him (Gen. 32:9-12). However, he still depended very
heavily upon his own devices to accomplish what he understood
to be the Lord's will for him. It is true that he was dealing
with a character that was volatile, fickle, sensitive, and proud.
There were reasons for thinking "gifts" might dissipate Esau's
anger. It is true also that he could not forget that the grudge
Esau bore was due largely to his own lying and trickery. Consciousness of all this made him ready to appease Esau. He knew
how to play upon the cupidity and the pride of men. His thinking
was obvious and his reasons were natural. Nevertheless, this
self-made plan reflected the characteristic fault of Jacob's
nature, trust in his own shrewdness to outwit and to supplant
others even by means unworthy of a pure faith in God.

Trust in trickery was doubtless another subtle temptation to
Jacob at this time. We are not told of any trick he planned, but
lack of opportunity for tricks was probably the reason why there
was no overt planning for such schemes. Trust in luck, trust in

---

11.   The author's translation.

the shrewd use of presents to accomplish an ulterior motive, and willingness to take advantage of another by trickery in case opportunity does appear are usually tied together in the nature of an ambitious schemer. The strong tendency of Jacob in the direction of all these spiritual evils was apparently the occasion for the severe chastening administered at this particular time by The Angel of Yahweh. Jacob, the spiritual heir of Abraham, returning now to his inheritance, needed discipline at this point above all else.

Redemption from these evils was accomplished by three lessons arising out of the necessity for a reconciliation with Esau. Each of these lessons was taught first by the encounter with The Angel of Yahweh. Then each one was accepted and applied in the meeting with Esau. Together these experiences turned Jacob from conceited, self-confidence, i.e., willful, and evil self-dependence, to faithful and obedient dependence upon the Lord. Those parallel features of the two encounters which were used in a marvelously telling way to teach these lessons were as follows: (1) an immediate encounter with no chance to run away; (2) a crippling injury to Jacob which made natural resistance useless; (3) a test of Jacob's personal attitude toward The Angel that opened the door of Jacob's heart for The Angel's blessing. The lessons learned through the chastening experiences were: (1) trust in The Angel's providential control under any circumstances; (2) trust in The Angel's ability to make his strength perfect in his servant's weakness; (3) trust in The Angel's ability to turn his surrender and his trust into means of effecting a reconciliation with Esau.

Trust in The Angel's providential control appeared as Jacob, helpless but still hanging on after he was crippled, said, "I shall not send you away unless you have blessed me" (Gen. 32:26).[12] All this trust appeared as he refused all Esau's offers of a guard for him and his possessions, putting all his hope of protection in The Angel's 'watchcare' over him.

What turned Jacob to this simple faith in The Angel?

All the day and most of the night before had been filled with feverish efforts to avoid a definite reckoning with Esau. Division of his company into two bands reflected a hope that one band at least would not meet Esau (cf. Gen. 32:8). Preparation of a very valuable present, sent ahead of his own company, divided into several parts with a space between parts, was intended to appease Esau's wrath and avoid any discussion of the wrong done and

---

12.   The author's translation.

atonement for it (cf. Gen. 32:20). Even during the night he was
racked by anxiety over the approaching meeting. Genesis 32:22
speaks emphatically of the fact that he got up "during the night"
to move his company across The Jabbok. Yet, as he carried over
all others, he remained behind (cf. Gen. 32:24). Possessions,
wives, and children were carried over, even Rachel and little
Joseph, and he was left alone. Could he have been thinking of
running away, leaving all others to their fate while he escaped
alone? Not that! Of course not that! Whatever else he was,
Jacob was never a coward. But there was a desperate struggle
in his soul, an overwhelming urgency that demanded a time alone
and with God. All he had done was not sufficient to give him
assurance. All he could think to do offered no sure hope. Doubtless he stood still in that hour and longed for a word from God.

And God gave it! The way was unexpected, mysterious, and
miraculous. That way was so strange that no attempt to explain
details appears in the account handed down to us. It is made
clear, however, that the mysterious person who appeared at first
as a man (cf. Gen. 32:24) was recognized by Jacob before their
struggle was over as The Angel of Yahweh, for he said afterwards,
" . . . I saw God face to face, yet my life was delivered" (Gen.
32:30). Thus Yahweh forced him to face another immediate encounter without opportunity for escape or chance to control the
circumstances in a way so as to avoid the crucial issue. Yahweh
used this encounter to teach several lessons that proved to be
essential in Jacob's dealing with Esau later, and the first of
these was reliance upon God's providential control. As he controlled Jacob in this struggle, so he used the transformed Jacob
to curb Esau in the struggle of personalities that ensued.

*Trust in the Lord's ability to make his strength perfect in
a believer's weakness* arose out of the crippling of Jacob when
The Angel strained the tendon of his hip severely. According to
Genesis 32:25, The Angel saw that "he did not prevail" over Jacob.
Evidently The Angel's observation did not mean that he lacked
power to crush Jacob physically, for a little later he did strain
his hip. It did mean that up to that point he had not stopped
him from struggling in his own strength.

We are compelled to understand the wrestling up to this
point as physical wrestling because the verb used to describe
it is restricted to the description of physical wrestling. This
verb is derived from the noun "dust." It is the equivalent of
our verb "get dusty," and its meaning can be visualized in the
wrestling of two boys in the yard, each trying to stay on top as
they roll and get dusty in the struggle. This verb stands in
sharp contrast to that from which the name Israel is drawn, for
that one is used to describe the mental and spiritual wrestling
of a prince with his sovereign as they deliberate in the council,

weighing affairs of state.   This one describes physical wrestling
only.

On the other hand, in as much as The Angel had the power to
crush Jacob utterly but did not use his power to that extent, we
are led to see that he approached Jacob in physical form and
became the aggressor in a physical encounter in order to put
Jacob in a fix wherein he could make Jacob realize his spiritual
weaknesses and accept the spiritual strength arising out of complete surrender and dependence upon The Angel's guidance.   Jacob
was still resisting, still thinking that by his own resistance to
every form of opposition he would conquer; so The Angel made that
kind of resistance obviously futile by crippling him. By this The
Angel reduced him to a suppliant. And by this The Angel prepared
him to face Esau in the strength of trust that God's strength can
be made perfect in a believer's weakness, even as Paul learned in
another mysterious but blessed experience.   The only way a man
can prevail over God is in prayer (cf. Gen. 32:28).

*Trust in the Lord's ability to use his surrender to the
guidance of The Angel and his prayer for The Angel's blessing as
means of effecting the reconciliation with Esau* arose in response
to a simple test The Angel made after Jacob was crippled.   He
said, "Send me away, for the daybreak has come" (Gen. 32:26).

Was The Angel afraid of the full light of day? Oh no! The
urgency was Jacob's rather than his.   Esau would be breaking camp
with the coming of daylight.   Jacob needed to hurry in order to
be at the head of this company as the two groups came together.
This would be Jacob's crisis.   Trust in God's guidance could
strengthen him for it but not remove him from it.

Was The Angel unable to break away from Jacob and to go when
he pleased? Remember that the physical phase of this encounter
was now over.   Jacob's resistance was now broken.   What then was
the purpose of this request? The key lies in the word "send
away."   It is close to the idea of "giving Godspeed."   It signifies sending away with approval and with prayer that the close
spiritual union that existed previously shall continue as if
there were no separation.   This is the kind of dismissal a god-
fearing host gives at the departure of a honored guest, or loving
parents give to a departing daughter who has become a bride.   In
other words, The Angel was asking for a token of Jacob's love and
an assurance of Jacob's remembrance as he departed.

Jacob's declaration that he would give that parting token of
love and remembrance only after he was blessed by The Angel did
two things.   It recognized The Angel as God.   It also pleaded for
his blessed control over all Jacob's life, as truly when not seen
as when seen.   This prayer, therefore, was the expression of a

surrendered, a transformed, a dedicated, a trusting Jacob.

Recognition by The Angel of the transformed nature of Jacob was shown by his declaration that Jacob would be called Israel from this time onward (cf. Gen. 32:27,28). First The Angel made him recognize and confess his former nature by admitting that his name was Jacob or Supplanter (One Who Supplants). Then The Angel declared, by the use of the new name, that henceforth he would be Israel, He Who Strives With God or Prince With God. The striving that had been misdirected in the old nature would be purified and utilized in the new by fellowship with God.

When The Angel deflected Jacob's request that The Angel tell him his name, he left Jacob to draw his own conslusion. He, of course, observed that Jacob's request for a blessing inferred the proper conclusion concerning his character. When he proceeded to bless Jacob, the blessing confirmed the conclusion Jacob had already drawn. Jacob implied it when he named the place of the wrestling *Peniel*, or The Face of God. Jacob reviewed it when he identified The Angel with The (One True) God according to our special text in Genesis 48:15,16. The prophet Hosea stated it explicitly when he said, ". . . he had power with God: yea, he had power over The Angel . . ." (Hos. 12:3,4).[13]

The new Jacob, the real Israel, appeared in every phase of his meeting with Esau. In his leadership, out in front, alone, and unafraid, he was Prince With God. In his extremely courteous respect for Esau, in his warmly emotional welcome of him as a brother, in his insistence that Esau accept his gift as a token of friendship, and in his insistence that he proceed with no other protection than the protection of God, he was truly Prince With God.

When Jacob saw Esau coming "and *with him* . . . four hundred men" (Gen. 33:1),[14] he arranged his family, then "he himself passed on before them . . ." (Gen. 33:3). There he was, one lone man, with women and children and undefended possessions behind him, facing four hundred fierce warriors of the desert and Esau. That took courage! And it was a courage born of faith that The Angel was overruling this experience as surely as he did that at *Peniel*.

Jacob proceeded to bow down to the ground "seven times as he was drawing near unto his brother" (Gen. 33:3). Prostration of

---

13. *American Standard Version,* with The Angel capitalized by the author.

oneself was a symbol of respect due a ruler, and Esau was now a
ruler. Among their peoples there was no suggestion of cringing,
servile, fearful abasement in this ceremony. Moreover, Jacob
appears to have realized that courteous respect could be paid
to Esau's power without sacrifice of his own loyalty to Yahweh.
In no act or word did Jacob deny or compromise his faith, yet he
paid the full measure or respect to Esau. That was discretion.

There is nothing in the story, save the obvious fact that
Esau refrained from any word or gesture suggesting a threat, to
tell us what transpired in Esau's heart as Jacob came forward.
If we try to read between the lines, our interpretations are pure
surmise. It is not unreasonable, however, to suppose that Esau,
warrior that he was, recognized the courage manifested by his
brother and respected him for it. If Jacob had fled before hand,
he could have overtaken him. If Jacob had resorted to begging,
bribery, or cunning at this time, he would probably have despised
him, and a hatred he had previously thought of as justified might
have flared up again in an avenging flame to destroy Jacob. Now
he saw a different Jacob. He could recognize courage when he saw
it, though he could not understand the faith from which his brother's courage sprang. Whatever the motivating ideas were, he
responded with surprising magnanimity and brotherly emotion. In
view of that response we can say that the changes in Jacob
wrought at *Peniel* were the Lord's means of redemption in this
hour. As such the redemption of Jacob at this time was a *redemption from himself more than anything else.*

The embracing, the kissing, and the weeping followed naturally after each of the brothers recognized the strength that was
in the other. They differed still in their religious convictions
as day from night, yet each could respect the other in his place.
Doubtless it was good that they not be thrown together too much,
lest they clash. Though Jacob suggested visiting Esau later
(cf. Gen. 33:14), he did not go. So far as the record shows,
they met again only to bury their father (cf. Gen. 35:29). Nevertheless, on the level of merely human relations they could meet as
brothers. Moreover, release from the tension created by deep personal animosity, gave occasion at this time for such emotional
expression as Eastern peoples are accustomed to expect on the part
of men and women when long-separated relatives or friends meet.
Apart from the pressure of want or the clash of personal interests, this was quite natural.

The gift that Jacob had sent was at first declined by Esau.
Then Jacob insisted that he take it as evidence that he accepted

Jacob. Jacob said, ". . . thus you will accept me"(Gen.33:10).[15]
Acceptance of the gift would be solemn testimony to Esau's willingness to let bygones be bygones, to forgive whatever wrong
Jacob had done him, and to let there be peace between them. This
statement cleansed the present from any taint of bribery and made
it a token of mutual reconciliation. This indeed made Jacob's
dealing with Esau at this time a spiritual victory of the first
magnitude. In this the blessing of The Angel reached a climax.

Jacob's insistence that he and his company needed no such
guard as Esau offered (Gen. 33:12-15) likewise reflected his
faithful dependence upon The Angel. He did not say so to Esau.
Esau would not have appreciated faith like that. Any spiritually
minded soul, however, can see that this faith gave him the confidence that sustained him.

In all these things Israel, Prince With God, took the place
of Jacob, and this blessed character was the ideal with which God
sustained him afterwards. After the disgrace of Dinah, the blood
revenge of Simeon and Levi, and the utter dispossession of the
men of Shechem by all the sons of Jacob (cf. Gen. 34), the spiritual estate of all was at a very low ebb. Then God intervened to
call him back to Bethel (Gen. 35:1) and to restore his hope of
living up to this name (Gen. 35:10). It is an arresting fact that
the name "Yahweh" is not used in the account of these events.
While it may be impossible to offer any certainty in the interpretation of this fact, it is possible to consider this as a suit-
able explanation: the providential circumstance that was a clue
to Jacob's deliverance at this time was "the terror of God" that
prevented pursuit; thus the part God had in this series of events
was not so much the covenant making and covenant fulfilling of
Yahweh as it was a result of God's sovereign control of the
heathen in restraining their efforts at revenge. Restoration of
Jacob's hope was a part of the covenant fulfillments, of course,
but the account of that was a sequel to the main account in this
case. Anyway God did continue to hold up this ideal and to assure
him of its fulfillment.

4. The One Who Redeemed Him From Fears About Going Down
    into Egypt

Once more God revealed himself unto Jacob to redeem him from
what seemed to Jacob a dire threat. Though he decided he must go
down to Egypt because of the fear of starvation, he was possessed

---

15. The author's translation.

by many fears as he was driven step by step to make that decision.
Despite the message from Joseph that he was still alive and would
take care of him, he was still afraid. Had not Abraham gone down
under similar circumstances and fallen into serious trouble? Had
not Isaac been commanded by Yahweh not to leave the Promised Land?
Could he ever forget his fears that he would not be able to return from Paddan-aram? Even after he had started on his journey,
he paused at Beersheba and offered sacrifices unto the God of his
father Isaac (Gen. 36:1). Then God said "in the visions of the
night, . . . fear not to go down into Egypt . . ." (Gen. 36:2,3).

The things Jacob feared can be imagined easily. Some of
them may be stated this way: (1) fear of assimilation (was not
Joseph already an Egyptian, married to an Egyptian, with sons who
would be reared as Egyptians? How could the others avoid Egyptians
alliances and the immoral worship of Egyptian gods?); (2) fear
of separation from Yahweh (Could Yahweh, even Yahweh, control the
conditions in a foreign land, especially in a powerful, rich, organized, skilled, artistic, and seductive society like that of
Egypt, so as to prevent alienation of Israelites from himself?);
(3) fear of failure to return (Would not all these influences in
Egypt naturally lead to settling down there?).

The words of "The (One True) God,"[16] the God of his father,
gave direct answers to these questions, as follows:

(1) ". . . for a great nation I shall make of you there"
said there would be no such assimilation as would prevent increase
of Israelites as Israelites, identification and training of Israelites as Israelites, and eventually organization of Israelites
as a nation of Israelites. The emphasis in these words was upon
"a great nation" (cf. Gen. 46:3 in the author's translation).

(2) ". . . *I* shall go down with you to Egypt" said there
would not be a separation between Yahweh, The (One True) God, and
the chosen people in this time of their sojourn. The emphasis in
these words was upon *"I"* (cf. Gen. 46:4 in the author's translation).

(3) ". . . and *I* shall bring you up, yea, I certainly shall"
said that there would be no failure to return, for Yahweh himself
would guarantee it. In these words there was a double emphasis,
first upon *"I"* as in the preceding clause, then upon the verbal
action, the bringing up, or the causing to go up (cf. Gen. 46:4
in the author's translation). Thus was the answer made complete.

---

16. Gen. 46:3 in the author's translation.

Then Jacob was willing to be carried away from the land for a time, but only for a time. As he drew near to the time to die, he took an oath of Joseph that he would bury him in the burying-place of Abraham and Isaac. After Joseph swore so to do, "then Israel bowed himself on the head of his bed" (Gen. 47:31). *Bowed and submissive but waiting for the return!*

Conclusion: The Coverage of The Angel's Redemption

Looking back over all the experiences of Jacob, one can see that the redemption he described in Genesis 48:16 covered both the consequences and the causes of sin. The consequences are covered by the word "evil" in its application to ethical evil, the evil that arises in the heart of man, sin. Moreover, the redemption wrought by The Angel, the kinsman-redeemer of Jacob, is described here by a participle that portrays its continuous application in the believer's life. It covers that dramatic moment when a kinsman-redeemer assumes the responsibilities of another, his debts, his sins. It likewise covers the fulfillment of that guarantee in the changed life of the redeemed. It covers all evil, not merely the outward and obvious damage but also the personal weakness and the inward love of sinful living that caused the damage.

The payment of the ransom is the spectacular phase of redemption which we can dramatize briefly and simply. The following experience of a chaplain in the United States navy does so in a fitting and moving way:

> Years ago when I was stationed at the Naval Air Station in Oakland, Calif., the telephone brought an urgent appeal to visit the county jail. It developed that one of the petty officers on our station had been involved in an accident that resulted in the death of a man. The young sailor had been attempting to start his old car. He had ignored the stop sign as his car was being pushed. When he went through the stop sign, his car struck another, resulting in the death of a man.
>
> The original charge filed against the young sailor was a charge of manslaughter. After some days of investigation and consideration the charge of manslaughter was dismissed. The sailor came to trial for the violation of several traffic laws. I stood beside the young sailor as he stood before the judge. The judge talked with him for a while about the seriousness of his offense that had resulted in the loss of a

human life.

Because of his very fine naval record to
which I testified, and because there was no
malicious intent involved, the judge said to
him, "Son, we will dismiss the other charges,
but because of the gravity of the situation,
I must fine you the limit of the law on the
traffic charges. The statutes in these cases
say that the limit which can be imposed is a
$150 fine or 90 days in the county jail."

If the sailor had had to spend 90 days in
the county jail, the likelihood is that he
would have had upon his release a general
court martial in the navy. To be absent 90
days without leave in war time would have been
an extremely serious situation. The judge
pronounced the sentence. "In the light of
the gravity of the offense, I hereby sentence
you to the limit of the law in this case, $150
fine or 90 days in the county jail."

The sailor's shoulders sagged. The judge,
noticing the boy's reaction, asked "Son, do you
have $150?" Said the sailor, "No, your honor."
Regretfully, the judge shook his head and said,
"I have no choice."

In the back of the courtroom a timid little
woman stood up and advanced toward the bench.
"Your honor," said she, "I am the boy's mother.
I have $150. May I pay his fine?"

The judge smiled, as we all did, and said,
"Yes ma'am, you may pay the fine." She did.
She put her arm around the boy's shoulders.
He walked out of the courtroom free. Another
had paid his penalty.[17]

The fulfillment of the guarantee is the miraculously wonderful phase of redemption which we find running through all the
appearances of The Angel of Yahweh to Jacob. As we rejoice over
the payment of the ransom, so we need to retain a vision of the
guarantee. At Bethel, in Paddan-arm, on Mt. Gilead, at Peniel,

---

17. Grady C. Cothen, *The God of the Beginning* (Oklahoma
City, Oklahoma: The Messenger Press, 1955), pp. 46,48.

and at Beersheba this golden thread of promise tied all experiences together in a story of redemption that moves through one period of suspense after another to a climactic transformation of character at Peniel. This transformation is beautifully described by Charles Wesley in these words:

> My strength is gone, my nature dies;
>   I sink beneath thy weighty hand;
> Faint to revive, and fall to rise;
>   I fail, and yet by faith I stand.
> I stand, and will not let thee go,
>   Till I thy name, thy nature know.[18]

11. GLIMPSES OF GOD

AS

THE ONE TRUE GOD OF JUDAH AND JOSEPH

Genesis 44:16, 45:8; Hebrews 12:9,10

Introduction: The Disappearance of a Vital Distinction

In Judah and in Joseph great spiritual changes and great spiritual victories were wrought. The faith of Abraham, Isaac, and Jacob did it. Neither of these was the firstborn, but the faith of Abraham, Isaac, and Jacob made them leaders among their brethren.

When Joseph said to Pharaoh concerning the interpretation of Pharaoh's dreams, ". . . that which *The* (One True) *God is about to do* he has made known to Pharaoh" (Gen. 41:25),[1] he used a definite article with the title "God." Ordinarily Joseph used "God" without the article. When dealing with Pharaoh's butler and baker he used "God" (cf. Gen. 40:8) without it. When assuring Pharaoh that the interpretation of this dreams would come from God, not from him, he used "God" (cf. Gen. 41:16) without it.

---

18. Charles Wesley, "Wrestling Jacob," in *The Old Testament and the Fine Arts* (New York: Harper and Brothers, 1954), p. 84.

1. The author's translation.

Therefore, when he afterwards added the article four times while explaining the interpretation of the dreams (cf. Gen. 41:25,28, 32), he had a definite purpose in doing so. The emphases he gave to the phrase containing "The God" (Gen. 41:25,28) show that the distinction meant a great deal to him. When he said, according to Genesis 41:32, ". . . indeed the thing is *established* by The (One True) God, and The (One True) God is hastening to accomplish it,"[2] he made it clear to Pharaoh that to him "God" meant "The God," the only one who could do this thing, *the only one who was truly God*.

The disappearance of the distinction Joseph made is no little matter. Those translating the Old Testament into English have tried to handle the situation at this point by using a capital "G" with "god." That, however, leaves Joseph's use of "god" in Genesis 40:8 and 41:16 exactly like his use of it in Genesis 41: 25,28,32. Since capital letters to distinguish proper nouns were not in use in Joseph's day, and the word "god" was plural so far as grammatical form was concerned, there was nothing in Joseph's use of the word without the definite article to say whether he meant it to apply to the many gods of Egypt or to the God of his fathers. In other words, our translations give no recognition to Joseph's choice of circumstances in which to make obvious the distinction which was so important to him. When he did choose to speak in unmistakable terms, his use of the definite article carried an inescapable implication that all the gods of Egypt were false gods. And Pharaoh was considered one of them! Begotten by a god, the embodiment of a god, he was a god to Egyptians! To have made this distinction clear prior to the time Joseph chose would have been considered by Pharaoh blasphemy and treason. At the moment when Pharaoh was extremely grateful for a miraculous interpretation of his dreams and for wonderfully wise advice based upon them, The (One True) God gave Joseph a rare opportunity. And Joseph had the courage, tactfully but surely, to bear testimony to his faith. To lose sight of the evidence highlighting this dramatic and inspiring scene is a serious loss.

Brown, Driver, and Briggs in their *Hebrew And English Lexicon*, which has been recognized in our day as the major lexicographal authority in this field, have interpreted "God" with the definite article as meaning "the (true) God."[3] This interpretation fulfills all requirements except for recognition of

---

2. The author's translation.

3. Francis Brown, *et al.*, *opus citus, supra*, p. 43.

"The" as being a part of the title as truly as "God." Even as
"God" was the ordinary title "The God" was the special title,
with the definite article an essential part of it. Even as when
"The" is part of a legal title today, it is due to be used and
to be capitalized.

Translators have driven themselves into many inconsistencies
in handling this special title. The Greek translators in The
Septuagint, the first translation, used the definite article but
used it in all cases, thereby blurring the original picture.
Aramaic and Latin translators did not have a definite article
in their languages, and they did not even attempt a circumlocu-
tion to keep the distinction alive. Others on down to today,
including authors of the *King James Version,* the *Douay Version,*
the *English Revised Version,* the *American Standard Version,*
Moffatt's New Translation, An American Translation, and the
American Revised Version, though varying among themselves at
places, have left the picture blurred.

In addition to the instance cited, there are instances scattered through Genesis in which the special title appears, always
with a significant application to its context. It is found in
the mouths of Isaac, Jacob, Joseph, Judah, and God himself.
Moreover, the author of Genesis describes God as The One True
God "with whom" Enoch and Noah "walked" (Gen. 5:22,24, 6:9).
When he described those who caused great confusion among the
godly because they married without consulting God, he still
called them "the children of The (One True) God" (Gen. 6:2,4).
The God who saw before The Flood that "the earth was corrupt"
(Gen. 6:11) and the God who dealt with Abraham in ways peculiarly
vital to his faith (Gen. 17:18, 20:17, 22:1,3,9) was called "The
(One True) God." In other words, the author of Genesis took the
special title brought into use by later patriarchs and told us
that the same God had dealt with the saints who lived before them.
All the way through the course of history The (One True) God
worked to sustain and to teach the men of faith. It is not
strange then that the special title appeared without special
explanation of it is Isaac's blessing (Gen. 27:28), in Jacob's
specially significant blessing (Gen. 48:15,16, cf. chapter XI
of this work), in the confession of faith which Joseph signified
to his brothers while they still thought him to be an Egyptian
and which he used to impart some faint glimmer of hope even as
he was taking Simeon as a hostage (Gen. 42:18), in Judah's great
confession of sin (Gen. 44:16), in Joseph's noble assertion concerning God's use of his own suffering to preserve the life of
others (Gen. 45:5-8), and in God's easing of Jacob's fears as he
started into Egypt (Gen. 46:3,4). It is strange, therefore, that
we should let the meaning of this significant usage slip away
from us.

The words of Judah in Genesis 44:16 and the words of Joseph in Genesis 45:5-8 have a highly exalted importance for this study of faith. These words, with their background in the lives of these men, furnish remarkably instructive observations concerning those ways of God with his children that make him to be The (One True) God. First, he is described by Judah as the one providentially controlling what happened to him and his brothers in Egypt so as to punish them for the guilt of their iniquity in selling Joseph, and his confession is shown to be the seed out of which come other remarkable changes in spirit. These changes are the spiritual profit produced by the punishment which The (One True) God metes out to his children. Second, he is described by Joseph as one permitting him to suffer in order to preserve the life of others. This likewise is a providence of The (One True) God. Thus Judah and Joseph left this title as the distinctive title for Yahweh in their experiences. Yahweh makes his judgment begin "at the house of God" (I Peter 4:17).

1. The One Who Turns Punishment to Spiritual Profit

Judah's words, when interpreted in the light of their background and their fruit, furnish a view of three spiritual changes that were taking place in the heart of Judah and his brothers when he spoke. These changes were in their early stages only at the time of speaking. However, because he believed even then that the providence of God had brought them face to face with punishment for selling Joseph, he was prepared afterwards to understand that all the spiritual changes made evident in this highly dramatic hour were wrought by the providence of God. Their expectation of punishment was merely an occasion for the Spirit of God to work in the hearts of these men. The changes wrought in their hearts were results of this inner working of the Spirit of God. The means used by him were spiritual influence and guidance working in connection with sovereign control of circumstances, and we call these means as a whole providence. Three enlightening illustrations of this providence appear, as follows: (1) the turning of expectation of punishment into conviction of guilt; (2) the turning of conviction of guilt into longing for justification; (3) the turning of longing for justification into willingness to sacrifice one's self for another.

Turning expectation of punishment into conviction of guilt appears in the fact that Judah's statement was made in answer to an insinuation by Joseph that he had learned of the theft of his cup by divination. Joseph had just said, "Did you not know that such a man as I can divine?" (Gen. 44:15). This question implied that the cup had been stolen, the facts were known, and punishment was inevitable. Judah's first answers were groping and hopeless, as he said, "What can we say to my lord? What can we speak?

Yea, with what can we justify ourselves?" (Gen. 44:16a). No
matter how false the charge, his expectation of the punishment
was fixed. Then suddenly Judah's convictions slipped into gear.
Many strange developments, accumulating since the time of their
first visit and the leaving of their money in their sacks, were
pressing him to a conclusion. He dillydallied no longer with the
minor question of punishment for the theft of a cup, though it
was said to be a cup for divining. He spoke firmly out of the
depth of his conviction as he added, "The One True God has accomplished the punishment for the iniquity of your servants . . ."
(Gen. 44:16b).[4] And his words assert in response to Joseph's
challenge that anything Joseph might do, or whatever had happened
to demand it, was merely permitted by The (One True) God in order
to accomplish his own purposes, not the working of the gods of
Egypt.

The primary meaning of the verb translated here as "accomplished" is "attain to." "To attain to a knowledge," in the
sense of "finding out knowledge" or "discovering knowledge," is
a very frequent application of this verb. Accordingly the words
"found out" and "discovered" prevail in our English translations.
In this text, however, this verb cannot mean "found out" or "discovered" in the sense of "learned," for God had known all the
facts of their iniquity from the beginning. The use of such
terms, therefore, leaves us with an enigma.

The key to the meaning of the verb here lies in its relation
to "iniquity." The word translated "iniquity" can refer to
iniquity, to the guilt of iniquity, or to punishment for iniquity.
Judah's statement recognized the fact that he and his brothers
had been brought face to face with the guilt of their iniquity in
selling Joseph and with punishment for it. Furthermore, Judah
was telling Joseph that the providence of The (One True) God,
rather than Joseph's professed divining, had accomplished the
punishment for the iniquity of his servants.

Their iniquity had been rooted in hate (cf. Gen. 37:4), because Joseph, in his early years, had reported the evil deeds of
some of them to their father. The fact that Jacob loved him more
than any other of his children and had shown his preference by
giving him a fine coat aggravated the tension between them.
Moreover, Joseph's dreams of pre-eminence kept their hate smould-
ering in jealousy (cf. Gen. 37:8,11). Therefore, they actually
conspired to kill him (cf. Gen. 37:20). Reuben tried to save
him (cf. Gen. 37:21,22). Judah managed to turn the others from
their murderous purpose by a suggestion that they sell him as a
slave and avoid having their brother's blood on their hands
(cf. Gen. 37:26,27). All of them, except Reuben, were parties
to the cruel selling of him into slavery. All of them were parties afterwards to the hypocritical and heartless deception

practiced on their father. When they dipped Joseph's coat in
goat's blood and sent it to Jacob, leading him to think Joseph
had been killed by a wild beast (cf. Gen. 37:31-35), each one was
particeps criminis.

All along the way between that day of cruel hypocrisy and
this day of solemn realization of guilt, their consciences had
gnawed away at them. Now they hated themselves. When, at the
end of their first visit to Egypt, Joseph accused them of being
spies and held Simeon as a hostage, "they said, *one to another*,
"Surely we are *guilty* because of our brother, in that we saw the
distress of his soul, when he besought us, but we did not heed;
therefore, there has come *upon us* this distress.'"[5] Over and
over and over through the silent years similar thoughts had
doubtless passed through their mind. Finally their God found a
time, an occasion, a way to lead them to confess one to another
that they all felt the same way about the matter. At this time,
in prospect of Benjamin being held a slave for a crime of which
he alone was accused, not one of them made an attempt to escape
by justifying himself. ". . . they rent their garments, each one
loaded his ass, and they returned to the city" (Gen. 44:13).
When they fell to the ground before Joseph and listened with consent as Judah included all of them in his admission of guilt (cf.
"servants" in Gen. 44:16), they subscribed to his conclusion that
"The (One True) God" had brought upon all a punishment they deserved because of their sin against their brother long, long
before.

Turning conviction of guilt into longing for justification
appeared in Judah's words and example as he took responsibility
for Benjamin. These are reported in two places, first in the account of Judah's pledge to his father (Gen. 43:1) then in Judah's
recital of his pledge before Joseph (Gen. 44:32). It is profit-
able to examine these words carefully in both places.

According to Genesis 43:9, Judah was facing his father back
in Canaan. After Jacob had delayed sending his sons back to
Egypt as long as it was humanly possible, he finally said, "Go,"
without mentioning Benjamin. Judah told him the journey was useless without Benjamin. Still his father quibbled, blaming his
sons for admitting that there was another brother. Then Judah
said, "I shall be surety for him; *from my hand* you will demand
him. If I have not brought him back to you and have not set him
before you, then I will have sinned against you all the days of

---

5. Gen. 42:21, in the author's translation.

my life."[6] He used a condition taken for granted, which took for granted the return of Benjamin. He wanted to convince his father of his firm expectation that he would bring him back and set him in Israel's presence. Furthermore, his use of the word "sin" in his conclusion showed how deeply and conscientiously he contemplated any failure to do so. His words referred to this possible failure as a sin "against" his father. What a change! What a difference between this word and the message sent along with that bloody coat years before! The years between had seen a tremendous change in Judah. Doubtless his father's unquenchable grief over Joseph, his father's never fading affection, his father's faith, had penetrated his own soul. Now he cared for his father. Now he loved him. Now sin had come to have a meaning of which he little dreamed in his reckless days, and he hated it as his father hated it. Therefore, Jacob could accept his pledge, while he refused that of Reuben.

According to Genesis 44:32, Judah was facing Joseph. In the power of one whom he thought to be a ruler of Egypt, "even as Pharaoh" (Gen. 44:18)! Charged with a crime of which he was not guilty. Thinking still, and knowing that his brothers thought the same, that this calamity was being allowed to engulf them because The (One True) God was punishing them for sin done to Joseph! Despite the mystery and the wrong involved in the charge about the cup, which he saw no way to solve or to correct, his mind dwelt supremely on the desperate desire to fulfill that pledge to his father. He repeated it almost exactly, saying, "If I shall not bring him back to you, then I will have sinned against my father for ever." His statement of the condition made it a more probable one rather than one taken for granted. As one prisoner pleading for release of another prisoner, he could not take anything for granted. The best expression of hope he could possibly reveal was a more probable condition. But the burning desire to accomplish the release of Benjamin was also a hope that he could yet spare his father the loss of Benjamin. So it was with the other brothers. They silently accepted his condemnation of them all in a desperate effort to find what their love of their father made them believe was the only way out. The mind of each of them had been greatly, greatly changed.

The convictions of Judah at this point are not spelled out for us by any text. However, his references to sin in making his pledge to his father and in repeating it before Joseph are good ground for thinking that there was in him at this time a deep, deep longing for justification. He described the sin that would

---

6.   The author's translation.

be incurred by failure to keep his pledge as sin or blame that would last forever; so his conviction was really deep. He was never given to much talk about his spiritual experiences, being instead the strong, active leader that gave himself usually to action rather than talk. We are forced, therefore, to try to interpret his actions rather than his words.   There appears to be ample ground, however, for saying that he longed at this time to do what could be justified in his own conscience, in the eyes of his father, and in the eyes of God.

How far did Judah's thoughts go in the direction of New Testament teaching about justification? That is a question that cannot be answered on the basis of the evidence given us. This at least we can say: there was in his hart a longing, a hunger for a righteousness that comes to sinners from God alone. Jesus said, "Blessed are they that hunger and thirst after righteousness: for they shall be filled" (Mt. 5:6).

Turning longing for justification into willingness to sacrifice one's self for another appears as the sequel to Judah's confession. He suggested that all the brothers would bear responsibility for what had happened rather than Benjamin alone, but Joseph refused that idea. Seeing that Joseph was willing to accept the servitude of one as a satisfaction for the crime, Judah then made his great plea that he be allowed to be a substitute for Benjamin.

Judah's plea expressed the spirit of all the brothers. Even as they had accepted his leadership when he made himself a pledge for Benjamin back in Canaan, so they stood ready to help fulfill it. Not one of them tried to deny their guilt and to escape responsibility by denying any connection with Joseph's cup. If Benjamin was guilty, and perhaps they thought he was, still they must play the kinsman's part and provide a redemption price for him ---- somehow. When they first heard the charge, still unaware that the cup was in Benjamin's sack, they had said, "In case it be found with one of your servants, then he shall die, and *also we* shall be my lord's slaves" (Gen. 44:9). When they fell before Joseph, with Benjamin apparently doomed, Judah could still speak for them, saying, ". . . behold, we are my lord's slaves, both we and he with whom the cup was found" (Gen. 44:16). Even when Joseph emphatically offered to release all others than Benjamin (Gen. 44:17), not a man showed an inclination to go.

When Judah moved into his final and magnificent plea, the brothers were evidently "one with him" in willingness to sacrifice themselves to show the love they now had for Israel their father. They could not lead as Judah did, but each was in his place. They could not match the strength of Judah's spirit as he stood alone and drew near to the ruler of Egypt, as he courteously tactfully, skillfully, reasonably, persuasively, sincerely, convincingly, and powerfully pleaded that his life should be accepted as a pledge, a substitute, a sacrifice for that of his brother, but they did share in part his spirit. They could not picture as Judah did the unbearable grief of their father should they return without Benjamin, but they did love him so as to prefer to be slaves in Egypt than to watch his grief as they had in the past.

These words of Jesus fit right here: "Greater love hath no man than this, that a man lay down his life for this friends" (John 15:13).

2. The One Who Permits Innocent Believers to Suffer That
    They May Help Preserve the Life of Others

Joseph's key word in Genesis 45:8 is as follows: *Now, you* did not send me here, but The (One True) God . . . ."[7] This was the key to the entire interpretation Joseph gave of God's providential use of his life in Egypt, his slavery, his imprisonment, his interpretation of dreams, his rise to power, his plans for management in the years of plenty and in the years of drought, and his plan to bring all of Israel's family to Egypt. He was saying that only The (One True) God did exercise or could exercise providential control of events and that children of God should find in his dealing with wrongdoing and with suffering among them a balm that heals in both cases. Thus he was urging his brothers to find in this ground for thanksgiving rather than continuing to grieve over what they had done to him. That which they had done was wrong, but it could not be undone. Let them thank God that he had so overruled their wrongdoing as to turn the effect of it into the accomplishment of great good. This providence depended in part, though Joseph left his brothers to see it for themselves rather than his asserting it, upon Joseph's marvelously forgiving spirit, marvelous purity, marvelous wisdom and efficiency. Therefore, he gave his brothers three great reasons for thanksgiving, as follows: (1) the fact that God was using the suffering of an innocent one to preserve the life of others (Gen. 45:5,6); (2) the fact that God was using the suffering of an innocent one to make secure for Israelites a remnant (Gen. 45:7); 3) the fact that God was using the suffering of an innocent one to make Egypt a means of accomplishing these things (Gen. 45:8-13).

The turning of Joseph's suffering to the preservation of life is stated emphatically by the words "to preserve life" in

---

7. The author's translation.

Genesis 45:5. The benefits went out to Egypt and the peoples of
many other lands. These benefits exemplified the mercy and the
kindness of The (One True) God toward the just and the unjust.
It is good for the children of God to remember that their God
has never neglected this objective while fulfilling that which
Joseph magnified next. This one is served by much of the benevolence practiced in the world today by Jews and Christians, even
that done by the United States government and the United Nations.
Let missionaries who suffer so often and so much remember that
they are used to preserve life on a wide scale, sometimes the
lives of those who have persecuted them.

   The turning of Joseph's suffering to secure a remnant for
Israel is likewise stated with emphasis. In Genesis 45:7 the use
and repetition of the words *"for you"* does this. The "you" referred to Joseph's brothers, and the lesson applied to all true
Israelites. The lesson runs all through the Scriptures. It constitutes a principle in God's control of history that is a key
to scriptural interpretation of that control. Those prophets
who contemplated prophetically the dispersion of the Jews among
the nations of the earth made constant recourse to this interpretation. One of the finest illustrations of it appears in Isaiah
65:8, as he says, "Thus saith Yahweh, 'As the new wine is found
in the cluster, and one saith, "Destroy it not, for a blessing is
in it": so will I do for my servants' sake, that I may not
destroy them all.'" In other words, as Joseph said that The (One
True) God was securing for Israel a remnant in his day, so the
prophets continued to say that he would do always.

   The turning of Joseph's suffering into a means of making
Egypt an instrument for the accomplishment of these things is
said in many ways in Genesis 45:8-13. After the key word in
verse 8, used as an introduction, two emphases in verse 9 show
this interpretation. *"Unto him"* indicates that all that follows
was intended for Jacob in particular, explaining this new situation so that he could see God's purpose in it. "Thus" looks back
to the two purposes already described and introduces the explanation of God's way of fulfilling them.

3. The One Who Makes Judgment to Begin at the House of God

   The experiences of Judah and Joseph furnish excellent occasion for the admonition given by the Apostle Peter in these words

> For the time is come for judgment to begin at the
> house of God: and if it begin first at us, what
> shall be the end of them that obey not the gospel
> of God? And if the righteous is scarcely saved,
> where shall the ungodly and sinner appear? Where-
> fore let them also that suffer according to the

will of God commit their souls in well-doing
unto a faithful Creator.[8]

Those who have already passed through such trials can rejoice
in the assurance the hymn writer expressed on God's behalf in
these words:

> When through the deep waters I call thee to go,
> The rivers of sorrow shall not overflow:
> The flame shall not hurt thee, I only design
> Thy dross to consume and thy gold to refine.[9]

The refiner's fire that burns at the house of God is tended
by The (One True) God.

CONCLUSIONS

USES OF THE NAMES OF GOD

Introduction: All Names Apply To Yahweh

The first use of a name for God, according to the Biblical
account, was Eve's use of "Yahweh" as recorded in Genesis 4:1.
Both "God" and "Yahweh" appear frequently in the text prior to
that verse, but they were used by the author of Genesis, who
wrote long after the time of Eve. It remains true, however, that
by his quotation of Eve's own words, including the name "Yahweh,"
the author credits her with the first use of a name for God.
Moreover, the author's first chapter taught later generations to
understand that the one Eve had called Yahweh was God the creator (cf. chapter III of these studies). His second chapter taught
later generations that the one who revealed himself to Adam and
Eve as their creator, teacher, and benefactor was the one afterwards called by them both Yahweh and God. His full account,

----

8. I Peter 4:17-19 in the *American Standard Version*.

9. "K" in Rippon's *Selection*, 1787, "How Firm A Foundation,"
in *New Baptist Hymnal* (Nahsville, Tennessee: Broadman Press,
1926), No. 228.

accordingly, appears as an interpretation of the earliest revelations of God to man and also the earliest attempts of man to describe God.

Likewise "The (One True) God" is applied to Yahweh. It furnished a title that asserted his uniqueness and supremacy. Worshippers of Yahweh could use it when speaking with unbelievers to assert simply but clearly their belief concerning Yahweh. This was certainly used this way by Isaac, Jacob, Judah and Joseph (cf. chapter XI).

Likewise, all other names for God used by believers are applied to Yahweh. Because Yahweh was the author of the promises to believers and of the covenants with believers, and those promises and covenants made distinctions between believers and unbelievers, it was not easy for believers to talk about him to unbelievers. That fact gave natural cause for much variation between "Yahweh," "God," and "The (One True) God." Their words made it obvious, however, that in all cases they were speaking of Yahweh. Moreover, even in their own meditations, prayers, and worship there was occasion again and again for them to describe various aspects of the character of Yahweh. Thus "Lord Yahweh" was used by Abram to express his own acceptance of Yahweh's sovereign lordship (cf. chapter VI). Thus Abram was probably the first to use "The Angel of Yahweh" and did so in order to express his belief that Yahweh, who revealed himself in physical forms, was indeed one mode of being in which the sovereign God operated (cf. chapter VI). Yet he was obviously describing Yahweh. "El Shaddai," "The Fear of Isaac," and "The Redeemer" arose likewise out of great spiritual experiences with Yahweh, and they were used to describe Yahweh.

This use of all divine names to describe one and the same God reveals three other features of the Book of Genesis that characterize the book as a whole. These are: (1) incipient monotheism; (2) standards of moral purity; and (3) literary unity.

1. The Names of God Were Used to Indicate Incipient Monotheism

The teaching about Yahweh God makes use of the title "The (One True) God" to be a natural development in the thinking of worshippers of Yahweh. The facts of composition which support this statement are so smoothly woven into the stories that most readers find no occasion for stopping to examine them. The following, however, are clearly a part of the account: (1) no other than Yahweh is mentioned as God; (2) the use of the article "the" in the title "The (One True) God" seemingly originated as a denial of polytheism and was certainly understood that way by Isaac, Jacob, Judah, and Joseph; (3) Yahweh God is described as exercising sovereign control over life.

The absence of any mention of another than Yahweh as God is a fact that fails to challenge many today because they are accustomed only to literature based upon the true teaching of the Bible. Any comparison with mythology, however, makes this simple fact to be highly significant. There is no other literature describing early men and early religion like this literature. The multiplicity of gods in the myths of all lands is one of their most striking features. J. E. Manchip White said, ". . . , over two thousand gods were worshipped in Egypt at one time or another."1 This is, therefore, the first main fact which makes it quite unfitting to use the word "myths" as a description of the stories in Genesis.

The use of the article "the" in the title "The (One True) God" has been hidden from most readers of the Bible by the fact that translations have frequently failed to reproduce the article. The Greek Septuagint, the first translation, did produce it. The Latin Vulgate and the Aramaic Peshitta did not do so because "the" is not expressed in those languages in any case. Many translations in modern times follow in the footsteps of the Vulgate and the Peshitta in omitting the article even though "the" is expressed in the language used. Most German, English, Spanish, and French translations have left it out. Such omission has hidden the original use from the eyes of most readers of the Bible.

Old Testament usage in general shows that the Hebrews used "God" *(Elohim)*, with or without the article, as a description of The One True God. Because believers among them thought of God as one, they saw no need for the article unless some circumstances left their intention in doubt. When there was occasion for doubt, they added the article to keep their intention clear. Therefore, the appearance of the article in the days of Enoch and Noah appears to indicate that men of that day who believed in Yahweh found themselves facing circumstances which made it necessary for them to say explicitly that Yahweh only was God. A probable explanation arises from the context in the accounts of Enoch and Noah. This statement concerning mankind in Genesis 6:5, "the whole frame of their mind was nothing but evil continually," probably means that ideas about false gods were included in the evil ideas. There is no evidence of the existence of idolatrous images at that time. However, the corrupt mind and the wicked conduct of the people probably sprang, as they have during all times since, from doubt of Yahweh's teaching and the substitution

---

1. J. E. Manchip White, *Ancient Egypt* (New York: Thomas Y. Crowell Company, (n.d.)), p. 21.

for it of false ideas about God. False ideas about God, when
accepted as reasons for thinking evil and doing evil, become false
gods. Cain's hypocrisy in worship, misunderstanding about Yahweh's
forgiveness, and stubborn intention to do as he pleased opened the
way for the setting up of such false gods. The probability that
they furnished the occasion for this emphasis upon "The (One True)
God" is therefore a strong one.

The use of "the" in this case is not necessarily an assertion
of monotheism in its full meaning, but it is in line with it. We
need to observe that all these statements about God which are attributed to human beings at this time arose out of their experience. They are,therefore, simple and practical descriptions of
what their experiences meant to them. There is no attempt to
theorize about the infinite and the eternal. Thus the use of
"the" does not necessarily cover more than the conviction that
Yahweh was the only one dealing with men in this life who could
truly be called God. Monotheism is far greater than this. It
remains true, nevertheless, that this conviction was one that
could be developed into full-fledged monotheism. Furthermore,
every teaching about Yahweh in Genesis, including those of the
author of Genesis in chapters one, two, and three, are thoroughly
consistent with this one. Use of the definite article with "God"
by Isaac, Jacob, Judah, and Joseph asserted what believers had
believed all along. Face to face with polytheism, they asserted
their monotheism.

Sovereign control over all life by Yahweh God is assumed
throughout these stories. Assertion that he was creator does it.
His teaching about life, his curse of the Devil, his acceptance
of worship, his decision to destroy evil men, and his interference
at Babel do the same. His providential control over Egypt, as
revealed to Jacob (cf. chapter X), as asserted by Judah and
analyzed by Joseph (cf. chapter XI), do the same.

The possibilities opened by this assumption are lifted to the
centuple degree by the use of the title "God" *(Elohim)* which is
plural. Hebrew plurals are frequently used to express fullness or
plentitude (cf. "life" in Genesis 2:7,9), and the plural evidently
does so in this case. This one is regularly used with singular
verbs, as in Genesis 1:1,3,4,5,6,7,8,9,10,11,12,14,16,17,20,21,22,
24,25,28,29, 2:2,3; so it cannot be an ordinary plural indicating
several different gods. There is then a fullness of Godhood indicated by the title "God." Moreover, when the title "Yahweh God"
is used, Yahweh is described as participating in that fullness of
Godhood. "God Most High," "Lord Yahweh," and *"El Shaddai"* do the
same. The teaching in these names is closely associated with the
following statement of God in Genesis 1:26, "let us make man in
our image . . . ." Discerning readers are made to realize yet
more definitely that there is a connection between the fulness of

God's being and the development of man's soul which needs to be considered more and more carefully. This fullness is not stressed in connection with matter and with animals. The decree of God and the brooding of the Spirit of God was considered sufficient there. With the first reference to man this connection is brought out, and with reference to man it continues to be developed. Abraham's faith, Isaac's fear, Jacob's redemption, Judah's and Joseph's providence bear testimony to the same truth.

The use of "us" by Yahweh God appears again in these words in Genesis 3:22: "Behold, the man has become as one of us, knowing good and evil . . . ." The point of supreme interest in these words is the fact that "one of us" indicates inner distinctions within the "us." The statement is made without any attempt to explain how the "one" could include members each of which is distinguished from the other. Nevertheless, the following deductions from the account as a whole are warranted: (1) the plurals of fullness, both in "God" and in the "us," clearly indicate one essential being which cannot be divided against itself; (2) at the same time the "one of us" does indicate the existence of distinct modes of being within that one essential being.

When the author of Genesis put all of the stories together, he gave to the discerning student ground for several observations that bear upon this mystery. First, the God indicated by the single title "God" and credited with power to create is infinite in power and transcendent in being. Second, the God indicated by the double title "Yahweh God" and credited with revelations of himself to men, making himself perceivable to their physical senses, is limited in power and immanent in being. Third, there are references to a third mode of God's being, "the Spirit of God." This third mode is related to God by the title "Spirit of God" in Genesis 1:2 and also to Yahweh by the possessive pronoun in "My Spirit" in Genesis 6:3. This statement in Genesis 6:3 was attributed to Yahweh. Doubtless these added points deepen the element of mystery, for they unquestionably involve assertions concerning modes of being that cannot be analyzed and proved by man's reason. The intent of our present inquiry, however, is not to learn whether the teaching has been proved but what the teaching is. The point is that the author of Genesis teaches that God's revelations of himself, even from the beginning, have involved this mystery.

2. The Names for God Were Used to Indicate Standards of
   Moral Purity

The creation of the human soul in the image of God meant that its attributes were spiritual, for God is a spirit (cf. chapter I). The rise of moral consciousness meant the exercise of these spiritual faculties (cf. chapter II). Yahweh's judgment

upon sin revealed sin as being first of all doubt of Yahweh, then
desire for what Yahweh had forbidden, then disobedience to Yahweh's
moral standards (cf. chapter III). The worship of Yahweh, therefore, was a prayer for deliverance from the moral disobedience and
moral degradation involved in sin (cf. chapter IV). Its forgiveness, its fellowship, its covenants were conditioned upon deep and
genuine desire for moral purity (cf. chapters V-XI). That is
what Jesus described as hunger and thirst after righteousness.

This exaltation of moral purity is that which sets these
stories apart from mythology of all kinds. It makes an interpretation of Genesis 6:1-4 involving the marriage of angels with
human beings to be contrary to the evidence (cf. chapter V). That
sort of thing is mythology, and it is given no place in the worship of Yahweh. These stories use words and figures drawn from
the languages in which the myths were written; but that does not
make them myths. In these stories, those words and figures have
been freed from association with false gods and immoral ideas
(cf. chapters V, VI, VII). They have been purified by a change
of meaning accomplished through association with worship of "The
(One True) God" and through association with the moral purity of
the worship of Yahweh. The stories narrate acts of sin plainly
and fully, but they do so to condemn it and to preach redemption
from it. They never compromise with it. They never lose the note
of unshakable hope for believers, because their climactic message
is Yahweh's revelation of himself in redemption of believers (cf.
chapters VIII, IX, X, XI).

3. The Names of God Were Used to Indicate Literary Unity

Long and learned have been the charges that the use of Divine
names in the early chapters of Genesis is part of the evidence indicating the piecing together of various documents with many conflicting statements of fact in them and with conflicting teaching
about God. The preceding studies have led to the conclusion that
the full teaching, with revelation and response accepted as presented, leaves no ground for such charges. Now we seek to summa-
rize the evidence showing that both revelation and response are
so reflected by the use of the names for God as to indicate a
remarkable example of literary unity.

An outward mark of unity is found in the ten main headings
placed in the text by the author of Genesis. These appear in
Gen. 2:4, 5:1, 6:9, 10:1, 11:10, 11:27, 25:12, 25:19, 36:1, 37:2,
and their relevance is demonstrated by the outline accompanying
the author's translation of Genesis. It is always possible, however, that an author may use an outline and yet be inconsistent
in his teaching. The question of consistency is a supreme one,
and we must probe deeper into it.

Looking to the Biblical account for its answer to our question about consistency, we find ourselves facing two kinds of evidence. One kind describes God as revealing himself to man, making himself perceivable by their physical senses, walking and talking with them. The other kind describes man as using names, poetry, forms of worship, and prophetic utterances to record his understanding of his relations with God. There is an interplay between the revelation of God and the response of men, the revelation provoking various responses and the responses conditioning the further revelations. Only as this interplay is understood, step by step, does the evidence concerning consistency of the account as a whole become clear.

In the introduction, Genesis 1:1 - 2:3, the teaching reaches its climax in the assertion of Genesis 1:27 that God created every human soul in his image. This image, is, therefore, a revelation of God himself. No response of man is included in that story because that story is used as an introduction and all that follows is an extensive treatment of man's response. As pointed out in chapter I of these studies, the introduction was skillfully arranged so as to close with an explanation of God's purpose of man's development, leaving the account of his actual development to the stories that followed. Man's response to this particular revelation appears in Adam's recognition of Eve as having a soul made in the image of God (cf. chapter II). The human response appears again in Eve's recognition of her first child as a being having the image of God in him (cf. chapter IV).

The first major evidence of consistency, therefore, appears in the harmony existing between the teaching of Genesis 1:27 and those teachings concerning the human soul which follow immediately. These teachings that follow appear in Genesis 2:4 - 4:26, which the author set off by the heading in 2:4 as his first major division.

There is no conflict between the statement made in Genesis 1:27 and the account which indicates that Adam recognized in Eve a soul created after he was created (cf. Gen. 2:22,23). Likewise, there is no conflict between this statement and the account which indicates that the soul of Cain was created at a date yet later than that of Eve. The verb of Genesis 1:27, which was a perfect, was used to describe *a general fact*, a single and timeless truth, which may be seen as fulfilled in particular acts over and over and over again. An illustration appears in the use of a perfect in Genesis 36:2 to describe the fact that Esau married heathen wives. The author is not concerned for the moment about the separate acts of marriage but the single fact which brought grief to Isaac and Rebekah (cf. Gen. 28:6-9). In the same way Genesis 1:27 deals with the fact that all human souls are created by God.

That statement does not contradict in any way assertions involving separate acts of creation that occur at different times, even each time a child is born.

Similar features of these passages which have often been occasions for charges of inconsistency have been dealt with in chapter II of these studies. More thorough translation of the original text reveals that there is no ground for these charges provided one's faith can accept the accounts of the self-revelation of God as given.

Accordingly, use of the name "God" in the creation story does not conflict with use of "Yahweh God" in the story that tells of Adam's recognition of the soul in Eve. "God" describes the transcendent nature of God as creator. His omnipotence and sovereign control of all his creations were wrapped up in that name. The human responses, however, were called forth by the direct and immediate dealing of "Yahweh God" with his creatures. That is the story told by chapter two of Genesis and those following. He laid aside his infinite perfections and limited himself so as to reveal himself to human beings in a form that could be seen with their eyes and heard with their ears. The author of Genesis used the compound name first in Genesis 2:4 where the story began which recounts these self revelations in finite form. He does not say that Adam and Eve used the compound name, but he himself used it to indicate the identification of the immanent God who walked and talked with Adam and Eve with the transcendent God who created their souls. Afterwards the author of Genesis led readers steadily onward to that word of Eve concerning Cain in which she used the name "Yahweh." He credits her then with the first use of it. In other words, she coined that name. That was her response to the revelation of God when she realized that God had created a soul in her first child. Even as intelligent beings are in the habit of producing names to distinguish things and persons after they have had opportunity to know their distinctive qualities, so she named the God who had made himself known to them. He had given to Adam and Eve reasons for thinking of him as creator and as providential guardian of their souls. The name that stated her understanding of his part in making her child to possess a human soul was a natural response to his revelation of himself. Thus the author of Genesis wove together the accounts of revelation and response so as to teach that God who created and Yahweh of whom Eve spoke were one and the same. He used the compound name to describe that same one, and he thereby tied his stories together with a thread of teaching about God.

It is clear then that this teaching leads straight onward to the beginning and to the history of the worship of Yahweh. That worship is the response of all believers. The emphasis in the introduction was a general preparation for all of this.

In the second place, the author gave in Genesis 2:4-25 a skillful distinction between things made out of the ground and things not made out of the ground. He thus distinguished "the spirit of life" which God breathed into the body of man from the body which he had already made. He described the dawn of moral consciousness as a development of "the spirit of life." Also he described this dawn of moral consciousness as a response to the immediate presence, teaching, and aid of "Yahweh God."

In the third place, the author described that God who took the initiative in the salvation of Adam and Eve from sin (Gen. 3:8-19) as Yahweh God. The Devil did not use that name (cf. Gen. 3:1,5). Eve, presumably Adam too, lost sight of that God while listening to the Devil (cf. Gen. 3:3). According to the author, however, the word of hope for Adam and Eve was given by Yahweh God (cf. Gen. 3:9,13,14). The implications of the story are that Adam and Eve heard his words, treasured them, and passed them on to succeeding generations. There was no one else to pass them on. The only other explanation is that the story is a fictitious one invented by men of later generations to explain their own ways and beliefs. In that case there is no sufficient explanation for the beliefs of Seth, Enosh, Enoch, and Noah. In other words, revelation and response do not continue to dovetail into each other. In the author's way they do dovetail into each other, each explaining the other.

In the fourth place, the God who dealt with fallen mankind so as to lead a little company in the days of Enosh to use the name "Yahweh" in the invocation of a blessing from God was called "Yahweh" both by them and the author. The author continued to use the compound name (cf. Gen. 3:22,23) down to the point where Eve's first use of "Yahweh" is mentioned (cf. Gen. 4:1), then he also used the single name "Yahweh" (cf. Gen. 4:3,4,6,9,13,15,16). There is nothing to indicate that Cain ever grasped a true understanding of Yahweh's dealing with him. He was afraid of him and brought an offering as a mere appeasement of his wrath. He misunderstood Yahweh's rejection of his offering, and he developed a steadily hardening mistrust of him. Abel understood, and thus he prepared the way for worship of Yahweh. Adam, Eve, Seth, and Enosh went on into full-fledged worship of Yahweh. According to Genesis 4:26, Eve used "God" to describe him as the one so near that they could use his name to sanction, authorize, or confirm their petitions. That response to the providential dealing of Yahweh was indeed a crucial step in the relations between God and men. How could it have occurred except as a response to the God who revealed himself little by little to men? That response was a truly spiritual one. It was not idolatry, animism, superstition, worship of sun, moon, and stars, or any other of the unguided expressions of worship which have cursed the human race. How could it have developed except as a response to God himself?

In the fifth place, use of "The (One True) God" in connection with Enoch and Noah is presented as a response to Yahweh's
revelation of himself. Habitual response to God warranted the
statement that each of these walked with "The (One True) God"
(cf. Gen. 5:22,25, 6:9). Others who knew them marked them as
worshippers of Yahweh. This distinction caused them and their
kind to be known as "the sons of The (One True) God," (cf. Gen.
6:2,4). They were not identified with the Sethites as a whole,
though they came from among them. This characterization distinguished them for all mankind (cf. Gen. 6:1,2,3,4,6,7). It
warranted the description of those spared during the Flood as
Nephilim (perhaps Separated Ones), "heroes that were from of
old," and "men of The Name" (Gen. 6:4; cf. chapter IV). Moreover,
the name "Yahweh" is interspersed in the account of these things
sufficiently to indicate that God's providential control of his
world, not merely through the laws of nature and moral principles
but by intervention and miraculous overruling (cf. Gen. 5:29,
6:3,5,6,7,8), characterized him as Yahweh. This trust in God as
Yahweh made men worshippers of Yahweh.

In the sixth place, Noah worshipped Yahweh after the Flood
(cf. Gen. 8:20), and he identified "the God of Shem" as Yahweh
(Gen. 9:26); so the continuation of the main line of worshippers
of Yahweh is unmistakably marked. In the story of the Flood,
prior to the points just mentioned, the author switches backward
and forward between the names without specific reasons apparently;
however, the account reveals no particular reason for doing so or
not doing so. Perhaps the significant thing is that he uses
both, even within one verse in Genesis 7:16. At least the reader
is reminded that God is Yahweh and Yahweh is God. If it should be
thought that the variations observed indicate that the author used
different sources here, it must be concluded that he did so in a
way to indicate this identity of God Yahweh.

In the seventh place, Yahweh is the one who turned Babel into
confusion, according to Genesis 11:1-9. Since he is described as
coming down to observe (Gen. 11:5) and as scattering the people
abroad (cf. Gen. 11:8), the same kind of personal intervention in
human affairs is portrayed here as in the previous chapters.
Moreover, the purpose of this action as a continuation of Yahweh's
providential care for worshippers of Yahweh is indicated by the
heading "Generations of The Sons of Noah" in Genesis 10:1; by the
references to division and scattering that appear in Genesis 10:5,
11,14,18,20,31,32, 11:9; and by emphasis upon Eber or Heber, the
father of the Hebrews, in Genesis 10:21. By these things the
account is stamped as a continued history of the worshippers of
Yahweh.

All the stories of Genesis are thus tied together by the use of "Yahweh God," its parts, and their synonyms. "Yahweh, God Most High," "Lord Yahweh," "El Shaddai," "Fear of Isaac," "Redeemer" (of Jacob), and all other names for God used by believers represented the response of men to Yahweh's revelations of himself. It is the compound name "Yahweh God" that symbolizes this unity. It is the center from which all the revelations of God and all the responses of men are viewed.

Conclusion: Dependence Upon Faith

Yahweh's revelation of himself, even from the beginning, has depended upon faith for its reception. This was as true of Yahweh God in the Garden of Eden as it was of Jesus in the manger at Bethlehem. The objective revelations of Genesis were and are as definitely beyond reach of scientific proof as was and is the incarnation of Jesus.

Those who depend solely upon "historical evidence" are bound to interpret crucial points in these stories very much as Sigmund Mowinckel has interpreted Genesis 3:15. He says,

> It is now generally admitted by those who adopt the historical approach to theology that there is no allusion here to the Devil or to Christ as 'born of woman,' but that it is a quite general statement about mankind, and serpents, and the struggle between them which continues as long as the earth exists. The poisonous serpent strikes at man's foot whenever he is unfortunate enough to come too near to it, and always and everywhere man tries to crush the serpent's head when he has the chance.[2]

This conclusion makes the verse an observation of men and completely disallows the view that God was speaking.

Recognition of unity in Genesis obviously depends upon a faith that can accept the walking and talking of Yahweh with Adam and Eve, even the wrestling of The Angel of Yahweh with Jacob, as self-revelations of God. Granted that kind of faith, there is nothing in Genesis that does not become the harmony of intelligence and faith belonging to an interpretative genius who edits and explains the spiritual experiences of his ancestors. Without

---

2. Sigmund Mowinckel, *He That Cometh*, translated by G. W. Anderson, (New York: Abingdon Press, (n.d.)), p. 11.

that kind of faith, the very things that harmonize all else become
at their best anthropomorphic symbols of subjective thinking about
God and at their worst the superstitious and irrational rambling
of mythology.

The records of Genesis, when interpreted with acceptance of
the self-revelations of God as given, are excellent evidence that
the book was prepared by one great and faithful soul.   Accordingly he used oral and written traditions handed down from his
spiritual forefathers as the poetic passages and the genealogical
tables show. He made use of a vast store of knowledge, probably
acquired in Egypt as is shown by the vocabulary and the intimate
knowledge of Egyptian customs appearing in the Joseph stories. He
was the beneficiary of a very remarkable literary training, as
his skill in story telling shows. He reflected an insight into
the theological beliefs of the Hebrews which could have come from
no other background than that of the Hebrews. All of these, however, could not account for the unity appearing in Genesis were
he not a most earnest believer in Yahweh. Only a faith that
shared the failures and the blessings of his spiritual ancestors
could weave together the account of their development in faith as
it is done in Genesis. Only a faith that knew the heights of
faith could have described the foundations of faith as they are
described in the first three chapters of Genesis, no matter how
many fragmentary and faulty products of predecessors may have been
known to him.

Those who magnify the self-revelation of Yahweh may consis-
tently magnify the fact that they do so upon grounds of faith.
There are supporting evidences, yet such a revelation can be ap-
prehended only by faith. The consistency, the incipient monotheism, and the moral purity which appear as results of belief
by early men that Yahweh did reveal himself are impressive and
important. It remains true, however, that they are not historical
proof that Yahweh did then walk and talk with men, for myriads of
counterfeits have crowded their testimony out of the pages of
history. Faith that he did so reveal himself to men in the beginning opens a door of understanding to many accounts of later
revelation which appear in the Bible, yet it remains faith.

Why need one hesitate to exercise such a faith? A child
learns to trust a parent because of parental love and care, yet
the child is utterly unable to apply canons of historical evidence. Likewise a sinner becomes a child of God by trusting him,
and all the evidence that later experience supplies can never be
a substitute for that initial act of faith. Believers are happy
to find that all their experience is in accord with their child-
like faith, then to acknowledge that it was faith and could have
been nothing other than faith. Thus faith is first of all a
response to God. Afterwards faith secures a response from God

that is ground for reason; reasonable understanding strengthens
faith; yet, in spiritual experience neither can dispense with the
other. The two must needs go hand in hand forever.

Truths like those taught in these stories in Genesis prepare
the minds of believers for an understanding of truths pointed out
by John the Apostle in these words concerning Jesus:

> That which was from the beginning, that which we
> have heard, that which we have seen with our eyes,
> that which we beheld, and our hands handled, con-
> cerning the Word of life (and the life was manifested,
> and we have seen, and bear witness, and declare unto
> you the life, the eternal *life,* which was with the
> Father, and was manifested unto us); that which we
> have seen and heard declare we unto you also, that ye
> also may have fellowship with us: yea, and our
> fellowship is with the Father, and his Son Jesus Christ:
> and these things we write, that our joy may be made
> full.[3]

3. I John 1:1-4 in the *American Standard Version.*

DATE DUE
